Attainment's

EXPLORE world history

Don Bastian
Tom Kinney

EXPLORE world history

By
Don Bastian and Tom Kinney

Editing and fact checking
Shannon Booth
Elizabeth Ragsdale
Dan Hanson
David Nelson

Illustrations
Beverly Sanders
Heidi Barnhill

Graphic design
Sherry Pribbenow

An Attainment Company publication

Printed in the United States of America

ISBN: 1-944315-35-7

Attainment Company, Inc.

P.O. Box 930160
Verona, Wisconsin 53593-0160 USA
1-800-327-4269
www.AttainmentCompany.com

Contents

CHAPTER 1

Study Tools

A key to history

Let's Explore World History

A map made in 1689 in Europe.

World history is a big subject. It covers everything people did in the past. It's about what people made, where they lived, and who they knew. We use tools to help understand history. A map shows where a place is. A timeline puts events in order. An image records a moment in time. A graph and table organize data. These tools are used a lot in this book.

VOCABULARY

map		shows features of an area of land or sea
timeline	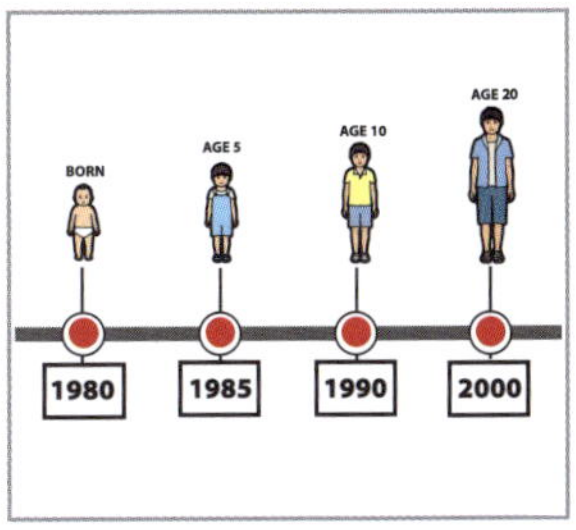	shows when events happen and the order they occur
image		a picture of people or objects
graph	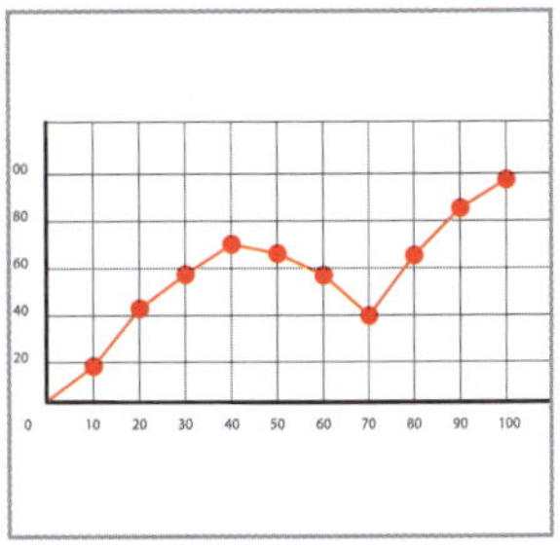	organizes data into a picture
table	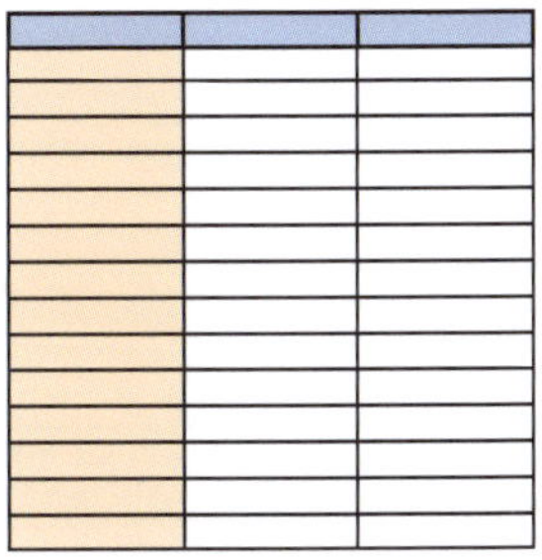	organizes data into rows or columns

Map

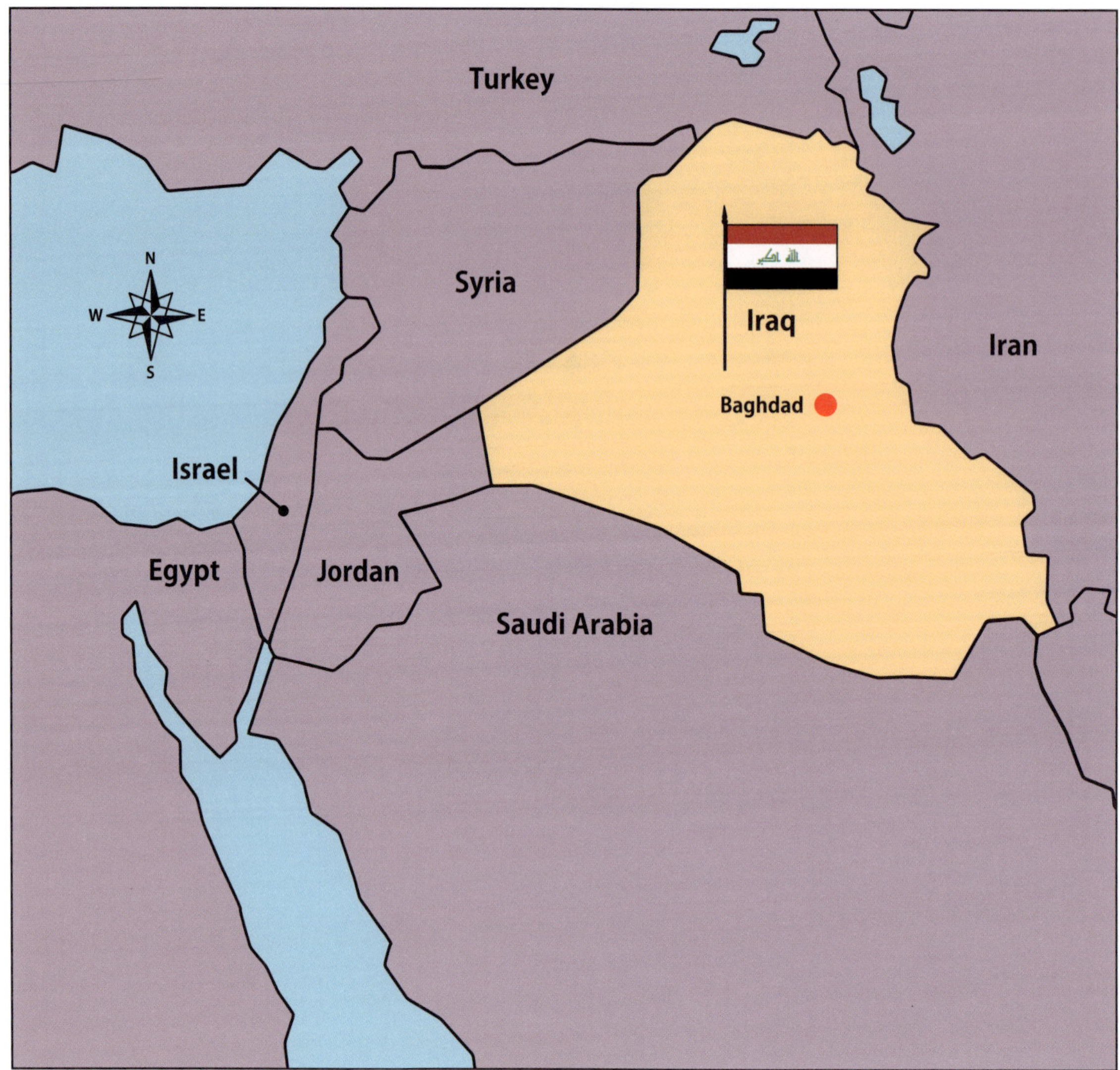

A **map** is a drawing of an area of land or water. A map can show a large area, like the world. Or it can picture one small town. This map shows countries in part of the whole world called the Middle East. The compass rose is in the blue area. It shows direction. Can you point to two countries that border Iraq?

Timeline

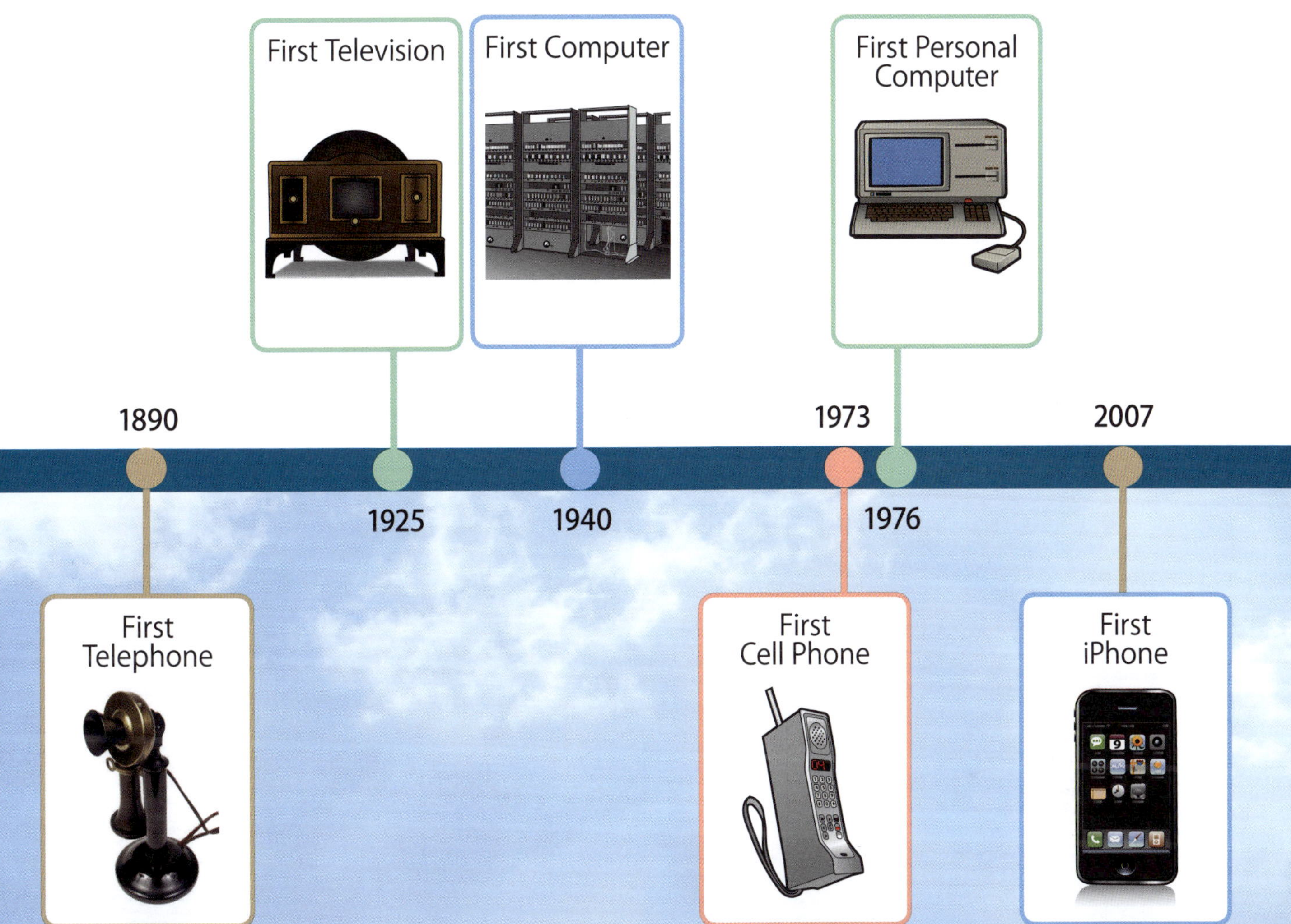

A **timeline** shows when events happened and keeps them in order. It also helps us judge how much time there was between events. Timelines can cover long or short periods of time. This timeline shows when things you use every day were first made. What event happened first? What two events occurred within three years of each other?

Image

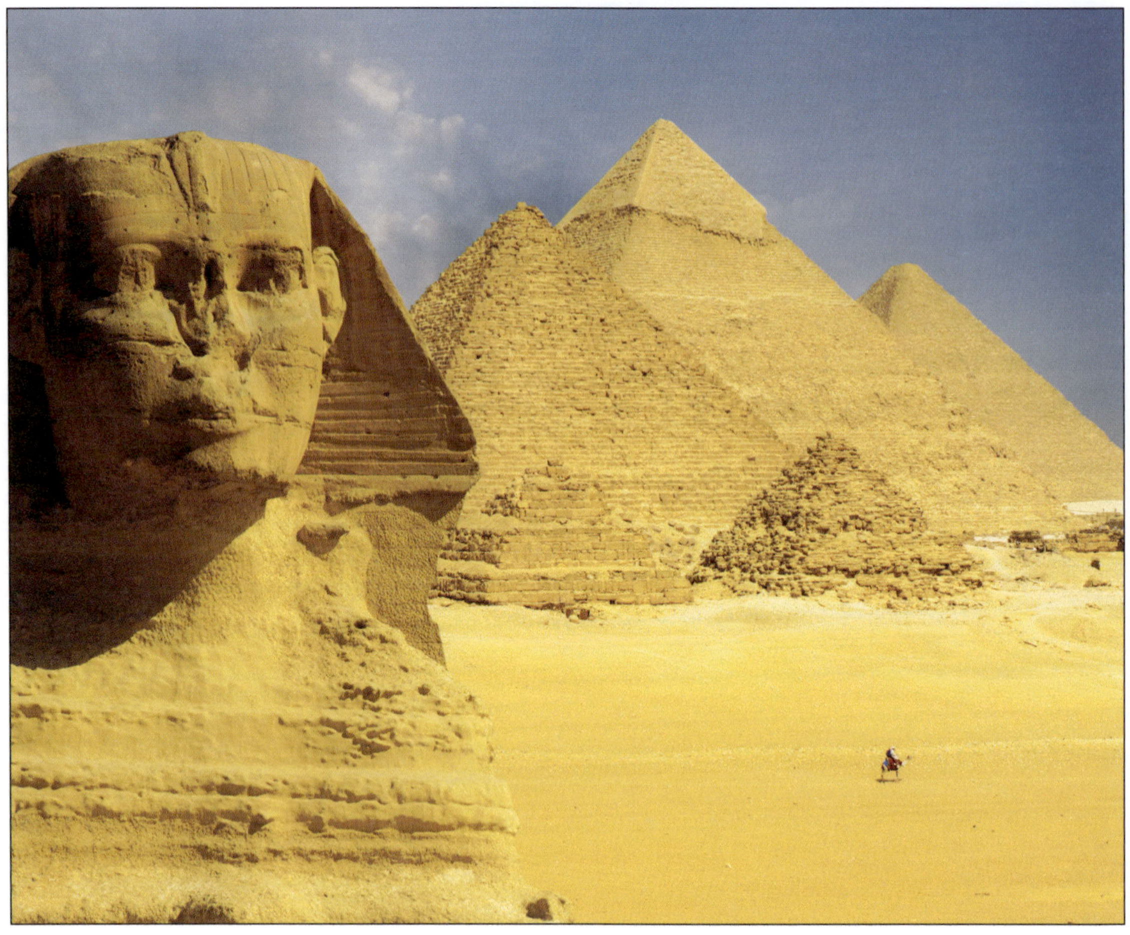

An **image** can be a painting, photo, sculpture, or video. A painting can give us clues to how people lived in the past. An old sculpture can tell us about ancient leaders. A photo lets us examine something we may never see in person. What does this photo show? Where do you think it was taken?

Graph

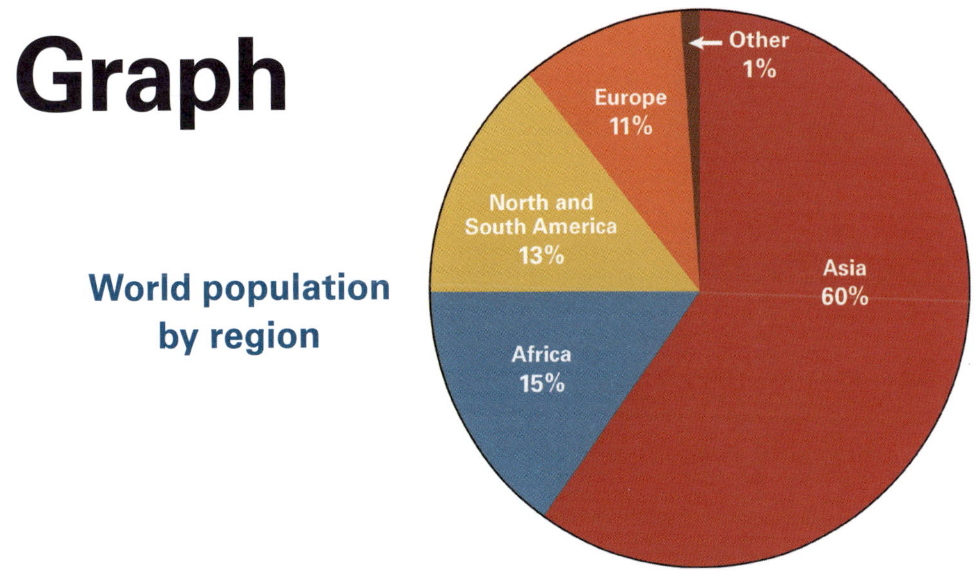

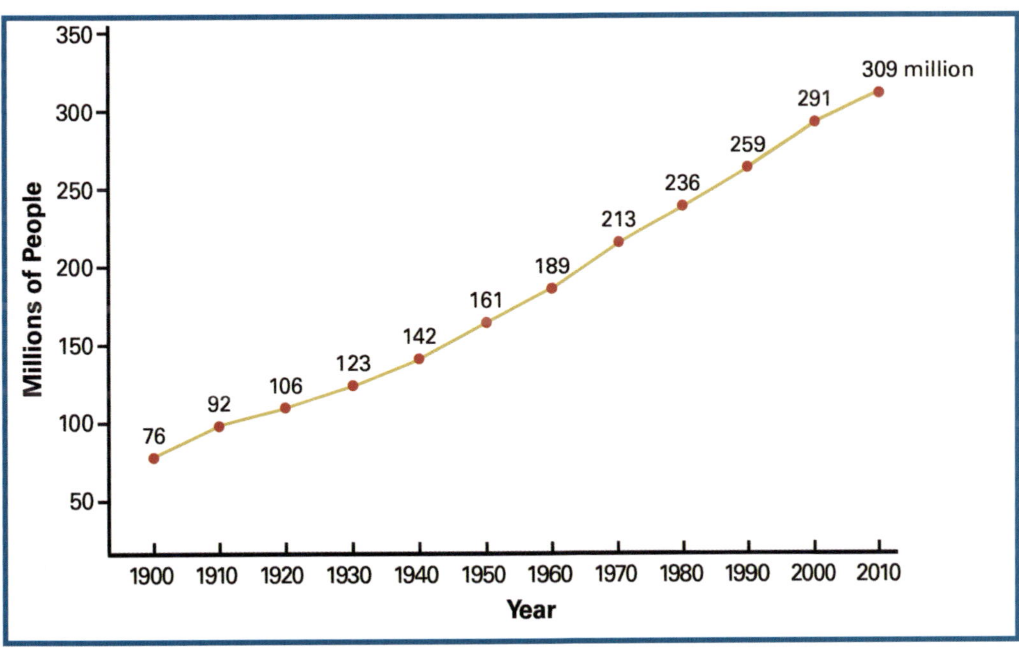

A **graph** is a picture that organizes data. A line graph has points along a line to show changes in amounts. A circle graph divides a round shape into sections. The circle graph above shows world population by region. Asia has the most people. What region is next? The line graph displays population in the United States from 1900. Does the population go up every year on the graph?

Table

CHINESE DYNASTIES		
Dynasty	**Dates**	**Duration in Years**
Xia	2070 BCE-1650 BCE	420
Shang	1650 BCE–1046 BCE	604
Zhou	1046 BCE–256 BCE	790
Qin	221 BCE–207 BCE	14
Han	202 BCE–220 CE	422
Sui	581 CE–618 CE	37
Tang	618 CE–907 CE	289
Song	960 CE–1270 CE	310
Yuan	1270 CE–1368 CE	98
Ming	1368 CE–1644 CE	276
Qing	1644 CE–1912 CE	268

A **table** organizes data into rows and columns. The table is a good tool to show complicated information. The table above lists Chinese dynasties. A dynasty is a line of rulers from the same family or group. The table shows when Chinese dynasties began and how long they ruled. What was the first dynasty? What Chinese dynasty ruled almost 100 years?

Examples of Study Tools in This Book

Map

Table

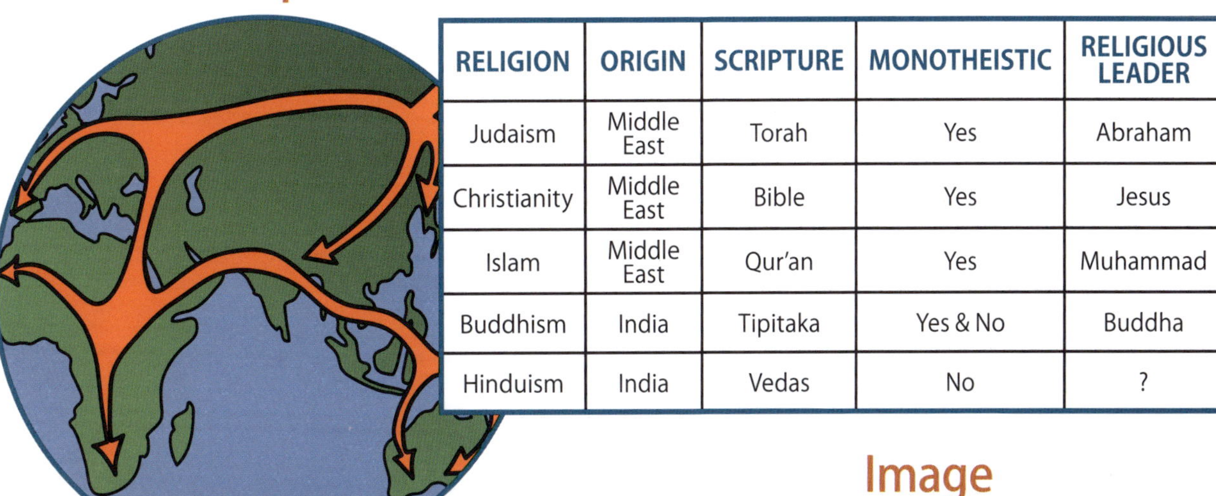

RELIGION	ORIGIN	SCRIPTURE	MONOTHEISTIC	RELIGIOUS LEADER
Judaism	Middle East	Torah	Yes	Abraham
Christianity	Middle East	Bible	Yes	Jesus
Islam	Middle East	Qur'an	Yes	Muhammad
Buddhism	India	Tipitaka	Yes & No	Buddha
Hinduism	India	Vedas	No	?

Graph

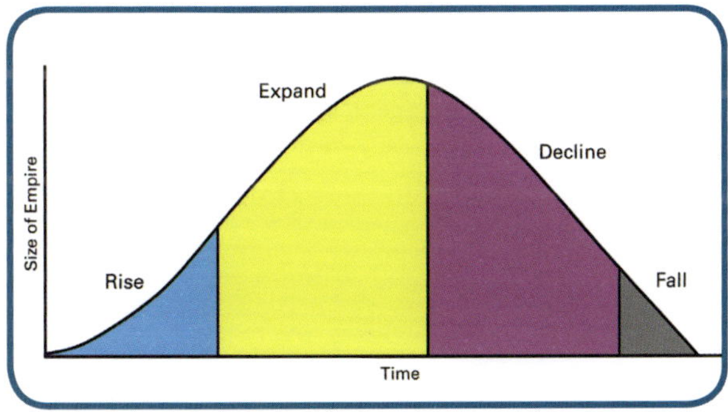

Image

Timeline

Hieroglyphics from Egypt

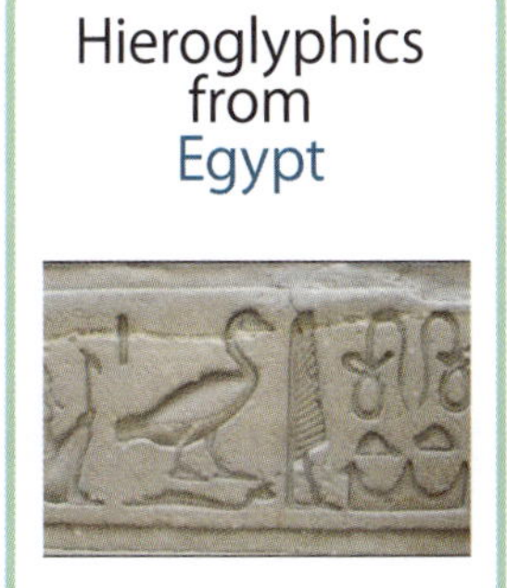

3200 BCE

Chinese Character Writing

1600 BCE

Confucius from China

500 BCE

Rosetta Stone from Egypt

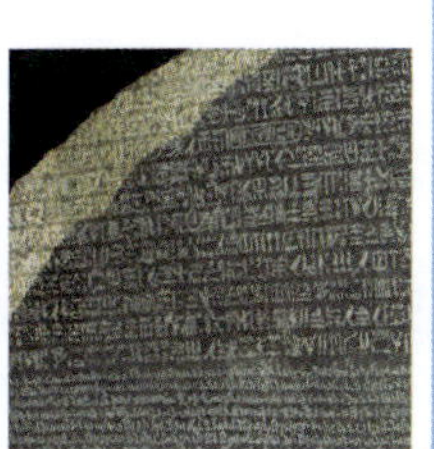

197 BCE

QUIZ

Circle the correct answer.

1. A ________ shows when events happen.

graph | timeline | image

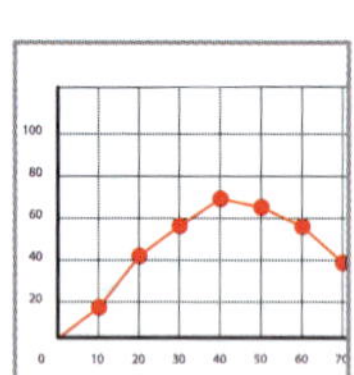

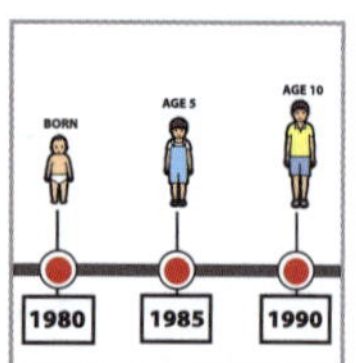

2. A ________ shows features of land or sea.

timeline | table | map

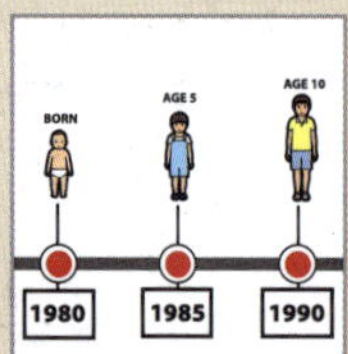

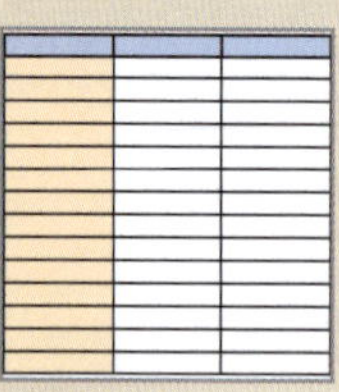

3. An ________ is a picture of people or objects.

image | graph | table

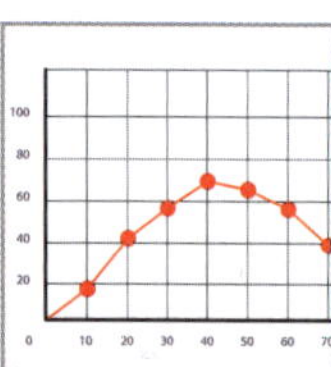

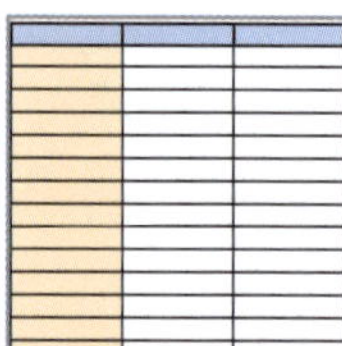

4. A ________ organizes data into rows and columns.

table | map | timeline

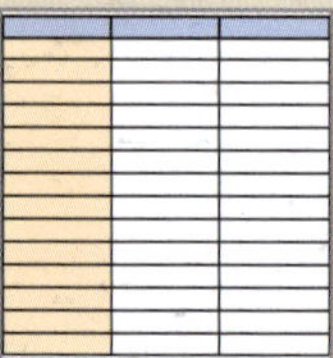

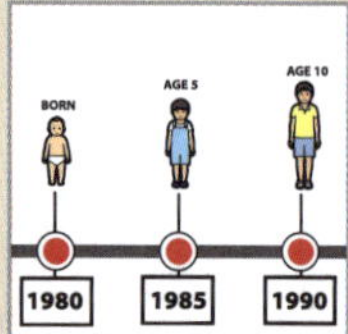

CHAPTER 2

Geography

A key to history

Human geography studies where and how people live.

Physical geography studies the natural features of Earth.

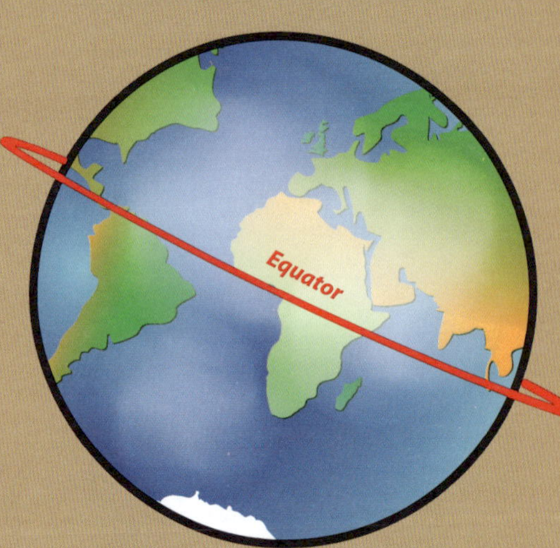

The equator is an imaginary line around the middle of the earth.

Geography changes over time.

Know the Continents

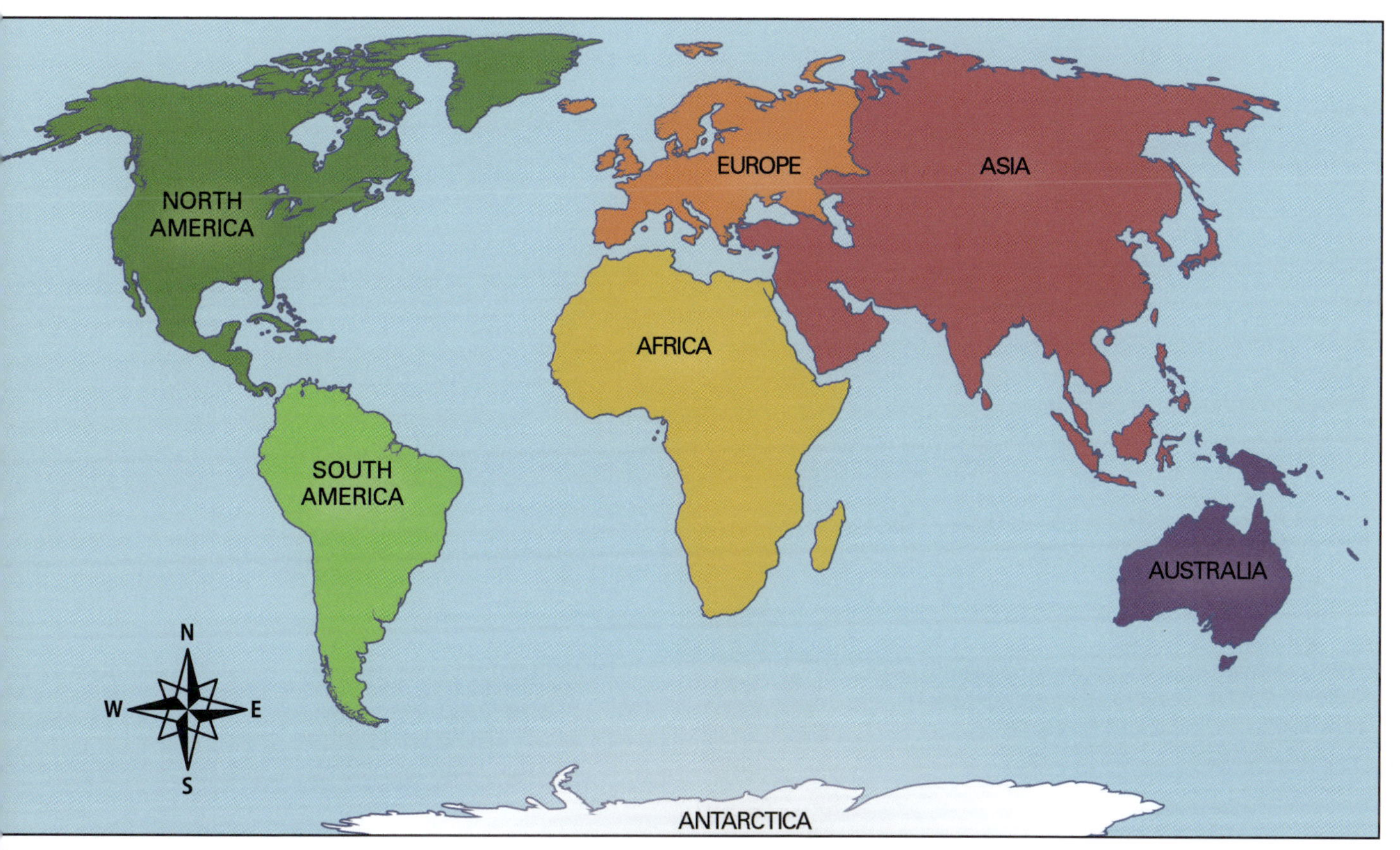

Locate these seven **continents** on the map:

Africa

Antarctica

Asia

Australia

Europe

North America

South America

VOCABULARY

continent		one of seven large land masses on Earth
ocean		a vast body of salt water
culture		a group of people sharing similar beliefs and behavior
equator		an imaginary line that forms a circ around the middle of the earth

An imaginary line on maps around the middle of the earth

___ ___ ___ ___ ___ ___ ___

VOCABULARY

climate	the weather conditions of an area
political map	a map that shows countries and their borders
population	all the people who live in an area
atmosphere	the air made of gases that surrounds the earth

The number of people who live in an area

__ __ __ __ __ __ __ __ __ __

Physical Geography

Physical geography studies the features of both land and water. **Oceans** cover most of the earth's surface. Oceans contain salt water, while lakes and rivers are made of fresh water. Land has many natural features like mountains and deserts. These features affect how we live. Big cities are often found near shorelines. Farmland is usually away from the coast where soil is good for growing plants.

Human Geography

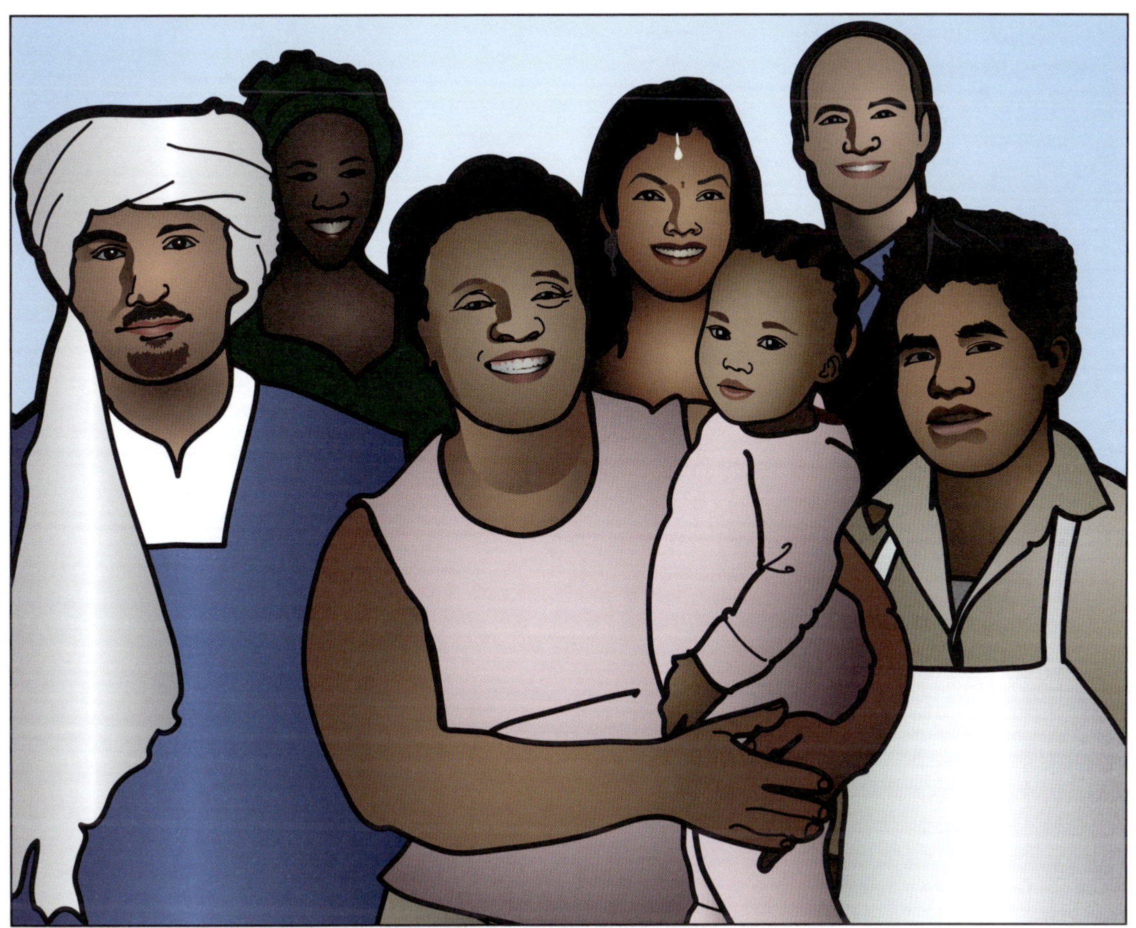

Human geography studies where and how people live. People have moved long distances throughout history. Most places have people living there. Humans have adapted to live in many different environments. People who live together often form a **culture**. People in a culture can share many traits, like the clothes they wear and the language they speak, or the religion they follow and the foods they eat. Different cultures often share the same area.

Geography Changes

A war makes many people move away from their homeland.

The physical geography of Earth is always changing. Continents only move a few inches every year. Over time mountains turned into hills. But human geography changes more quickly. People often move from one place to another. New countries and cities arise. Both kinds of changes, slow and fast, define what Earth is about.

Pangea was a supercontinent. It existed a long time ago. It contained all the land on Earth. The seven continents we know broke apart from Pangea. They drifted away very slowly. The continents continue to move today.

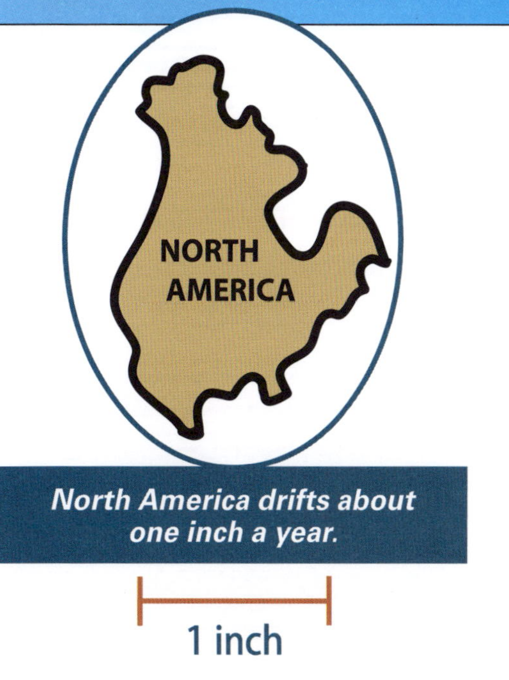

North America drifts about one inch a year.

Grid System

Globes and maps have lines that are not real. Geographers draw these lines to help us find places and to make traveling easier.

A latitude is a line that goes east to west, around the earth. The **equator** is a latitude that divides the earth in half. A longitude is a line that goes north to south, top to bottom. Longitude lines meet at the north and south poles.

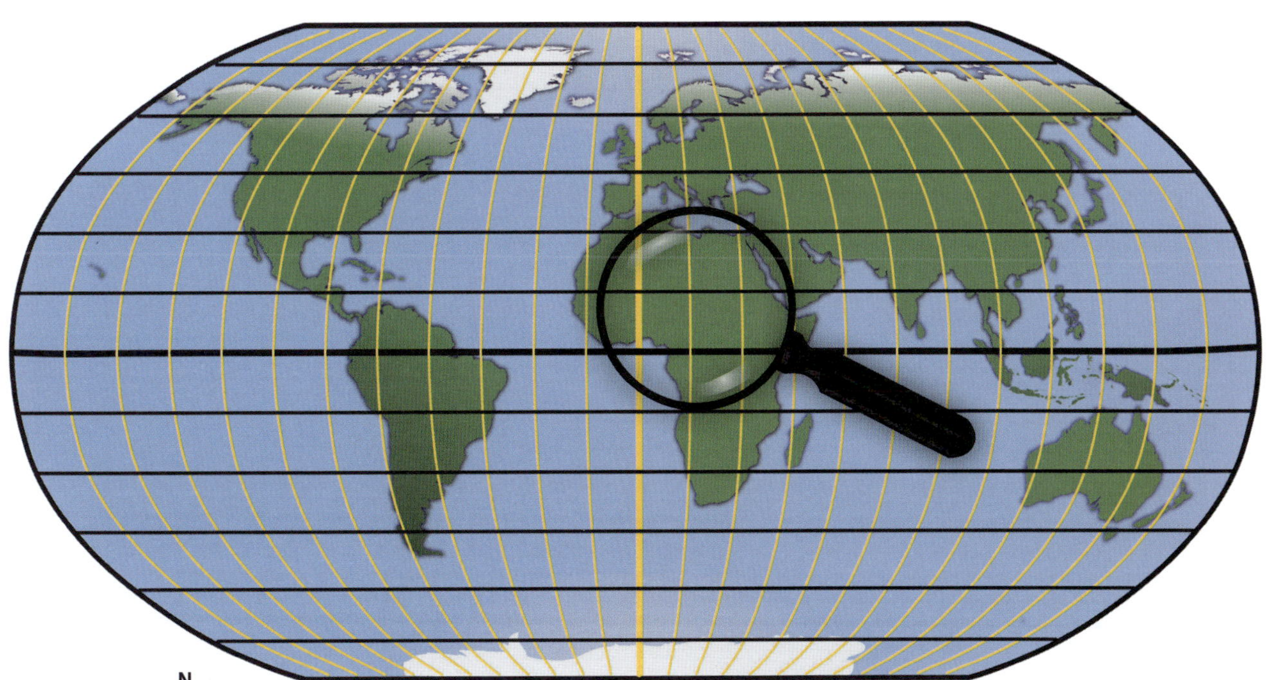

Latitudes are the **black** lines. They go east and west.

Longitudes are the **yellow** lines. They go north and south.

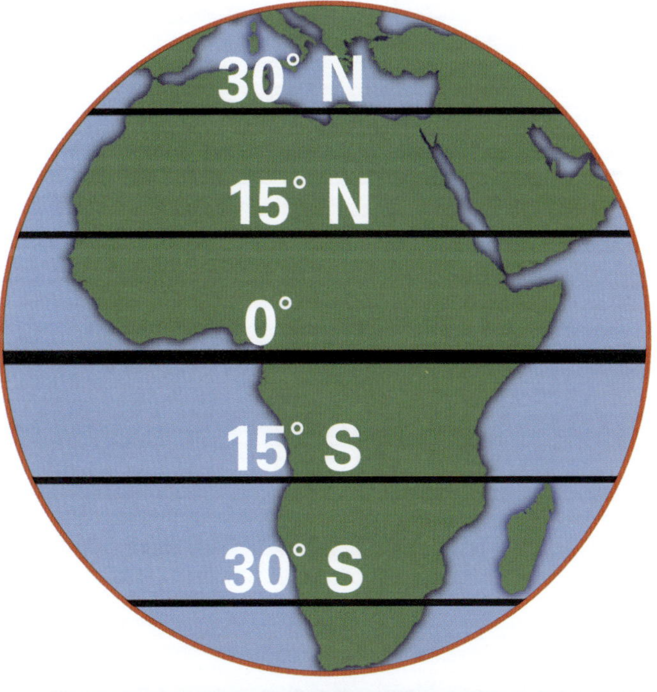

Longitudes and latitudes are measured in degrees, like temperature. The degree symbol is °.

Climate

The **climate** is the usual weather pattern of an area. Earth has many climates. The land, oceans, and heat from the sun work together to make climates. Hot and wet climates are found around the equator. The middle part of Earth gets more direct sunlight. Cold climates are far north and south because these areas get less heat from the sun.

Landforms

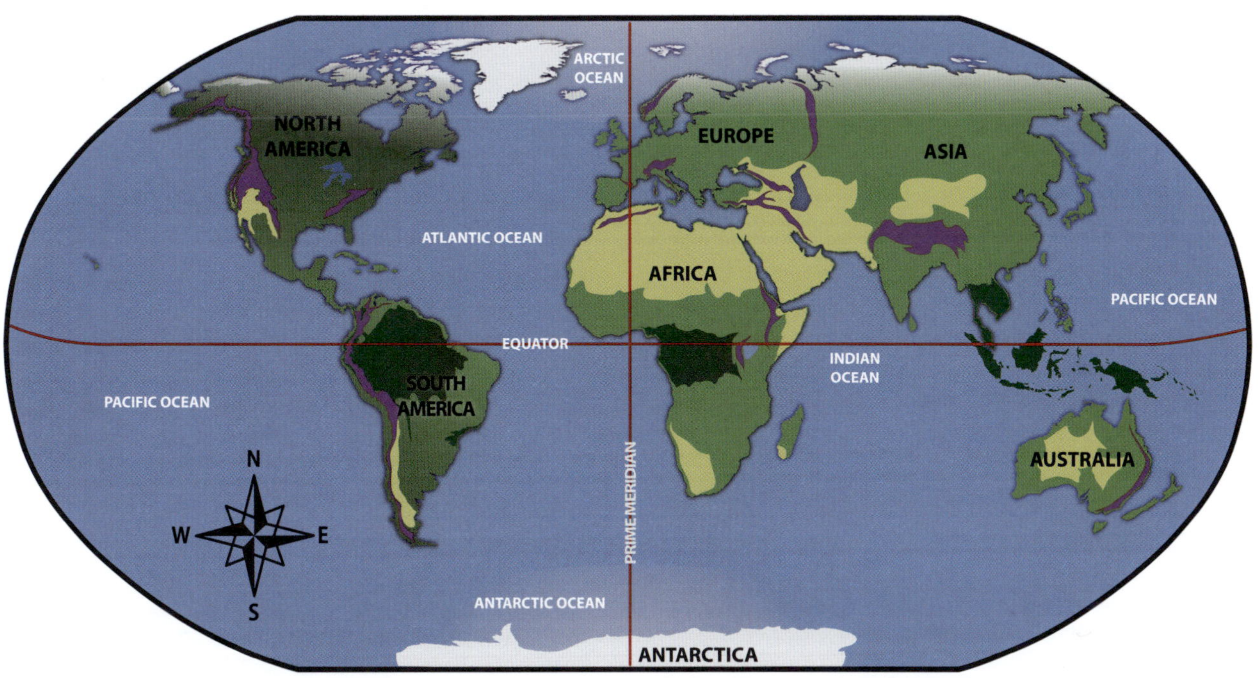

Key

- Mountains
- Water
- Tropical Forest
- Snow and Ice
- Desert

Landforms and climate are related to each other.

Deserts are dry. Tropical forests are hot and wet. Frozen areas are cold and dry. Mountains are colder than the surrounding lowlands. Why? Because the higher up you go, the colder it gets.

Political Map

Map of Europe, 1913

Current map of Europe

A **country** is an area with its own government and clear borders. Landforms like shorelines and mountains often form the borders. Countries have citizens who share a culture and a language. Countries come and go. Names and borders can change because of war or other events. Sometimes a territory breaks away to form its own country.

This political map shows countries or nations. See if you can locate these countries:

Italy	Iran
Greece	Syria
Egypt	Cyprus
Saudi Arabia	Israel
Iraq	Jordan

Where People Live

1		China	1,385,566,537
2		India	1,252,139,596
3		United States	320,050,716
4		Indonesia	249,865,631
5		Brazil	200,361,925
6		Pakistan	182,142,594

Population estimates from the United Nations, 2015.

More people live on Earth than ever before. The world's population is over 7 billion. A large **population** requires a lot of resources. It's hard for some countries to provide enough food and medicine for everyone. The population of countries varies because they can be of any size. In some countries people live closer together than in other countries.

Care of Earth

Geography studies show how the environment influences people. The environment includes the food we grow, the water we drink, and the **atmosphere** we breathe. People influence the environment. Pollution is a bad influence. Keeping the environment healthy is our responsibility. Using less and recycling are ways you can help the environment.

Climate Change

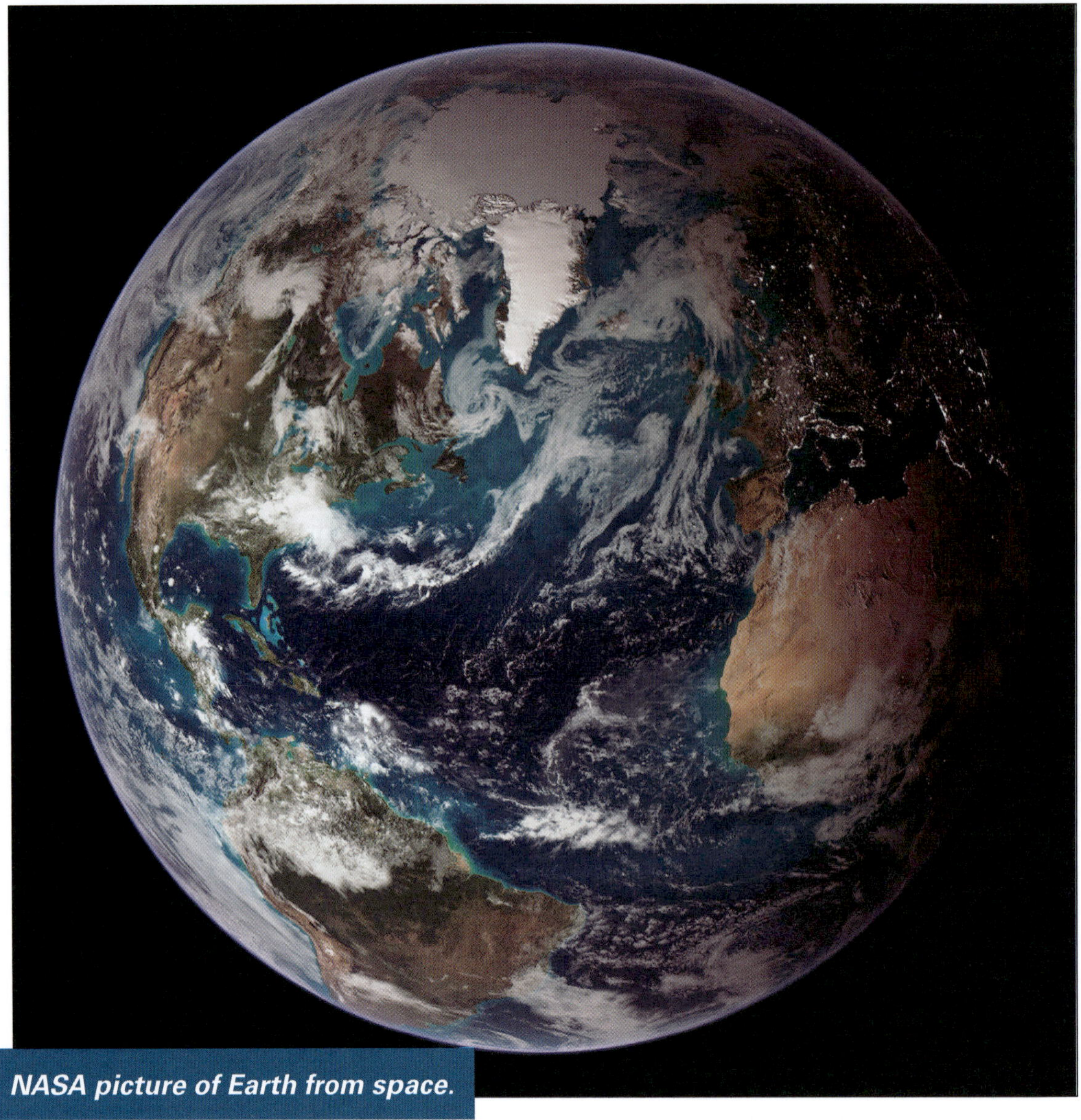

NASA picture of Earth from space.

Our climate may be changing. Most scientists say we are putting too much carbon into the atmosphere. A lot of carbon comes from burning fossil fuels, like gasoline. Fossil fuels were formed a long time ago from living plants and animals. Over time, they turned into oil and coal. We all share the same atmosphere. That's why climate change is a worldwide concern. Geography affects people, and people affect geography.

QUIZ

Circle the correct answer.

1. ________ studies where and how people live.

Human geography | Atmosphere | Ocean

2. ________ studies the natural features of Earth.

Culture | Physical geography | Climate

3. An imaginary line around the middle of the earth is the ________.

climate | continent | equator

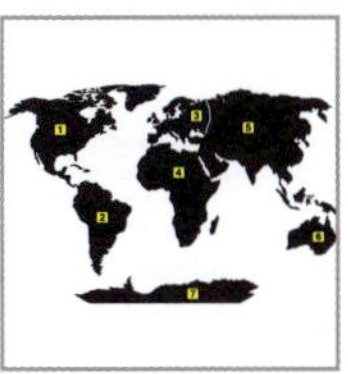
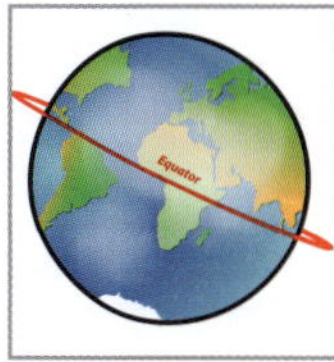

4. Both physical and human ________ change over time.

geography | nomads | Ice Age

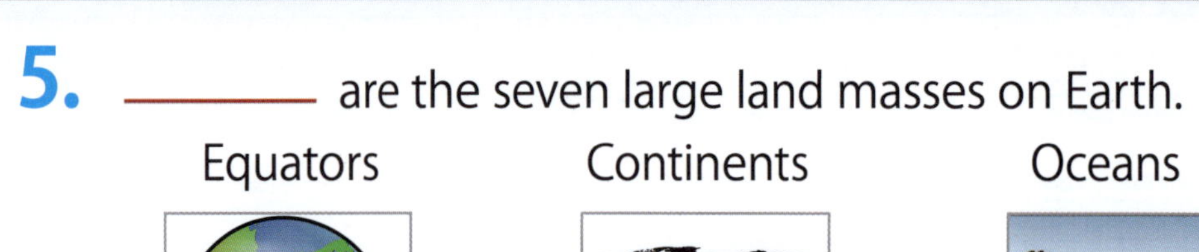

5. ________ are the seven large land masses on Earth.

Equators — Continents — Oceans

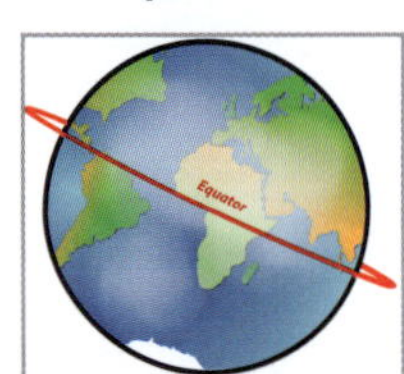

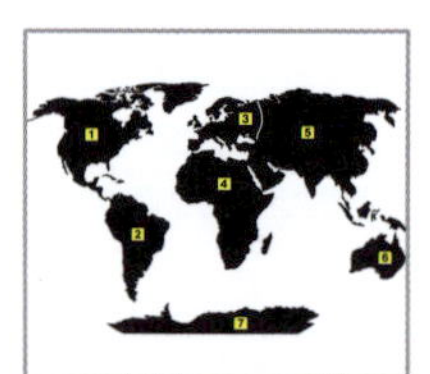

6. The weather conditions of an area are the ________ .

culture — atmosphere — climate

7. A map that shows countries and their borders is a ________ .

landform map — political map — space map

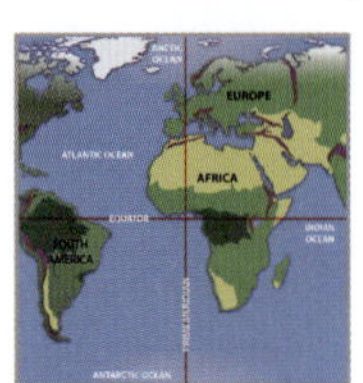

Write About It

CHAPTER
3

Early Humans

An era of history
50,000 BCE to 10,000 BCE

Early humans survived by hunting and gathering their food.

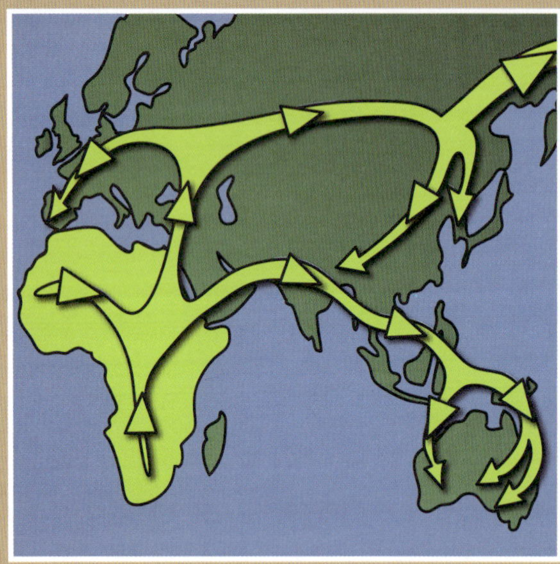

Early humans left Africa and moved throughout the world.

Early humans made stone tools to make their lives easier.

Early humans created beautiful cave paintings to express themselves.

Early Humans Timeline

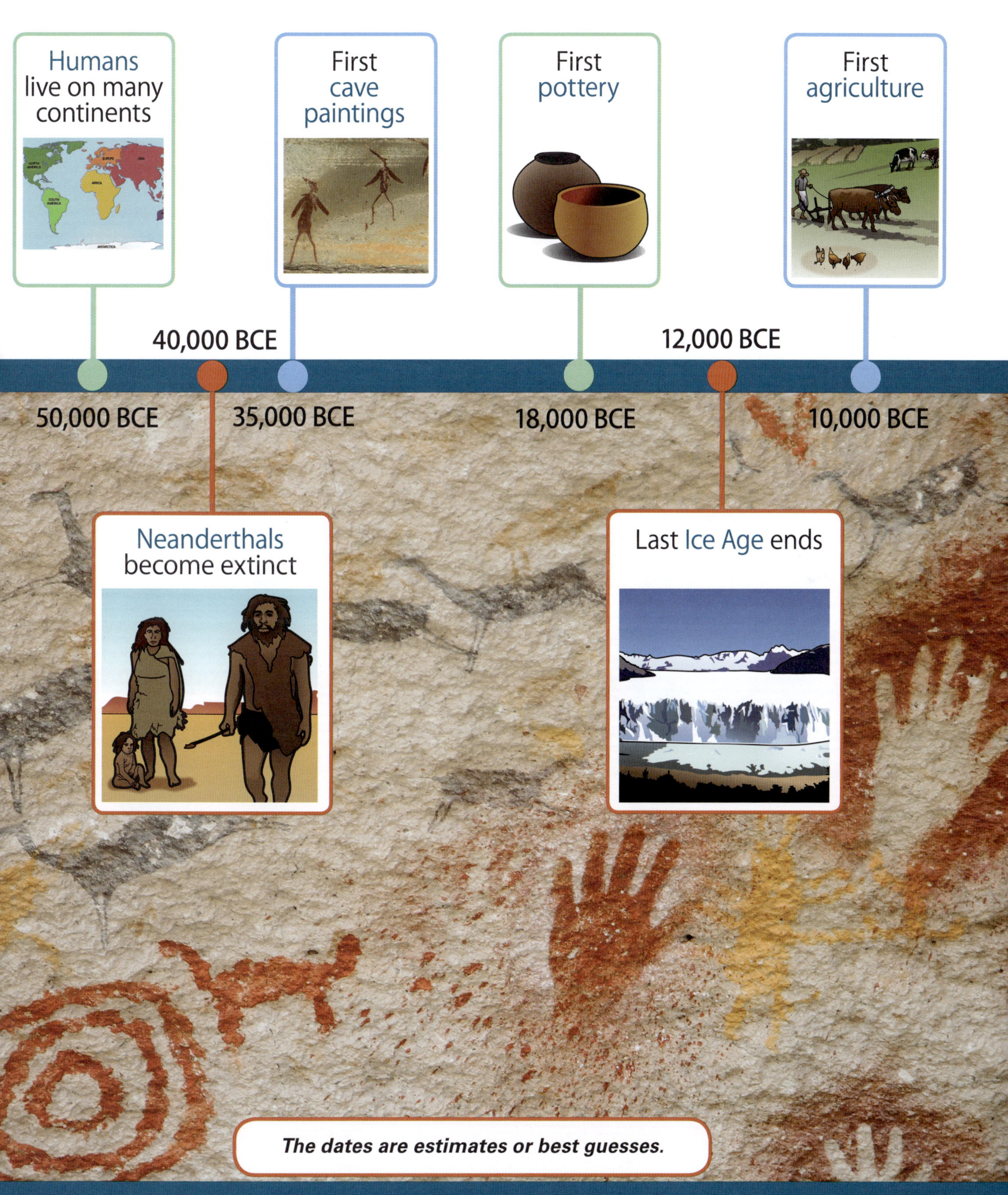

The dates are estimates or best guesses.

VOCABULARY

era	any period of time
nomads	people who often move from place to place
Ice Age	a very long time with an unusually cold climate
BCE	an abbreviation for Before the Common Era

People who regularly move around

___ ___ ___ ___ ___ ___

VOCABULARY

Neanderthal	a human species that went extinct
extinct	died out
DNA	genetic code found in cells
archaeologist	a person who studies old cultures and artifacts

Someone who studies ancient things

__ __ __ __ __ __ __ __ __ __ __ __ __

Early Humans

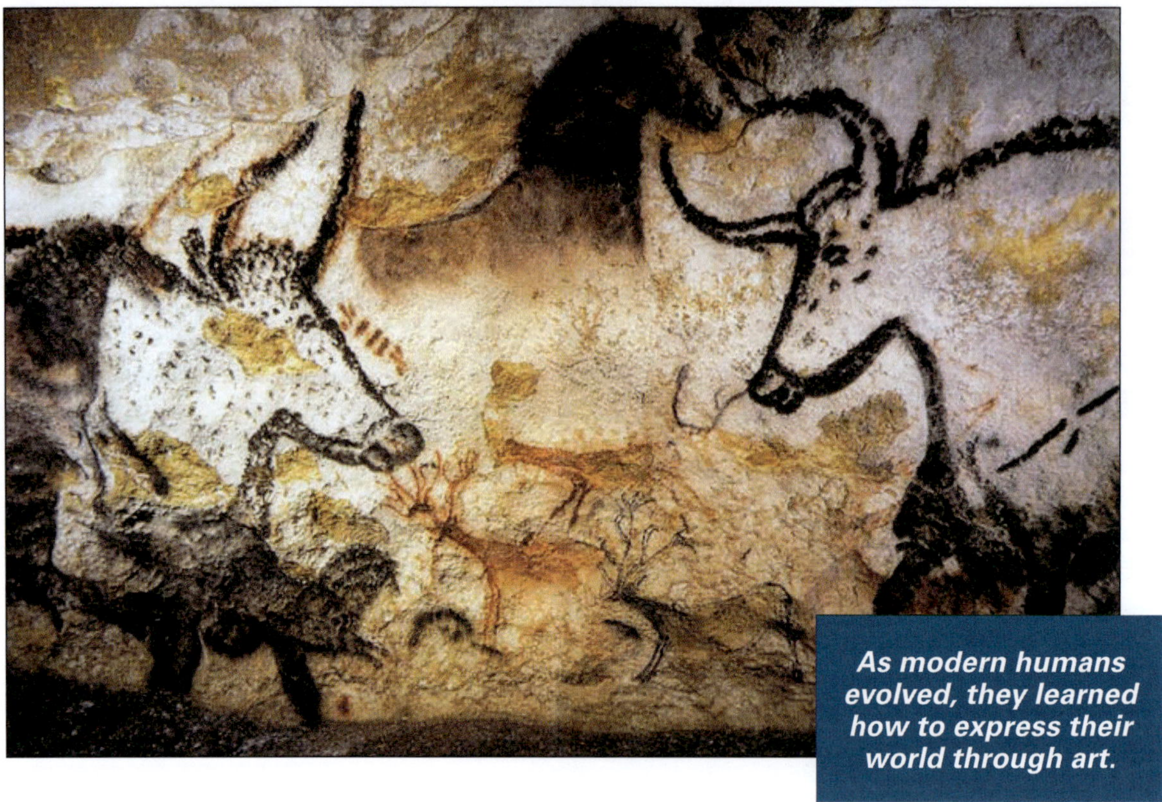

As modern humans evolved, they learned how to express their world through art.

This chapter covers the Upper Paleolithic **Era**. That was from 50,000 BCE to 10,000 BCE. People came out of Africa in family groups. They spread throughout the world. They learned to make stone tools to make their lives easier. Rock drawings are found from this era. For the first time people felt the need to express themselves through art.

Hunting is a common theme in cave paintings.

Early humans were **nomads**. They hunted and gathered their food. They often hunted large mammals, so they needed to plan and work together. The climate was cold then. It was called an **Ice Age**, but it slowly got warmer near the end of the era. This climate change hurt large mammals. Many of them, like the mammoth, died out.

Many mammals became extinct when the last Ice Age ended.

Planting Seeds

Planting seeds changed human history.

Early humans had a hard life. They were always on the move. They needed to find or hunt their food, and the animals they hunted were dangerous. It was an ice age so the winters were cold. But the climate slowly got warmer. The Ice Age ended. Then someone, somewhere in the Middle East, planted some seeds from a plant they ate. People started to grow their own food. That simple event changed history forever.

Out of Africa

Archaeologists believe our ancestors came from Africa. This is called the "Out of Africa" theory. People left Africa in small family groups, beginning as early as 150,000 **BCE**. First they moved into the Middle East. They kept moving until they populated all livable parts of the world. During the Ice Age, people could sometimes walk from continent to continent over land bridges.

Neanderthals

During this era there were other human species living besides us. The **Neanderthals** lived in Asia and Europe. They became **extinct** about 40,000 BCE. For a while our ancestors lived near the Neanderthals. Scientists believe some of them interbred with Neanderthals. The remains of Denisovans were discovered recently. They were another human species who lived in western Asia. They went extinct too.

DNA

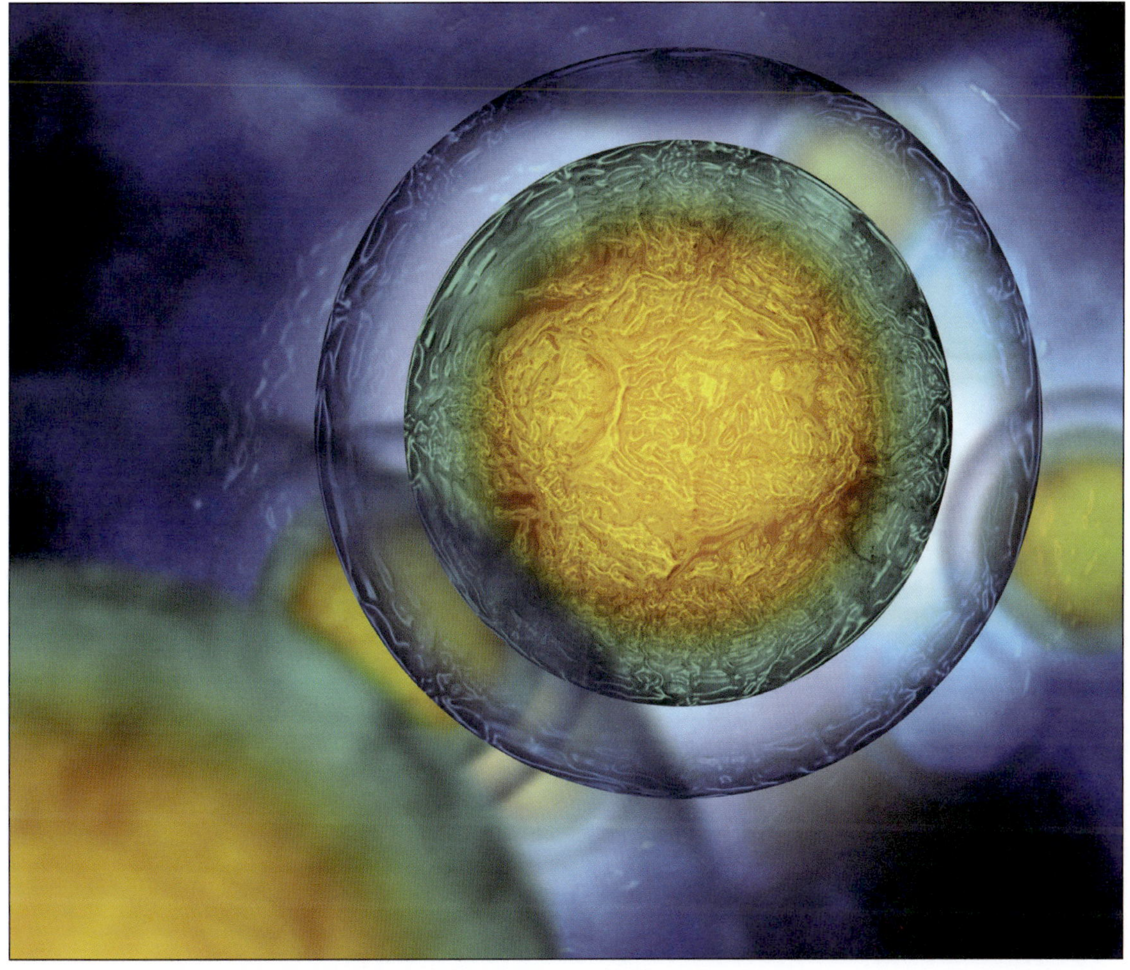

DNA is found in all living things. It gives the cells instructions for life. Scientists can sometimes read the DNA left in things that died a long time ago. By comparing DNA, they found that we are related to the extinct Neanderthals. DNA can show historians a lot, like when a culture lived, where they came from, and even what they ate.

Cave Paintings

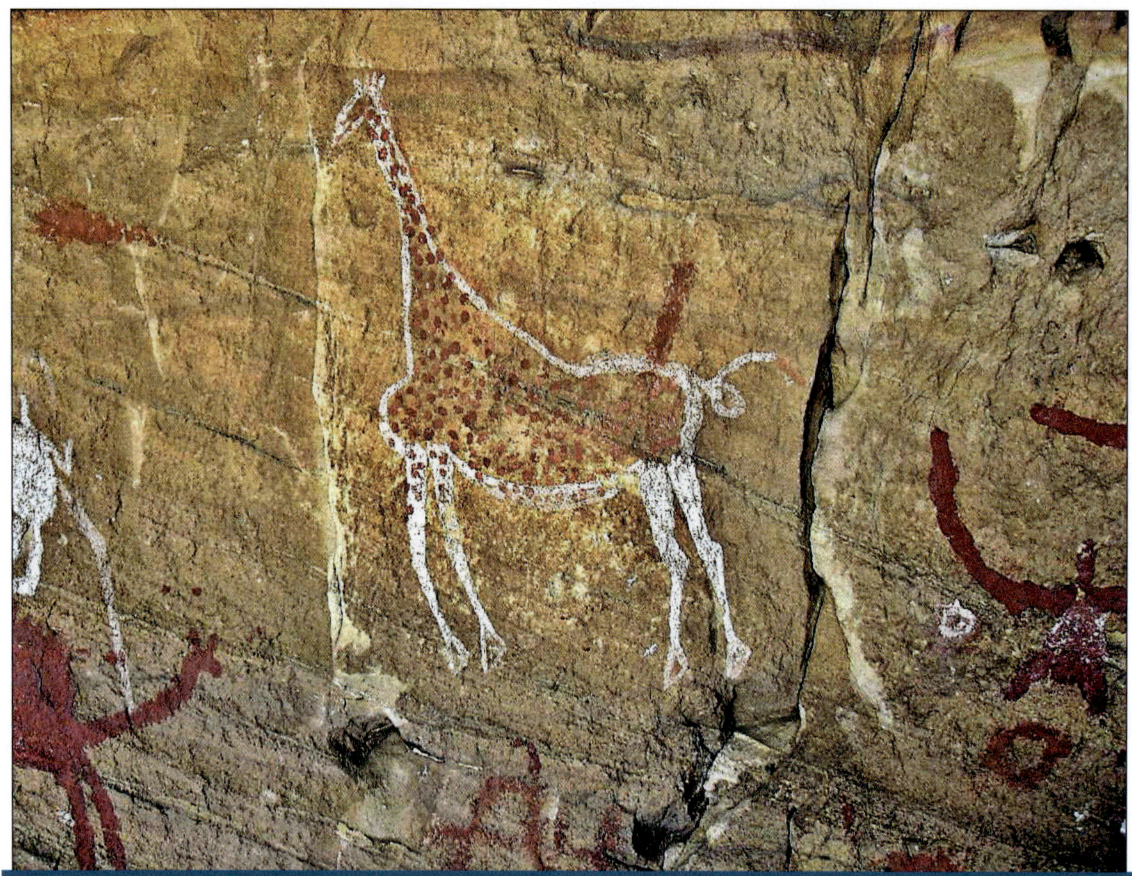

A reproduction of an ancient rock painting from Libya, Africa.

Cave paintings go back 40,000 years and are found all over the world. They are the earliest art forms ever found. Some were pictures of animals they hunted and animals they may have been afraid of. Paintings may also have been for religious rituals or to assure a successful hunt. Experts think their art was almost as skilled as modern painters.

Venus Figurines

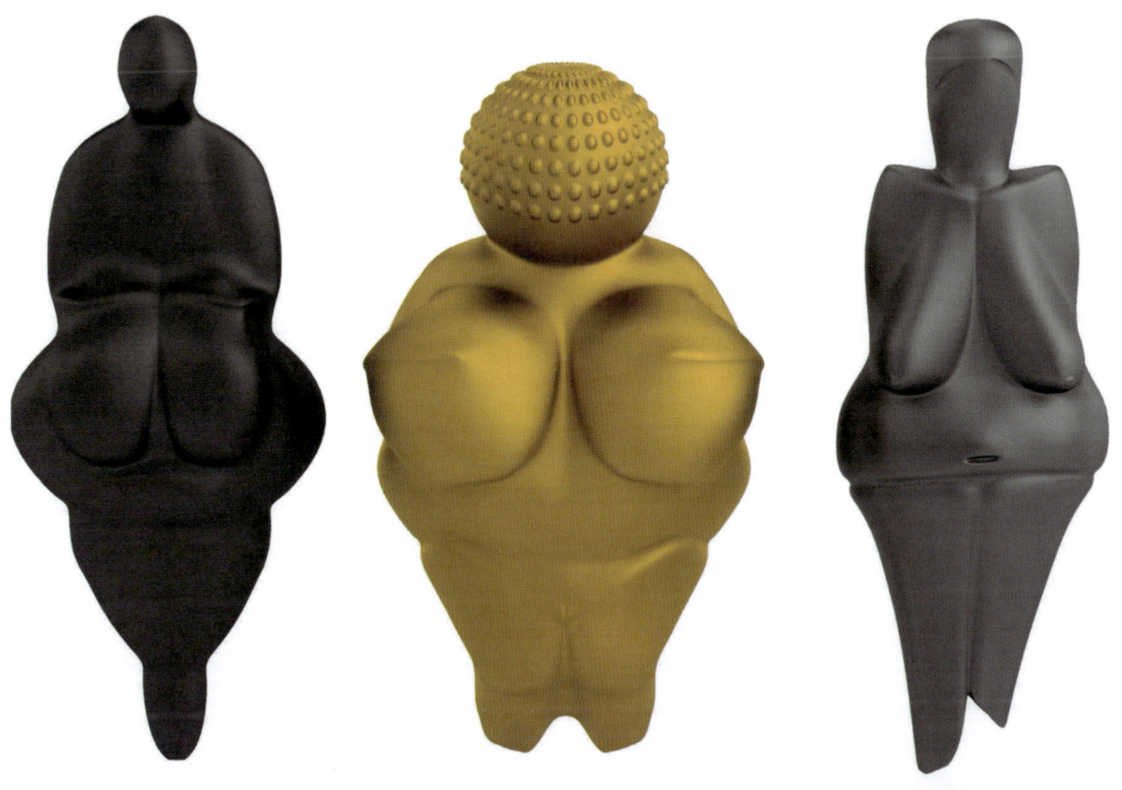

A work of sculpted art known as Venus Figurines.

A figurine is a small sculpture of a person. Figurines of women have been found in Europe and Asia that look very similar to each other. Some were made as early as 30,000 BCE. The sculptures show women with big bodies. Some are pregnant. Archaeologists are unsure if they are fertility goddesses or a form of magic. They are beautiful art and may be the beginnings of religion.

Tools

The development of tools by early humans was a big step. Spears and bows made them better hunters. Shovels made it easier to dig up food. Needles helped them fashion clothes from animal hides. The tools were made from materials they found, like stone or wood. Tools helped early humans survive.

Pottery

Pottery found in China was made around 20,000 BCE. Pottery comes from forming clay into a shape. It's then heated over fire to remove the moisture. That makes it hard. Pottery is an important invention. At first pottery was used to store and transport the food people foraged. When agriculture was invented, pottery stored the food they grew. That helped early humans save food for hard times, like droughts and winters.

Science of Archaeology

Archaeologists study the remains humans leave behind, like ancient buildings or human bones. Sometimes it is early human tools they find. Or it may be art of early humans, like their pottery and cave paintings. They want to know how people lived back then. But they also look at more recent things, like how modern cities have changed over time.

QUIZ

Circle the correct answer.

1. Early humans left ________ to settle the world.

Africa 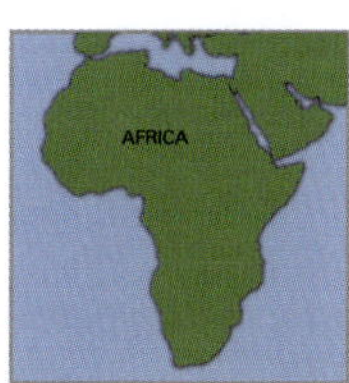

Antarctica 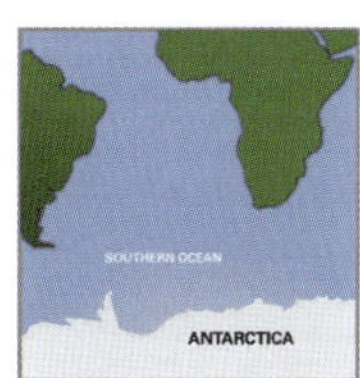

pottery 

2. Early humans survived by ________ their food.

cave painting 

hunting and gathering 

DNA

3. Early humans made stone ________ to make their lives easier.

DNA 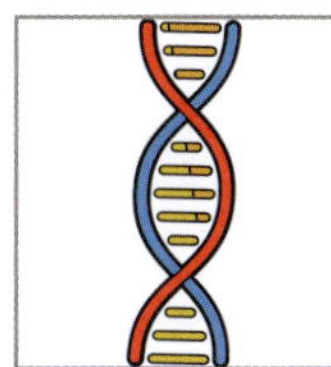

tools 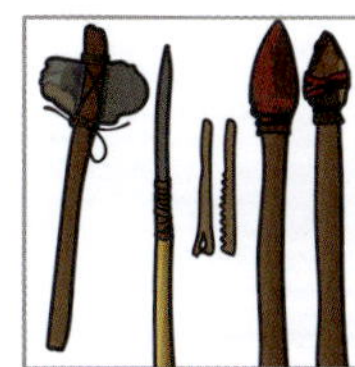

nomads 

4. Early humans created beautiful ________ to express themselves.

BCE 

Ice Age 

cave paintings 

5. An ________ is a very long time with an unusually cold climate.

archaeologists Ice Age nomads

6. ________ often move from place to place.

Nomads An Ice Age DNA

7. The ________ are an extinct human species.

pottery archaeologists Neanderthals

Write About It

CHAPTER
4

Agriculture

A theme of history

The invention of agriculture increased permanent settlements.

Agriculture developed worldwide around the same time.

Agriculture led to population growth.

Agricultural practices have improved throughout history.

Early Farming Timeline

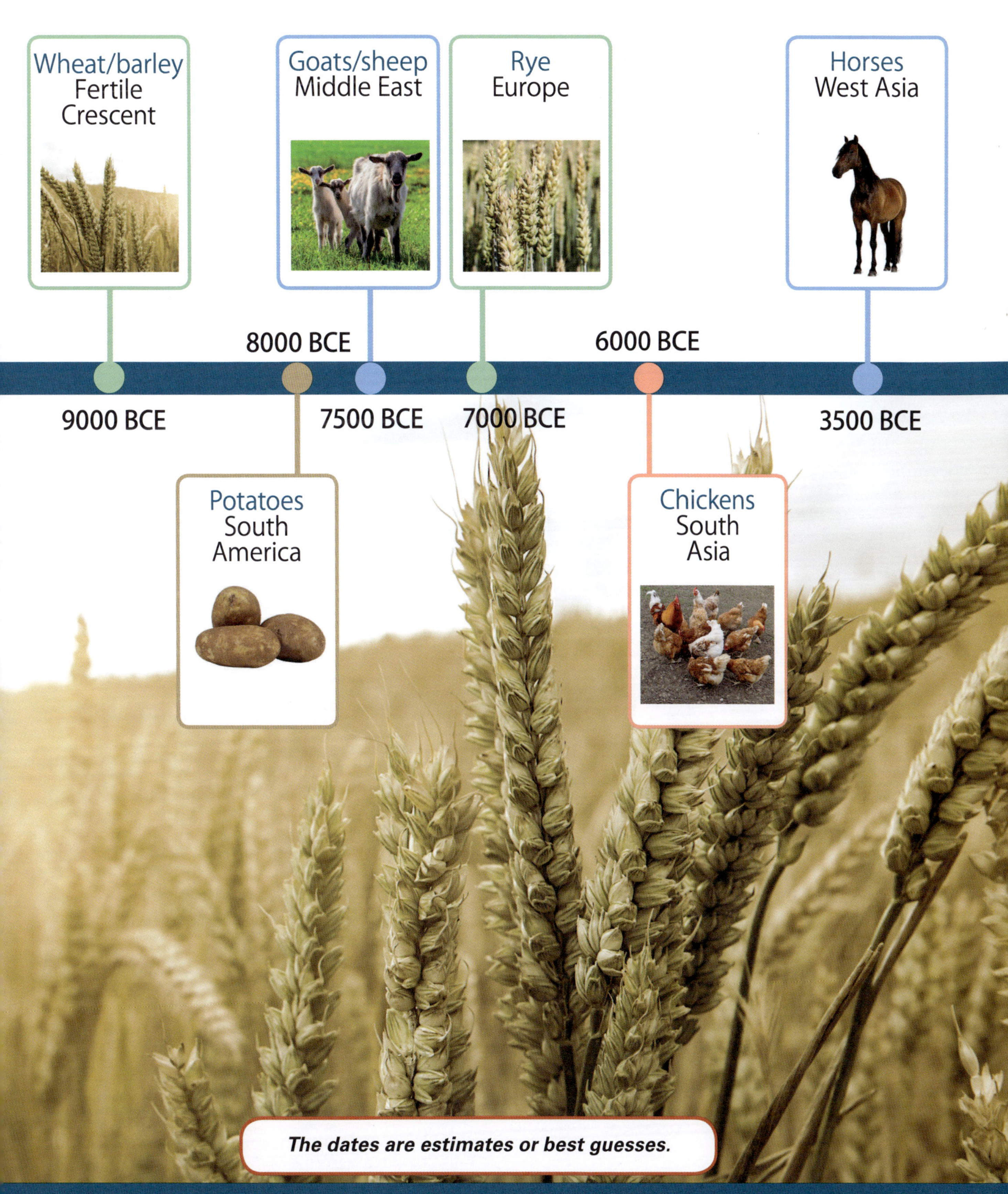

The dates are estimates or best guesses.

VOCABULARY

agriculture		growing plants and raising animals for food
surplus		something left over, like grain after a harvest
domesticate		to tame animals and plants for food or other uses
settlement		a small community of people who live in the same place

A community of people

___ ___ ___ ___ ___ ___ ___ ___ ___ ___

VOCABULARY

cultivate	 prepare and use the land for crops
irrigate	 to supply crops with water to improve the harvest
protein	 a nutrient in food necessary for survival
breed	 to control the offspring of animals

Getting the land ready for planting

___ ___ ___ ___ ___ ___ ___ ___ ___

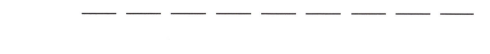

Agriculture

Agriculture changed how people lived. Hunters and gatherers became farmers. People could live in one place and not move around so much. They could store **surplus** food to survive winters and droughts. Surpluses allowed the population to grow. The first cities arose. Farmers could supply enough food so other people could do different jobs. People became builders, soldiers, and teachers.

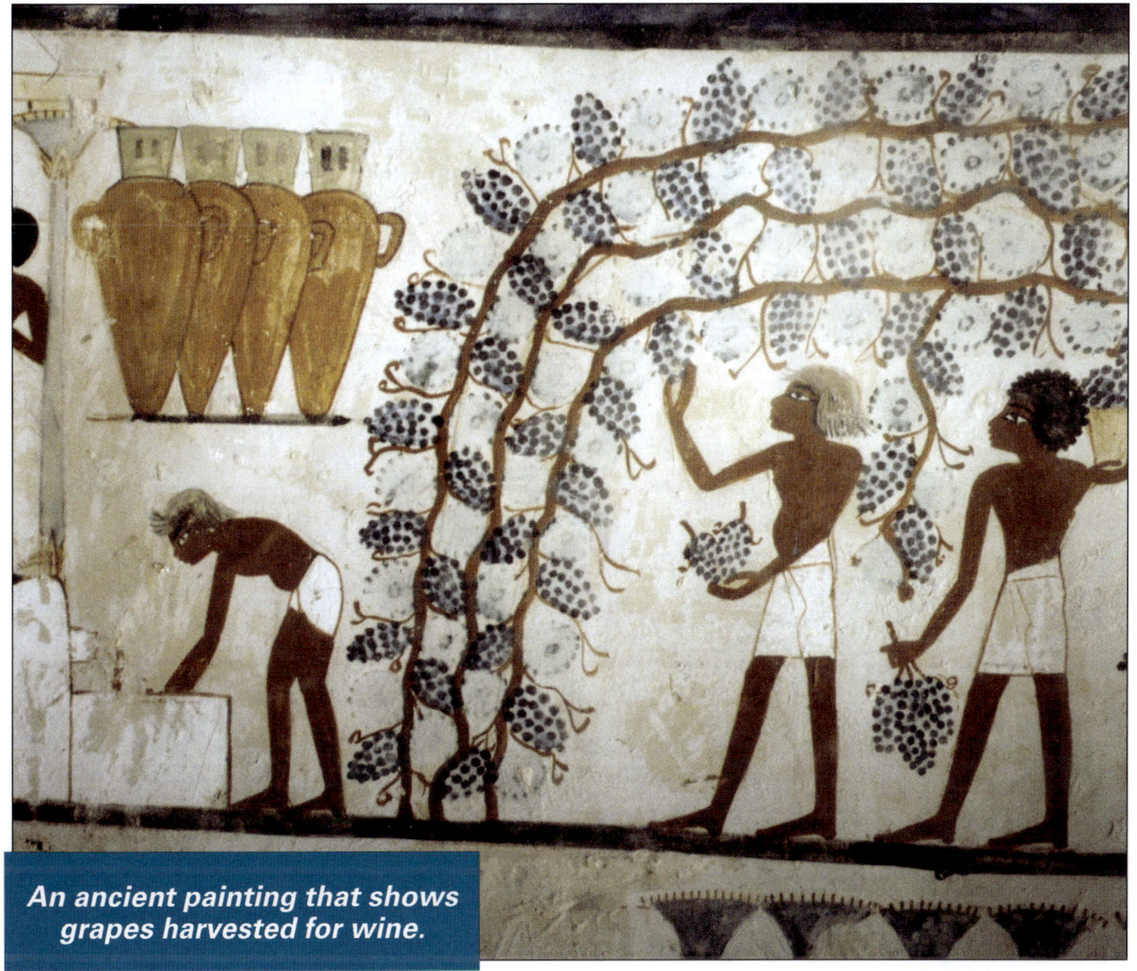

An ancient painting that shows grapes harvested for wine.

People knew how to find edible plants before they knew how to grow them. And they knew what animals were good to hunt. Slowly, over time they learned how to grow their own plants. They learned which animals they could **domesticate** for food. Domesticated animals were also helpful for transportation and doing hard work like plowing. By inventing agriculture people had better lives. They could accomplish more. Agriculture changed human history.

A Worldwide Invention

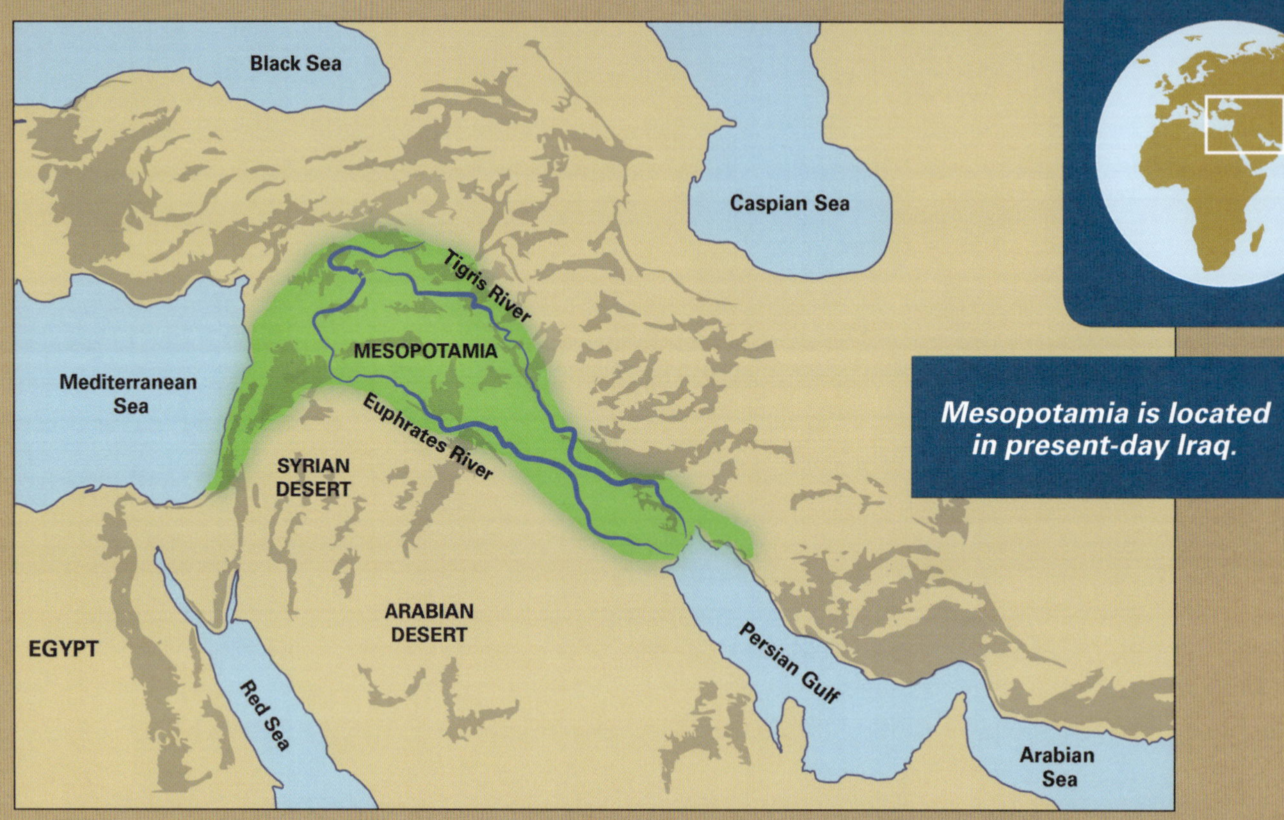

Mesopotamia is located in present-day Iraq.

The first **settlement** using agriculture was in the Middle East. It was called Mesopotamia. This culture **cultivated** grains and domesticated sheep. Their climate and soil were ideal for agriculture. That's why it was called "the Fertile Crescent." Mesopotamia is thought to have the first cities too. Agriculture quickly spread to other places nearby.

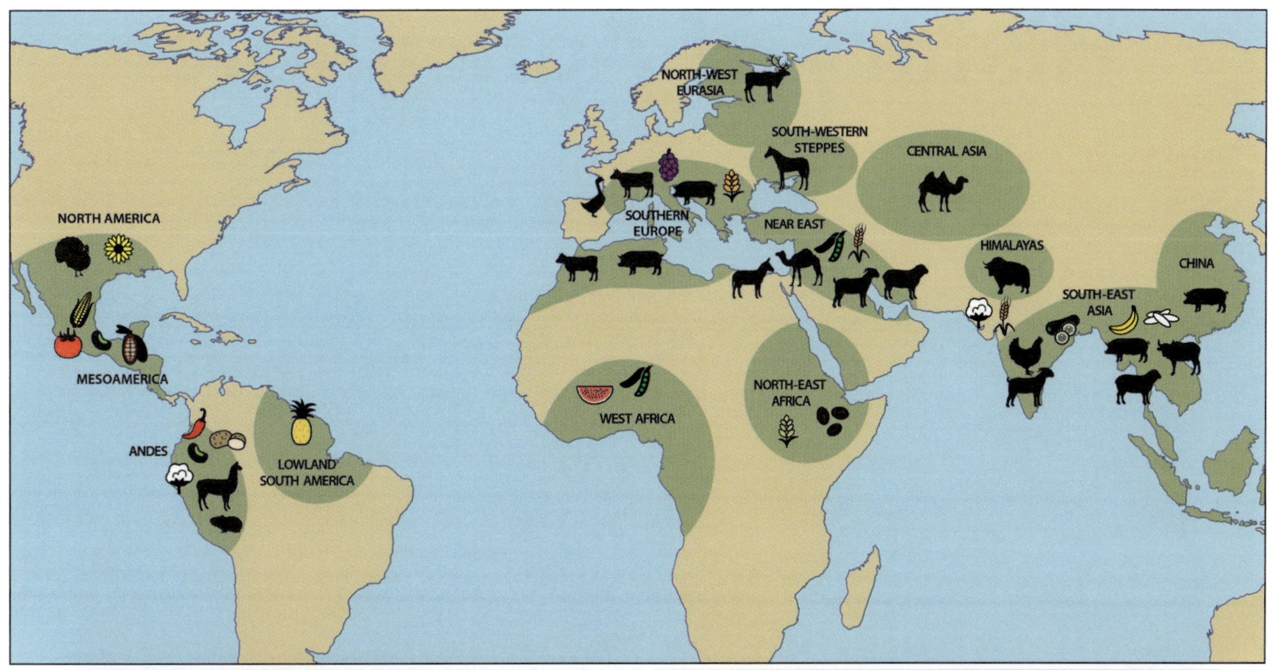

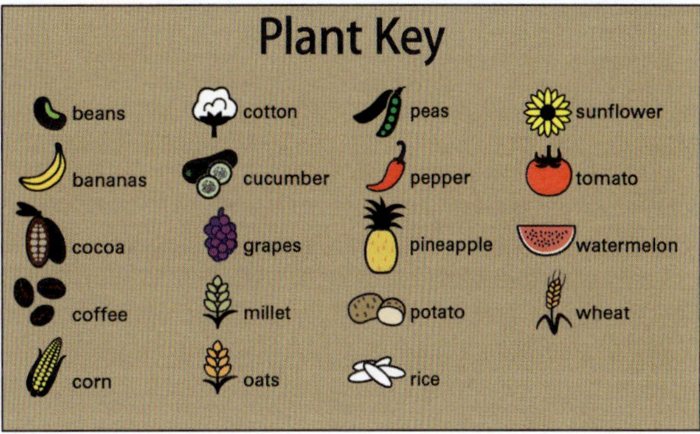

Other faraway cultures invented agriculture too. They used different plants and animals. China farmed rice. Potatoes were cultivated in South America. Chickens and pigs were raised in South Asia. Maize, a crop like corn, came from North America. Africa grew yams and peas. Farming included crops for food and cotton, silk, and wool for clothing. Horses and camels were used for transportation. Agriculture was a worldwide invention.

History of Agriculture

Agriculture began around 10,000 BCE. It became a common practice in cultures everywhere. Many inventions made farming easier and better. Early on people invented the sickle, shovel, and plow. They learned to use domesticated animals to work the fields. Today we plant and harvest with giant machines. And we transport food around the world to trade or feed the hungry.

Farming practices have changed too. The ability to **irrigate** land helped many early cultures to survive droughts. Irrigation continues today with powerful watering machines. Farmers learned to rotate their crops to prevent diseases, and fertilize to increase yield. Today the DNA of some crops has been changed to make them grow better.

Protein

Protein is a necessary nutrient for humans to survive. It builds body tissue and provides us with a fuel source. The first farmers chose the best grains and over time were able to increase their protein. More protein in our diet through animal domestication also helped the human community to grow and be healthy.

Grains

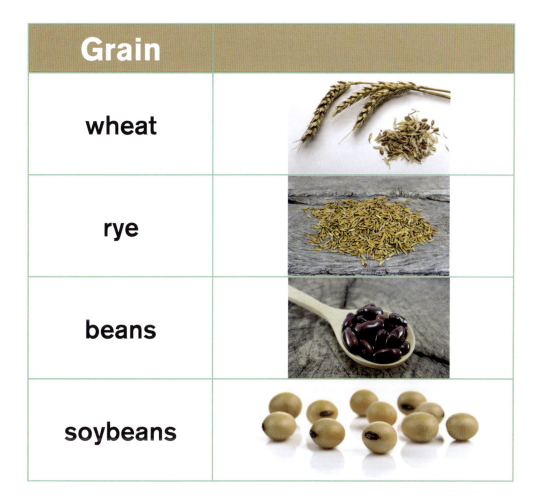

Grain	
wheat	
rye	
beans	
soybeans	

Grains are seeds that we harvest for food. They are left to dry and last longer in storage than other foods. Grains contain proteins that allow them to provide a constant food source through winter. And they're easy to transport. Grains have been very important to people throughout history. Today grains are popular in dishes like bread, breakfast cereal, and cookies.

Breeding Animals

Animal	Interesting Info
Cat	They were useful to protect grain storages.
Cow	They are useful for food, including milk and meat.
Chicken	There are more species of chickens than any other bird.
Pig	The domestication history of pigs is a mystery to archaeologists.
Goat	Goats were kept for milk and meat, and their dung was used for fuel.

Learning how to **breed** animals helped humans survive. People used cows, pigs, goats, and chickens for food. Horses and oxen were used for work and transportation. Dogs were used to hunt, fight in wars, and as watchdogs. Cats kept rats and mice from eating stored food.

QUIZ

Circle the correct answer.

1. Agriculture increased the size of permanent ________ .

settlements | Ice Age | maps

2. Agriculture developed ________ around the same time.

United States | worldwide | oceans

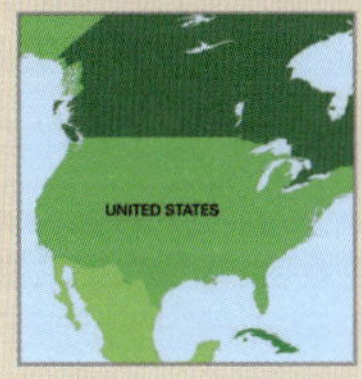

3. Agriculture led to a ________ increase.

population | climate | Neanderthal

4. ________ practices are still improving today.

Classical | Cavalry | Agriculture

5. Early farmers learned to ______ plants.

bronze | government | cultivate

6. To ______ an animal is to tame and breed it for food or work.

domesticate | cultivate | irrigate

7. ______ is an important nutrient for human survival.

Agriculture | Surplus | Protein

Write About It

CHAPTER
5

Early Civilizations

An era of history 10,000 BCE to 400 BCE

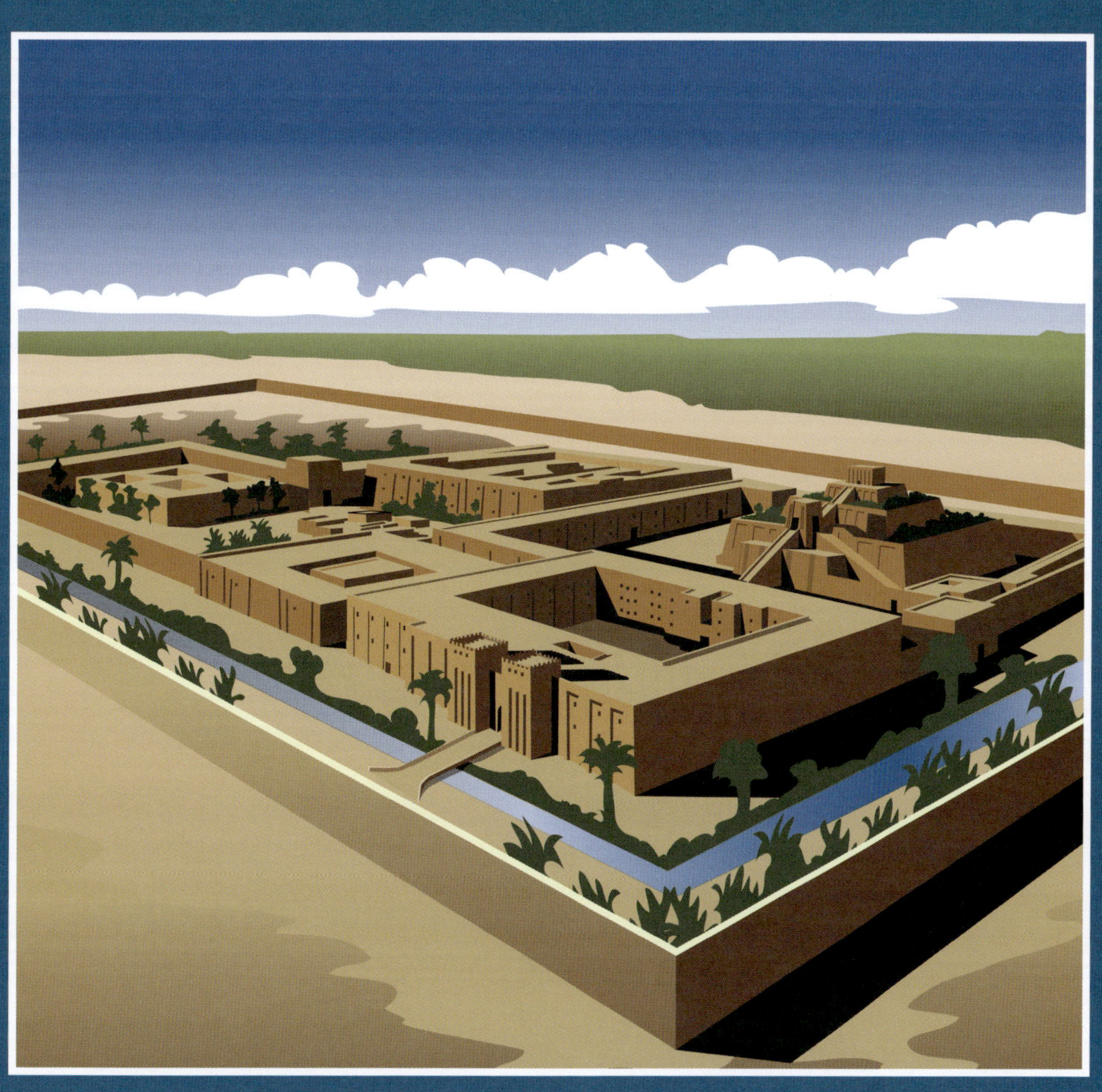

Four important civilizations arose in river valleys around the same time.

Governments were created to better manage larger civilizations.

The invention of writing helped early civilizations succeed.

Inventions of bronze and iron made for better tools and weapons.

Early Civilizations Timeline

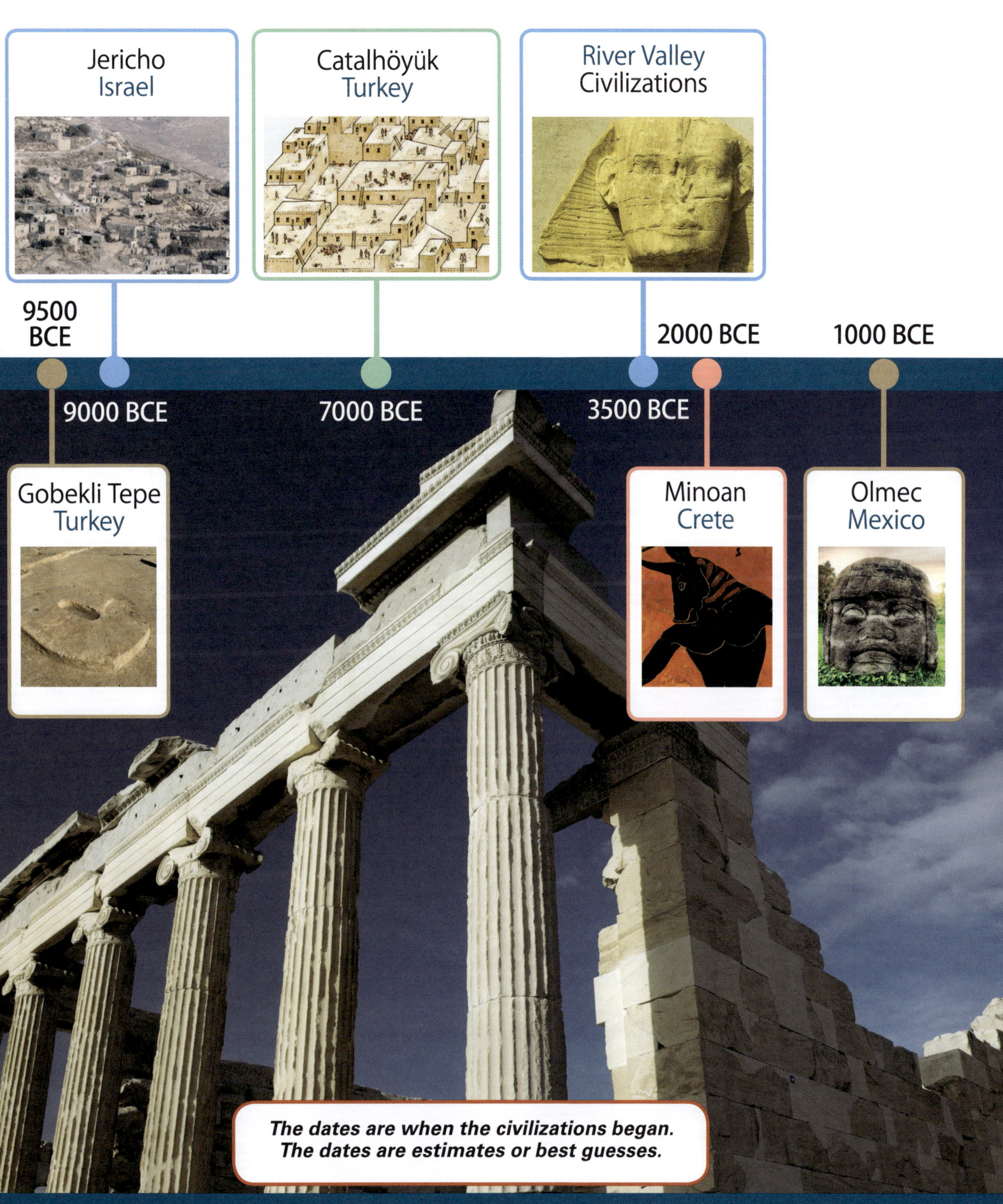

The dates are when the civilizations began. The dates are estimates or best guesses.

VOCABULARY

government		the power structure to represent, control, and organize a society
social class		a ranking of people in a society based upon their role, wealth, or job
city-state		a city and surrounding territories governed as one state
civilization		an advanced state of cultural and material development in a society

A ranking of people in a society

__ __ __ __ __ __   __ __ __ __ __

VOCABULARY

bronze		a metal made from copper and tin
iron		a silver colored metal stronger than bronze
fertile		land that's good for growing crops
pyramid		a large structure with a pointed top

A large building shaped like a traingle

___ ___ ___ ___ ___ ___ ___

Early Civilizations

In the beginning of this era people lived in small settlements.

When this era began, agriculture was spreading. People still lived in small permanent settlements. Then cities were formed. **Governments** were created to better manage them. Governments had **social classes** that included a ruling class and workers. The ruling class provided leadership and more safety. The working class did jobs like farming and building. After a while, rulers expanded their power to include nearby communities. They created **city-states**.

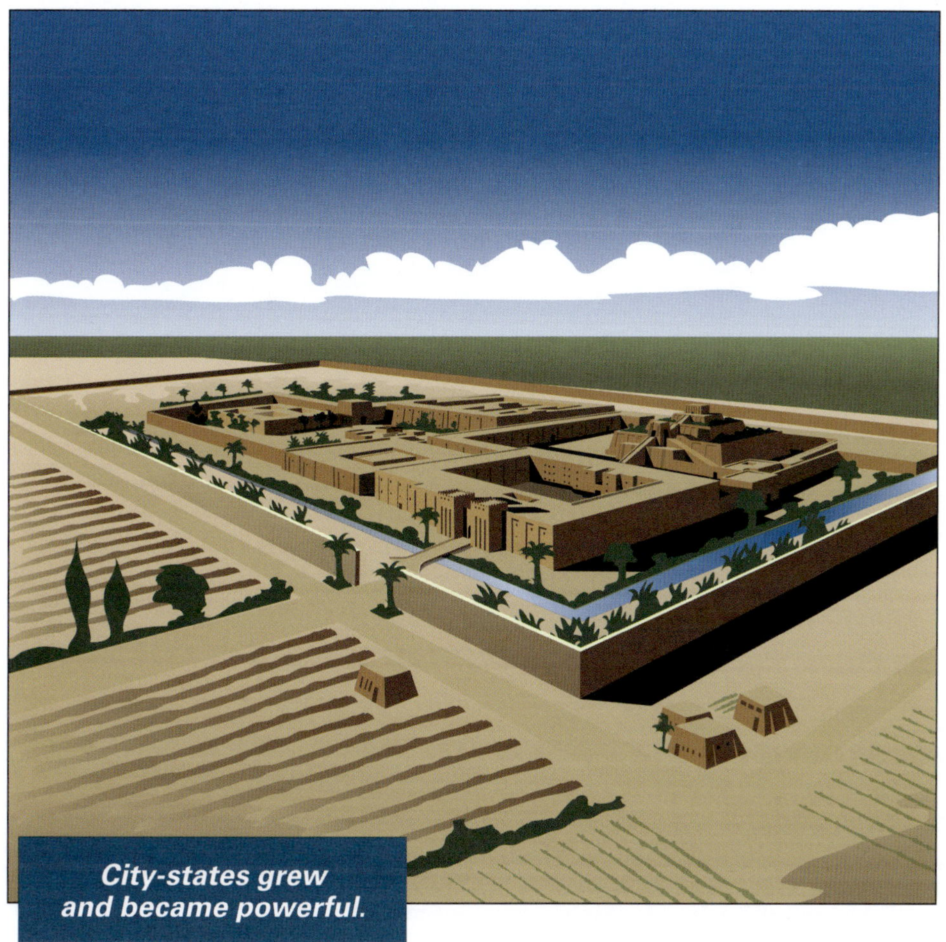

City-states grew and became powerful.

People learned to make stronger tools and weapons using metals found in the ground. These important inventions helped some city-states invade others. Empires were created. Empires controlled a large area and many communities. They could be cruel to the people they conquered. Sometimes they had slaves. During this era, cultures grew from small communities to empires.

First Words

Words are written above the carved images.

Writing was invented during this era. It helped early **civilizations** grow and prosper. With writing they could communicate ideas over time and distances. They could record how many animals they owned and how much grain was harvested. The first writing used small pictures. Later, alphabets were developed.

Bronze Age

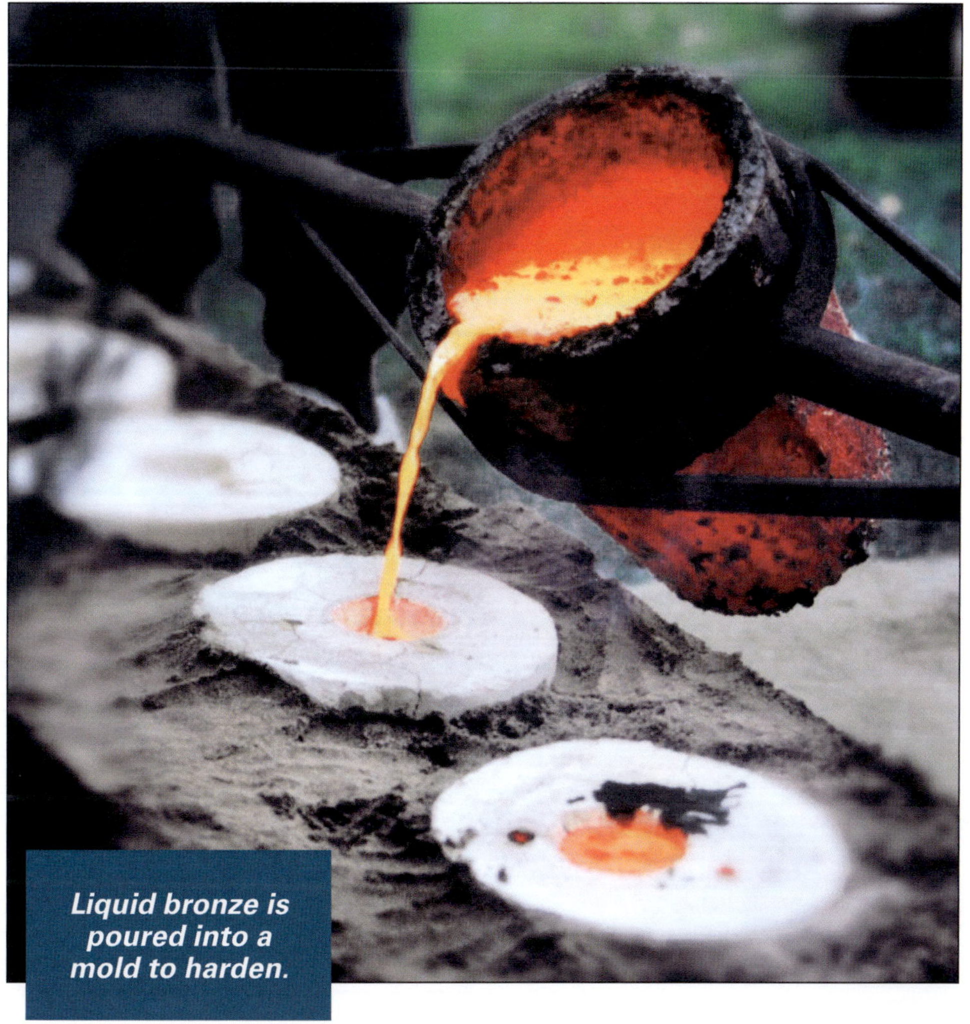

Liquid bronze is poured into a mold to harden.

For thousands of years people made tools and weapons with the materials around them, like stone. Later, they learned to pound copper into jewelry or pots. But copper was a soft metal. **Bronze** was made by mixing heated copper with tin. It made strong tools and weapons. This invention was so important that an era is called the Bronze Age. Later, **iron** was used to make even stronger things.

Large Settlements

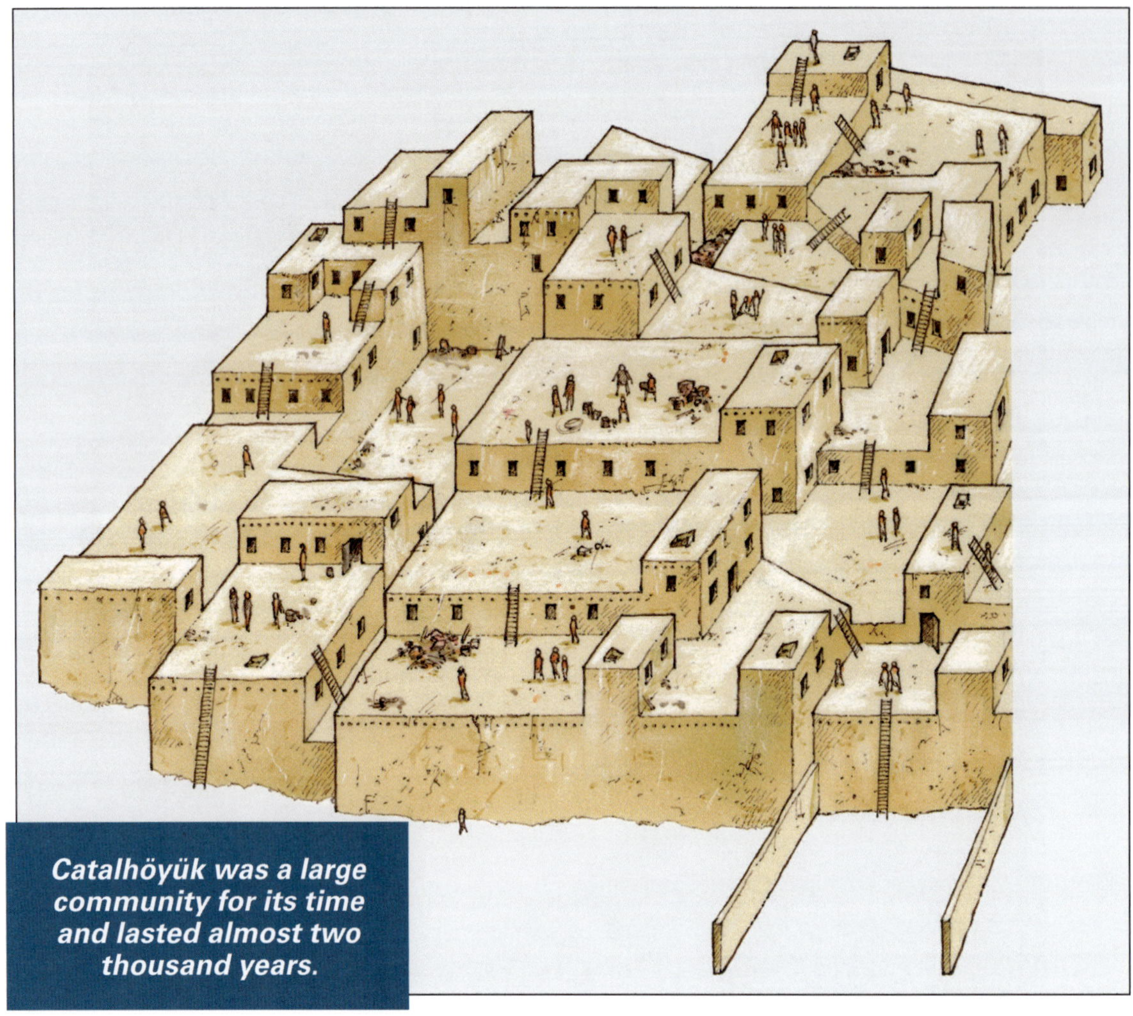

Catalhöyük was a large community for its time and lasted almost two thousand years.

In the beginning of this era large settlements appeared all over the world. Some did not have agriculture yet. Two were in present-day Turkey. Gobekli Tepe was the first. Archaeologists think it was a religious center. People performed rituals. Catalhöyük began later. It lasted for about 2000 years. As many as 10,000 people lived there. Their houses had doors in the ceilings and were beautifully decorated.

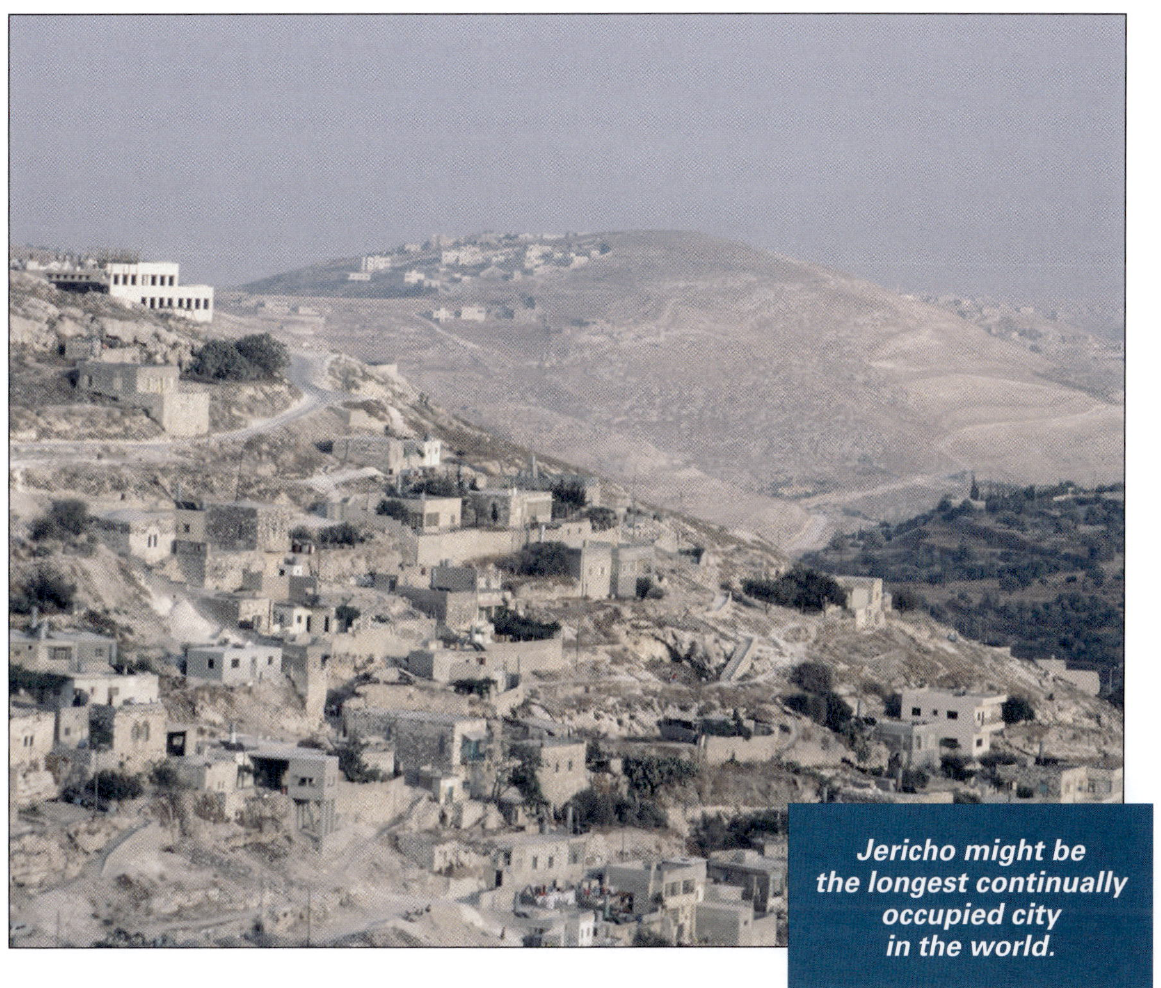

Jericho might be the longest continually occupied city in the world.

The Pengtoushan culture began in China around 7500 BCE. Their rice may have been the first domesticated. If so, they were among the earliest to discover agriculture. Jericho in the Middle East was settled before Pengtoushan. It's located along the Jordan River. The Battle of Jericho—when the attackers blew trumpets and the walls came down—is a famous story. Jericho is still a city today. It's been continuously occupied since 9000 BCE!

River Valley Civilizations

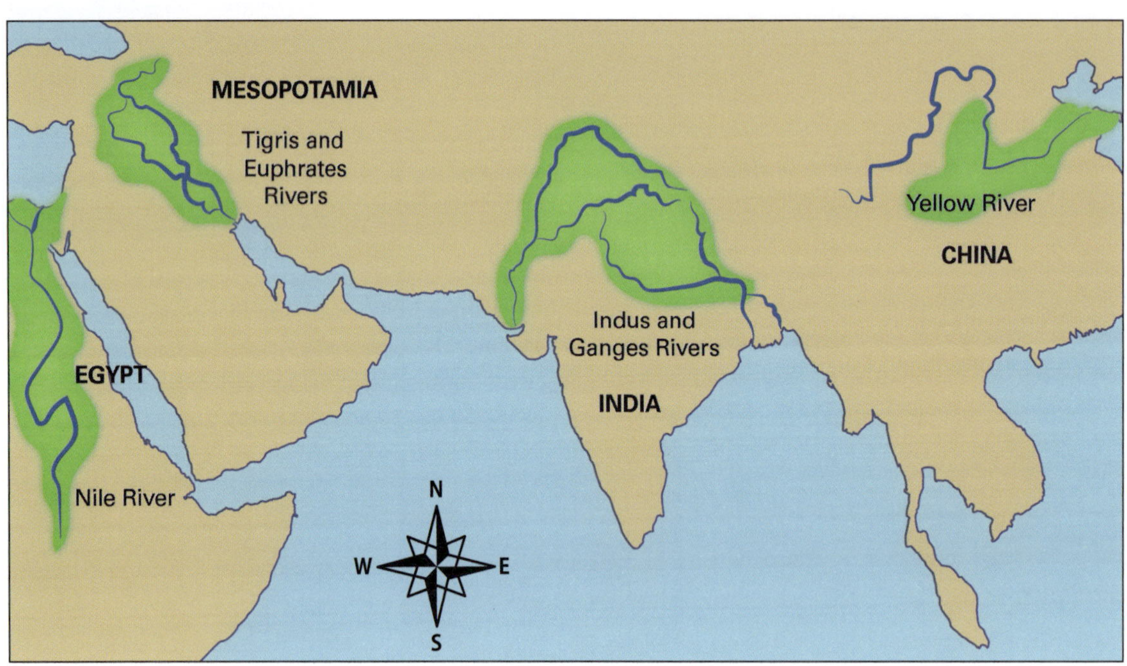

These four civilizations arose in river valleys around the same time. They invented their own writing. They had cities with a government and social classes. Sometimes they had slaves. They had a military with metal weapons. They traded goods like grain and copper. Rivers helped with transportation. Most importantly, river floods made the soil **fertile**, so they could grow enough food to support their large population.

Egypt

Egyptians had a long-lasting empire. They benefited from fertile soil and regular flooding of the Nile River. They developed hieroglyphics to write. They recorded taxes and military successes. They built great monuments like the **pyramids** and the Sphinx. The pharaoh was a god-king ruler. Upon death, the pharaohs' bodies were preserved for religious reasons. You can still see their mummies today in museums.

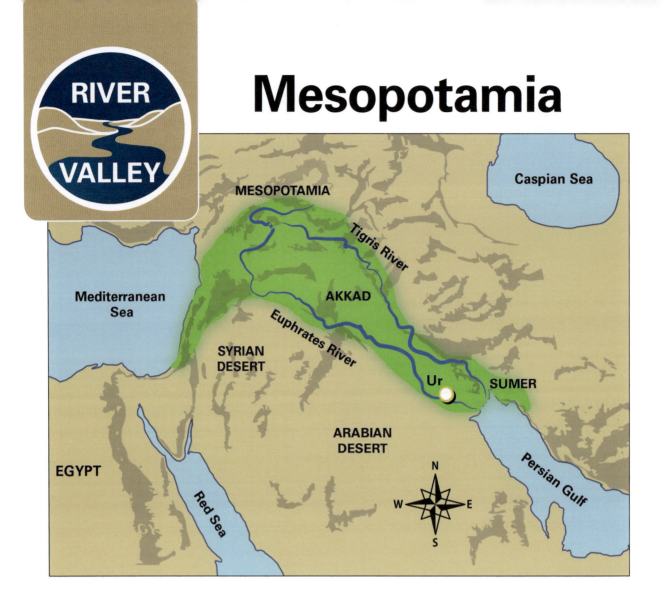

RIVER VALLEY

Mesopotamia

Mesopotamia is the land between two rivers. It was a great area to grow wheat. Many cultures have lived there. Writing was invented in the Sumer region. Sumerians built great cities like Ur. A neighboring city-state Akkad conquered Sumer in 2300 BCE. Together they formed a powerful empire. Later, Hammurabi from Babylon ruled Mesopotamia. He's known for Hammurabi's Code, a set of written laws.

Indus Valley

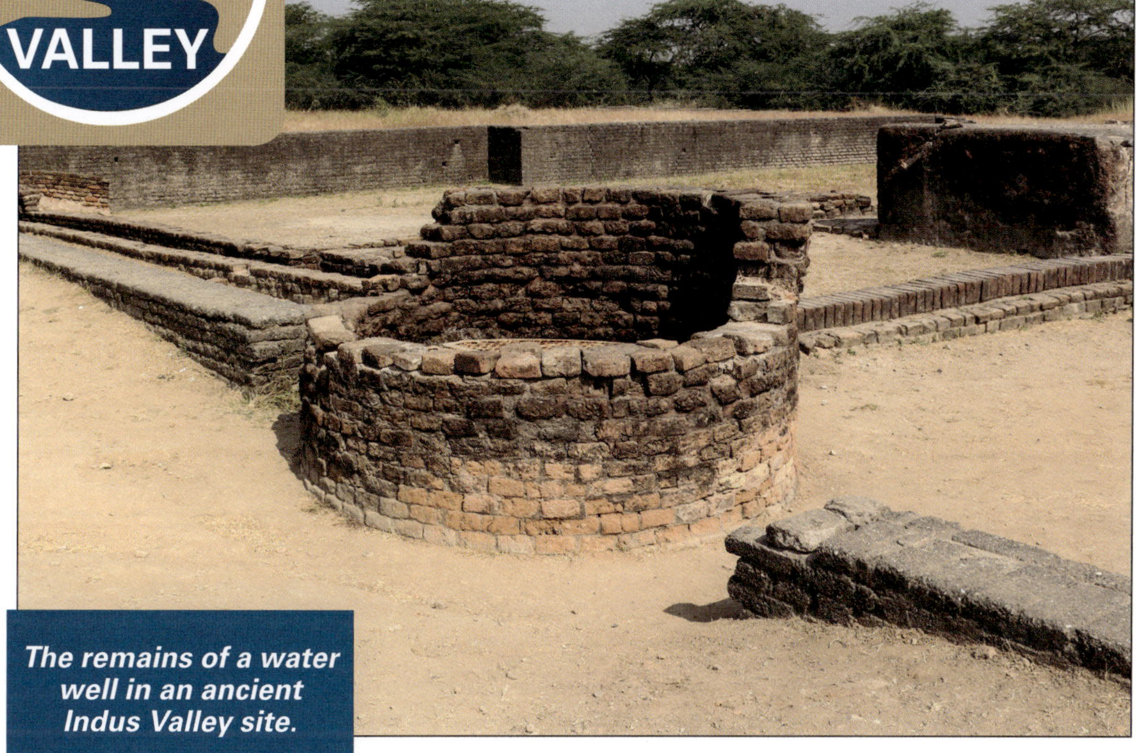

The remains of a water well in an ancient Indus Valley site.

Indus Valley rivaled the Egyptian and Mesopotamian cultures. Of the three, the Indus Valley culture covered the most land. It was known for its remarkable sanitation and the world's first flush toilets. It had a healthy trading relationship with the Sumerians. Later, the civilization mysteriously declined. It was forgotten until archaeologists discovered artifacts in Pakistan about 100 years ago.

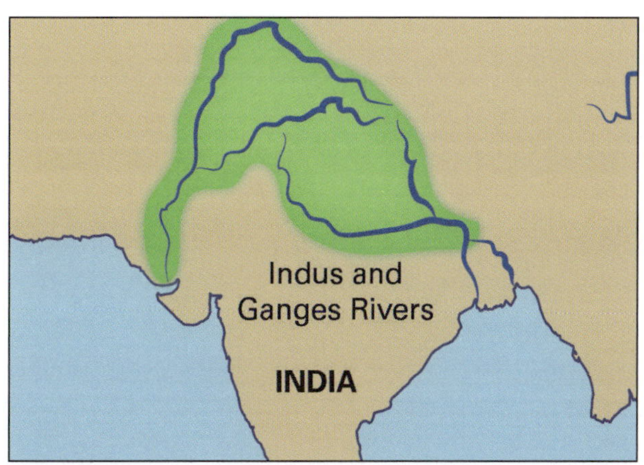

Yellow River

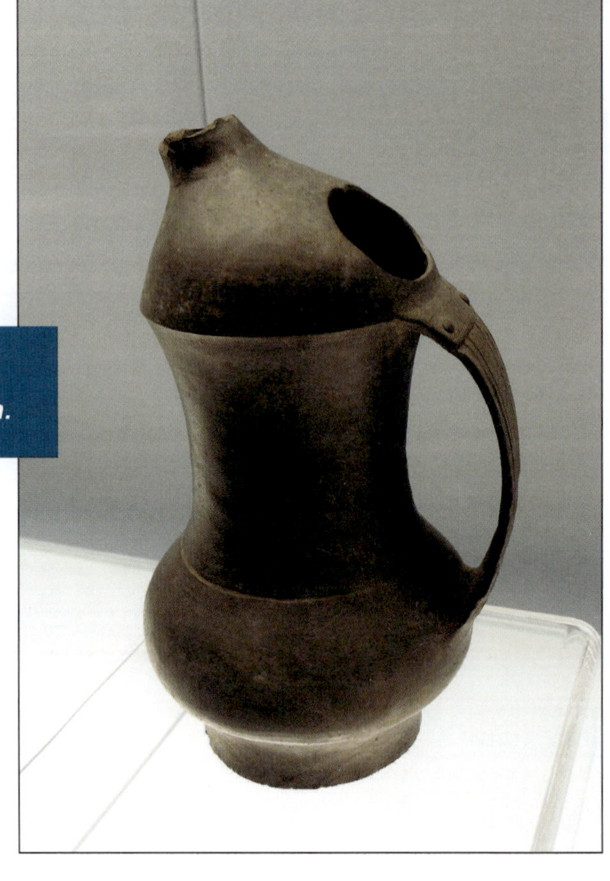

Early pottery made in China.

Cultures lived in the Yellow River valley of China before 3000 BCE. They had agriculture, cities, and writing later on. The Longshan culture was known for beautiful pottery. The Xia was the first Chinese dynasty in 2070 BCE. A dynasty is a long period ruled by one family. It was followed by the Shang Dynasty. Their writing is similar to what's used in China today. The Shang had cities surrounded by big walls, royal palaces, and burial tombs.

Minoan

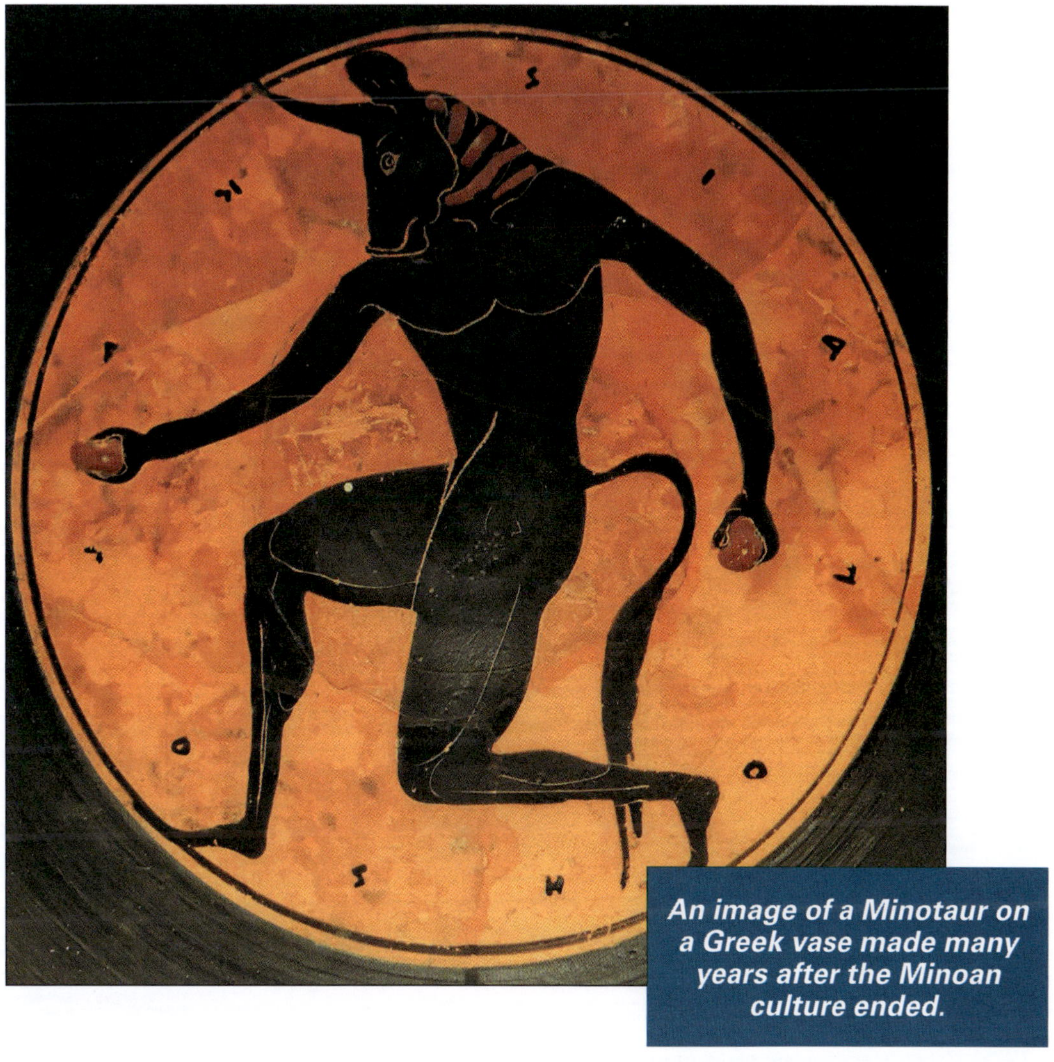

An image of a Minotaur on a Greek vase made many years after the Minoan culture ended.

Minoan culture was the first advanced civilization in Europe. It was based on the island of Crete. The Minoans were known for being peaceful and having a large fleet of ships for trading. They spread technologies, like making bronze, to many places in Europe. They invented their own writing. The Minoans were known for their legends like the Minotaur, who was half man and half bull. A huge volcano eruption weakened their culture.

Olmec

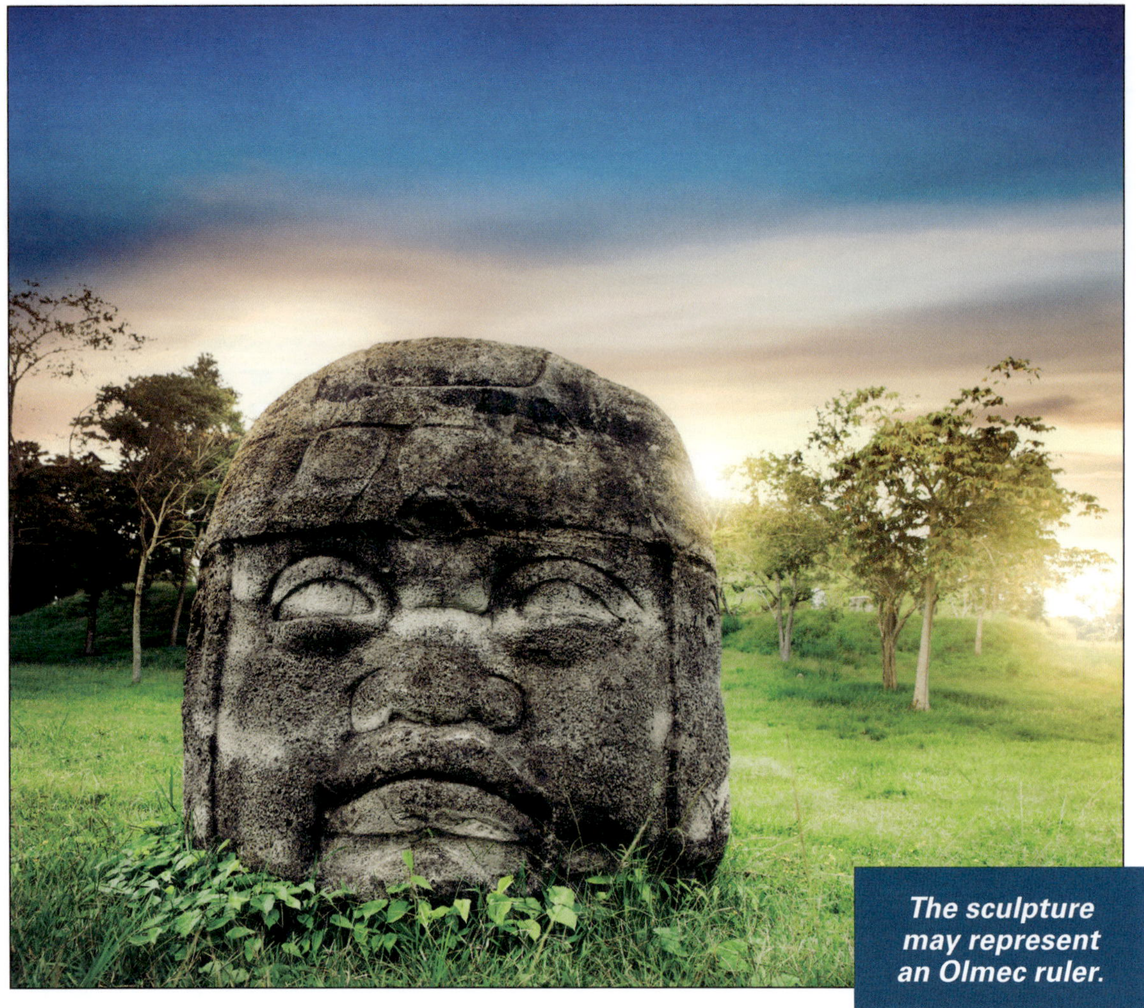

The sculpture may represent an Olmec ruler.

The Olmec were the first advanced civilization in Mexico. They settled in a fertile area. They grew enough food to support a large population. The Olmec were very good at carving. They are famous for large stone sculptures of human heads. They also carved channels from stone to drain water long distances. They made beautiful figurines of clay. It's believed the Olmec influenced later cultures, like the Maya and Aztecs.

QUIZ

Circle the correct answer.

1. ______ was a River Valley civilization.

Ocean | Olmec | Egypt

2. Better ______ were needed to manage larger civilizations.

pyramids | fertile | governments

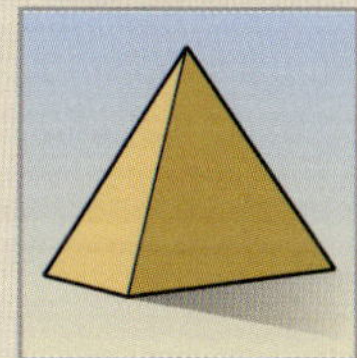

3. ______ helped civilizations record information.

Writing | Century | City-States

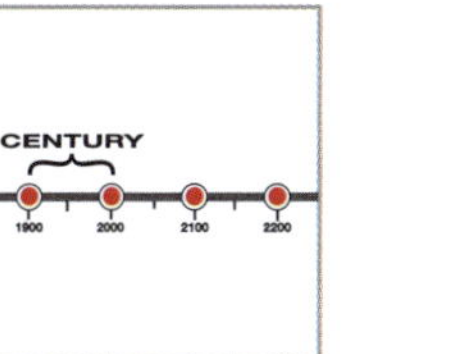

4. ______ made stronger tools than stone.

Settlements | Bronze | Ice Age

5. Crops grow better on ________ land.

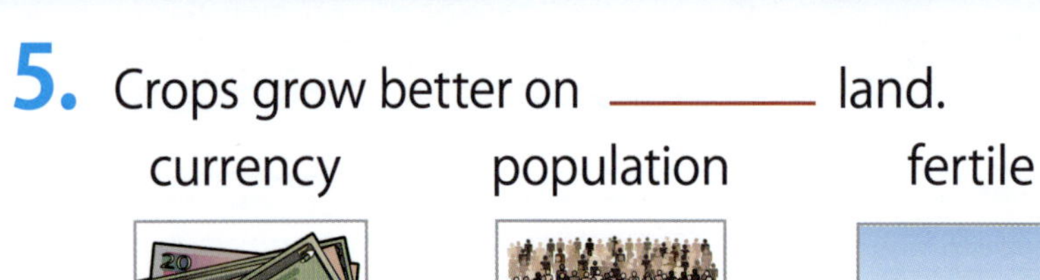

currency population fertile

6. ________ is a ranking of people in a society.

Social class City-State Agriculture

7. ________ makes stronger tools than bronze.

Stone Iron Protein

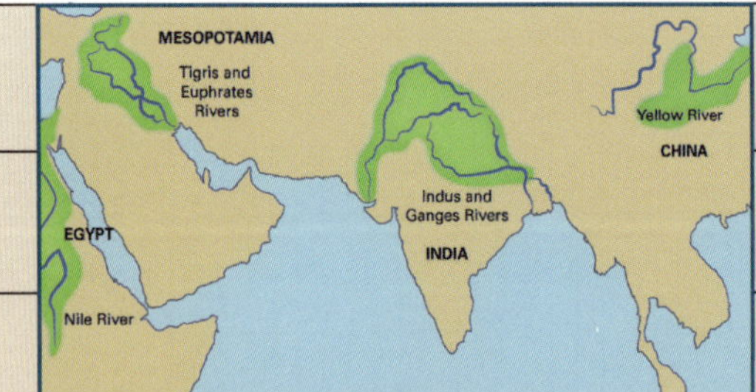

Write About It

CHAPTER 6

Writing

A theme of history

Prehistory ended with the invention of writing.

Early writing used pictures and symbols.

ABCDEF
abcdef

The use of an alphabet improved writing.

Writing helped governments enforce laws.

Writing Timeline

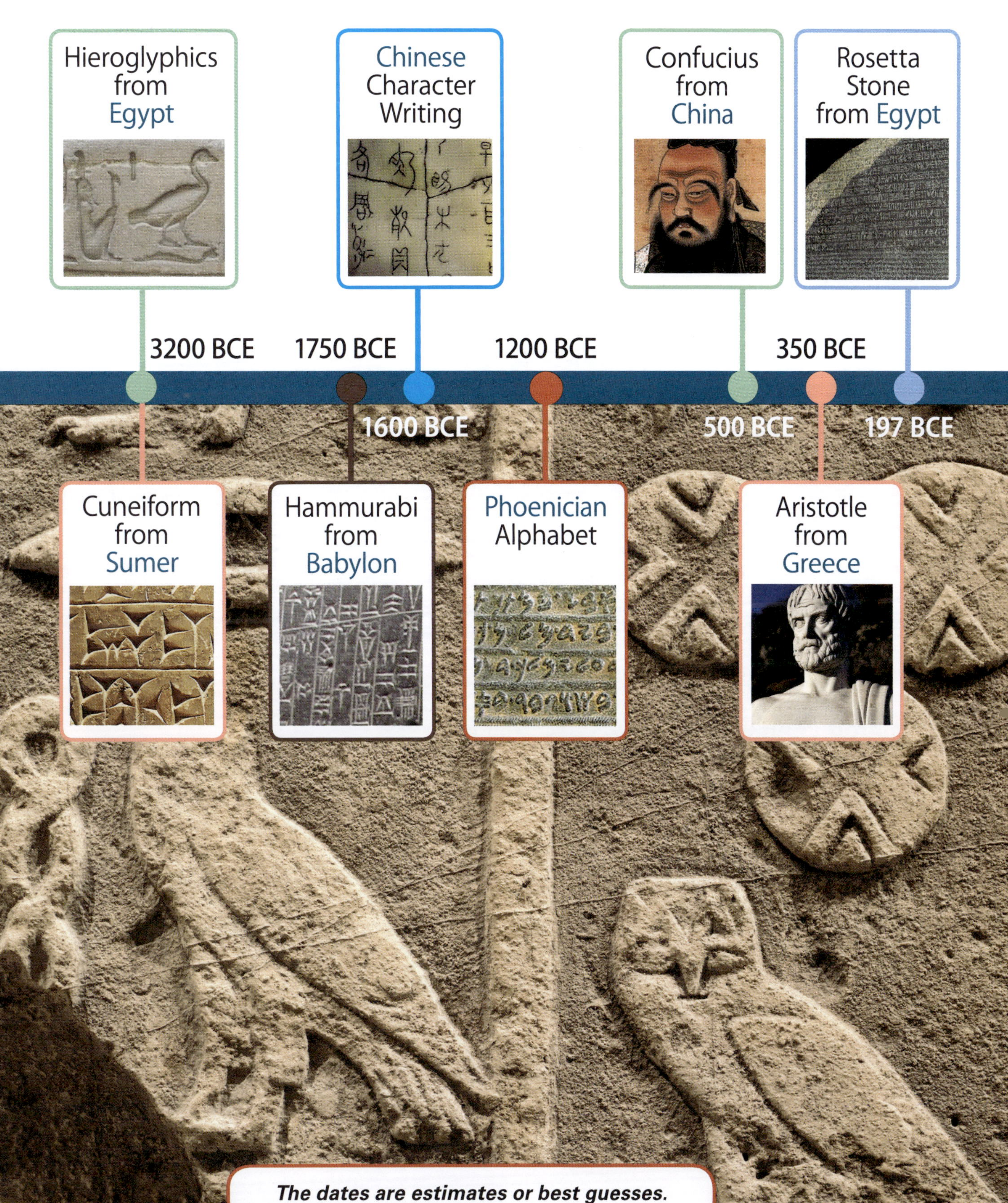

The dates are estimates or best guesses.

VOCABULARY

writing		producing words that can be read and understood by someone else
prehistory		the time before writing was invented
document		a piece of written material that provides information
hieroglyphics		a writing system used in ancient Egypt

Words that someone else can read and understand

___ ___ ___ ___ ___ ___ ___

VOCABULARY

cuneiform		a writing system used in Mesopotamia
stylus		a small tool used for writing or drawing
alphabet		letters of a language that are arranged to make words
scribe		a person who writes information down

Someone who writes

___ ___ ___ ___ ___ ___

Writing

Early forms of writing used pictures and symbols.

Like the invention of agriculture, several civilizations invented **writing** about the same time. **Prehistory** ended with the invention of writing. Historians can study prehistory only by examining artifacts. Writing gives historians a new source of information. But ancient writing is hard to understand. Still today, we can't read Indus Valley, Minoan, or Olmec writing.

Ancient cultures used scribes to write information down.

Historians know that writing helped cultures develop. Important information could be saved and shared. Earlier forms of writing kept records, like how many cows you own. As cultures became more complex, they created **documents** to record taxes and write down rules. And leaders wanted to record their heroic stories. Victories in war were a common theme in early writing.

Rosetta Stone

The Rosetta Stone has the same information written in three different ways.

Hieroglyphics was the writing system of ancient Egypt. It used symbols and pictures to tell stories. Historians couldn't understand these stories. Then in 1799 an ancient stone was discovered in Rosetta, Egypt. The stone had the same information written in different ways. One part was written in hieroglyphics, another in Greek. Historians understood Greek. Now we understand hieroglyphics too.

Code of Hammurabi

Written laws and rules have played an important role in world history. Before writing, governments would tell citizens the laws. Having scribes write them made it easier for citizens to understand and follow the laws. The most famous early written laws are called the Code of Hammurabi. Hammurabi was a ruler of the Babylon city-state in Mesopotamia. The laws were written on four large stone monuments in about 1750 BCE.

Photos of the Code of Hammurabi.

Cuneiform

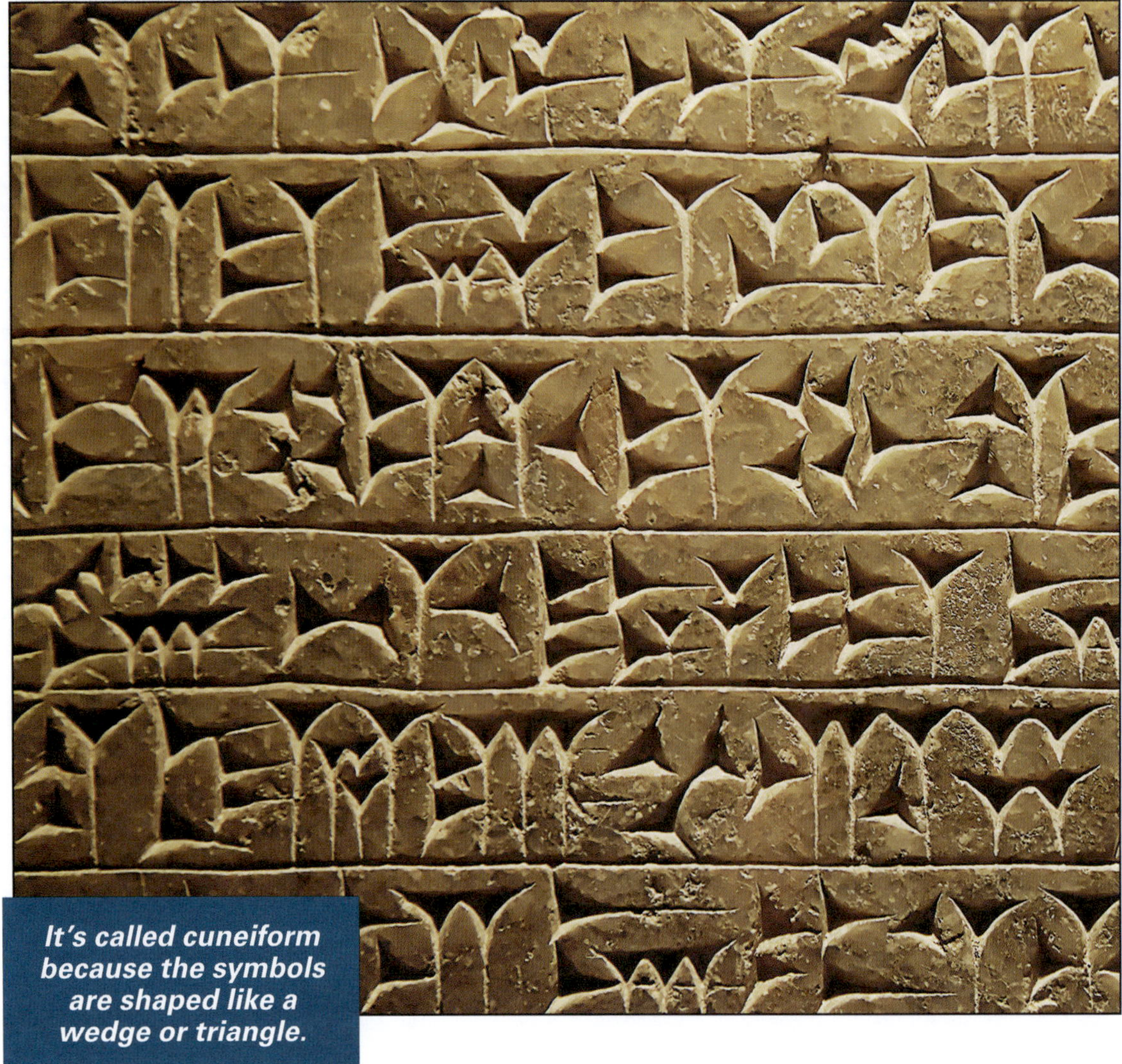

It's called cuneiform because the symbols are shaped like a wedge or triangle.

Cuneiform was the writing system in ancient Sumer in Mesopotamia. Like hieroglyphics, cuneiform used symbols to represent objects and sounds. They wrote with a **stylus** on wet clay tablets. When the tablet dried it would harden. Many samples of their writing have been found and translated. Cuneiform writing spread to many cultures and lasted for thousands of years.

Writing in China

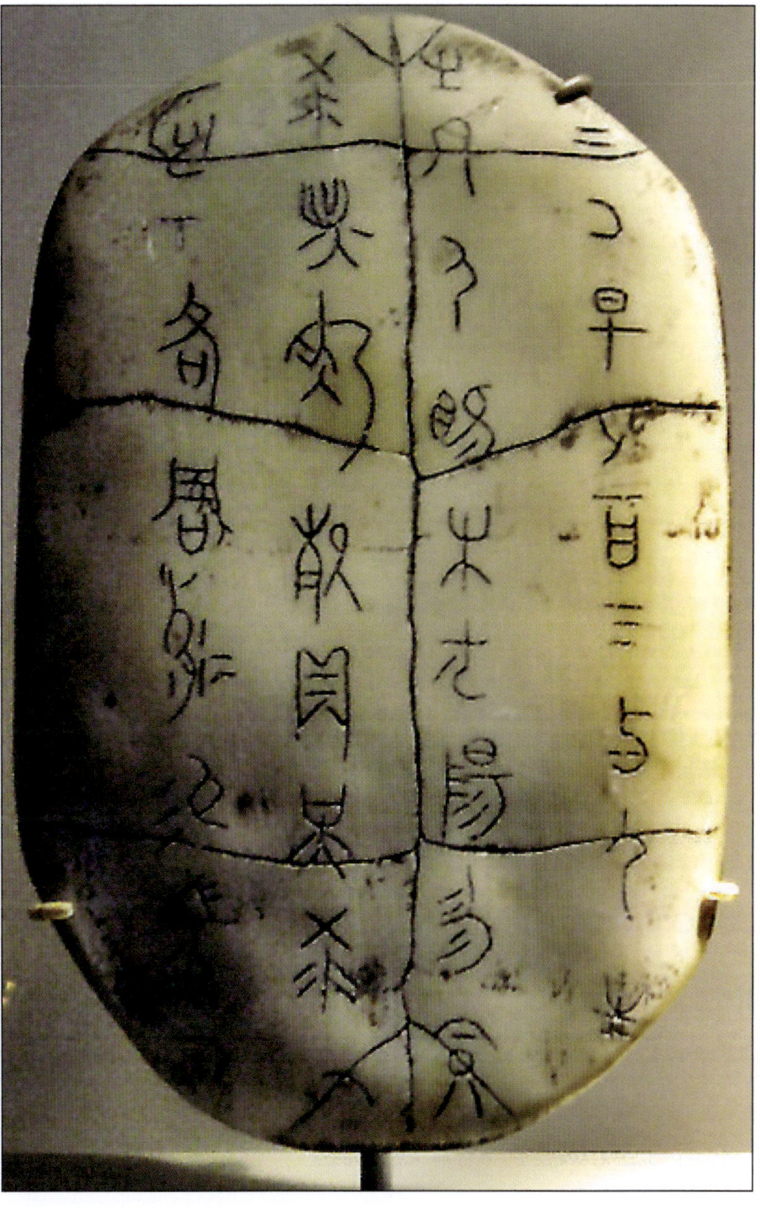

A copy of ancient Chinese writing on a tortoise shell.

The Chinese have been using the same writing system longer than any culture. It began in the Shang Dynasty around 1650 BCE. That writing is similar to what is used today. Chinese writing doesn't have an alphabet. They use characters instead. Chinese writing spread to many cultures in East Asia. Japan and Korea use a similar system today.

Phoenician Alphabet

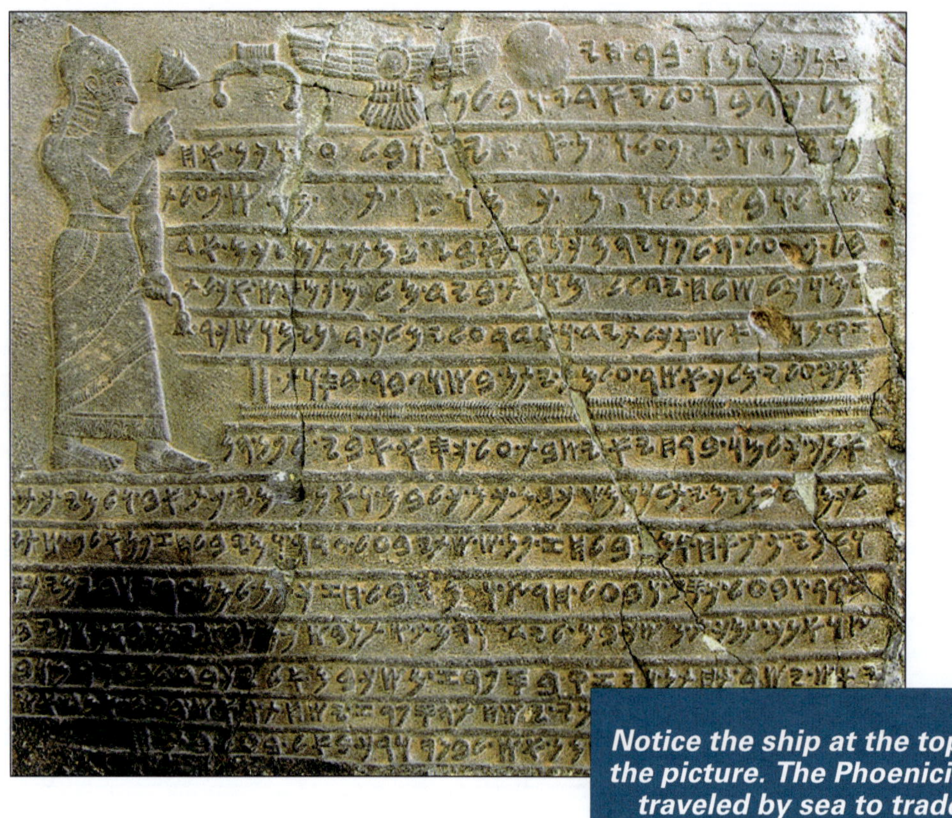

Notice the ship at the top of the picture. The Phoenicians traveled by sea to trade.

Around 1200 BCE the Phoenician **alphabet** was invented. It was the beginning of modern writing. It led to the first true alphabet. The Phoenicians were great traders. They traveled the Mediterranean Sea by ship. As they traded their goods, their writing style was learned by many cultures. It was used in Asia, Africa, and Europe. The Phoenicians didn't invent the alphabet. They just spread its use.

Greek Writing

The remains of an ancient Greek outdoor theater.

The Greeks improved the Phoenician alphabet. They used it to write the Greek language. It's called the first true alphabet because it added letters for vowels. The Greeks were great writers. They wrote about philosophy, politics, and science. They also wrote a lot of plays for the theater. Going to the theater was very popular in ancient Greece. Many ruins of their theaters survive today.

Aristotle, a Greek writer and philosopher.

Rule of Law

Confucius was a Chinese philosopher around 500 BCE. His teachings about family loyalty and respect for elders were written down by **scribes**. Confucius is given credit for the Golden Rule. His teachings are still studied today.

A painting of Confucius from 1790 CE.

The Magna Carta is another example of the importance of written laws. It was signed by King John of England in 1215 CE. It was the first document to guarantee rights to citizens.

QUIZ

Circle the correct answer.

1. ________ ended with the invention of writing.

Agriculture | Rituals | Prehistory

2. ________ used pictures and symbols for writing.

Hieroglyphics | Currency | Trade

3. The use of an ________ improved writing.

iron | tax | alphabet

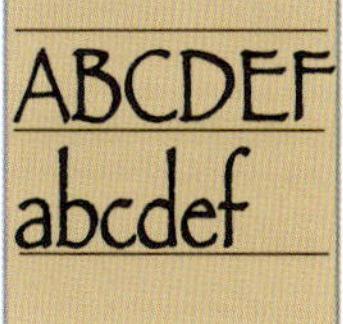

4. ________ helped governments enforce laws.

Bronze | 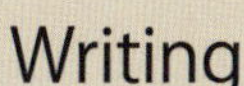 Writing | Geography

5. A ________ is a piece of written information.

century | military | document

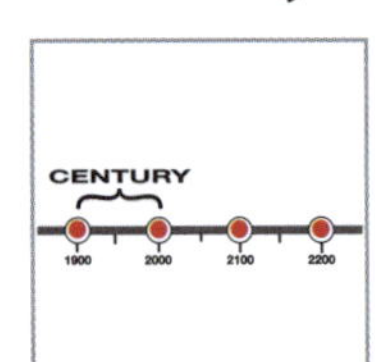

6. ________ was a form of writing invented in Mesopotamia.

Cuneiform | Tax | Protein

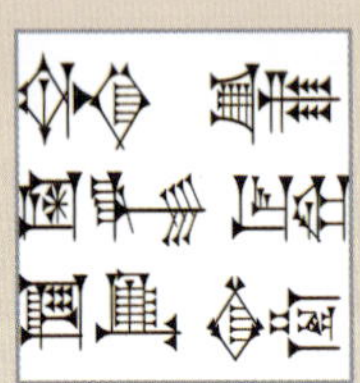

7. A ________ writes down information.

Neanderthal | stone | scribe

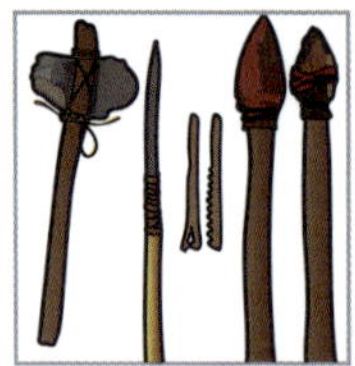

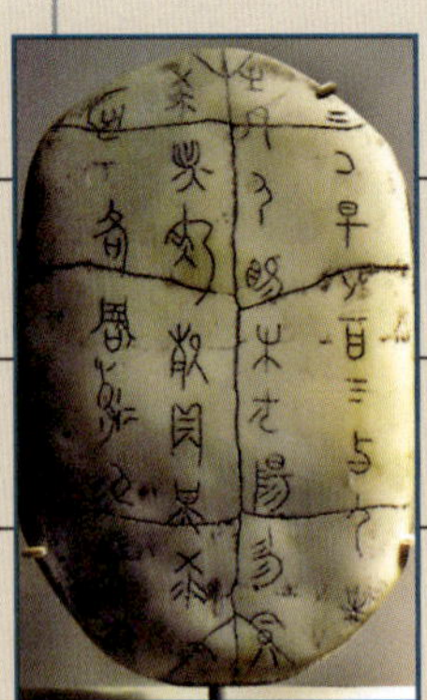

Write About It

CHAPTER 7

Classical Empires

An era of history 400 BCE to 500 CE

Classical empires controlled large areas and populations.

Classical empires had strong militaries.

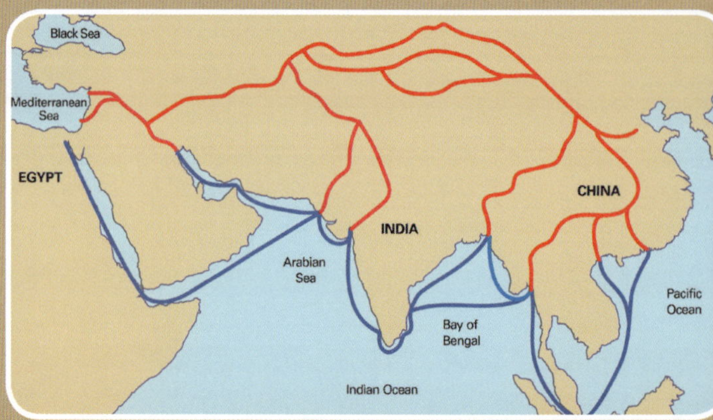

Classical empires traveled long distances to trade.

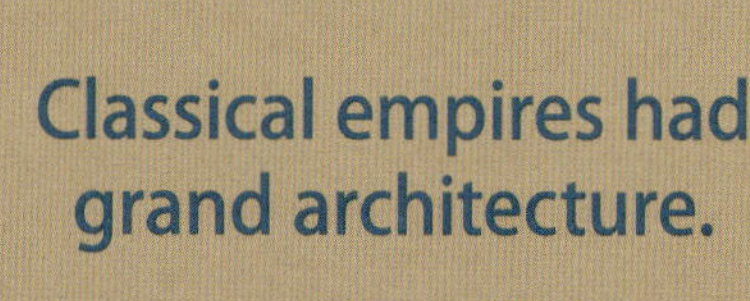

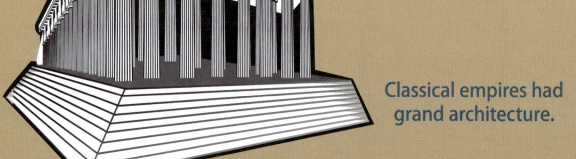

Classical empires had grand architecture.

Classical Empires Timeline

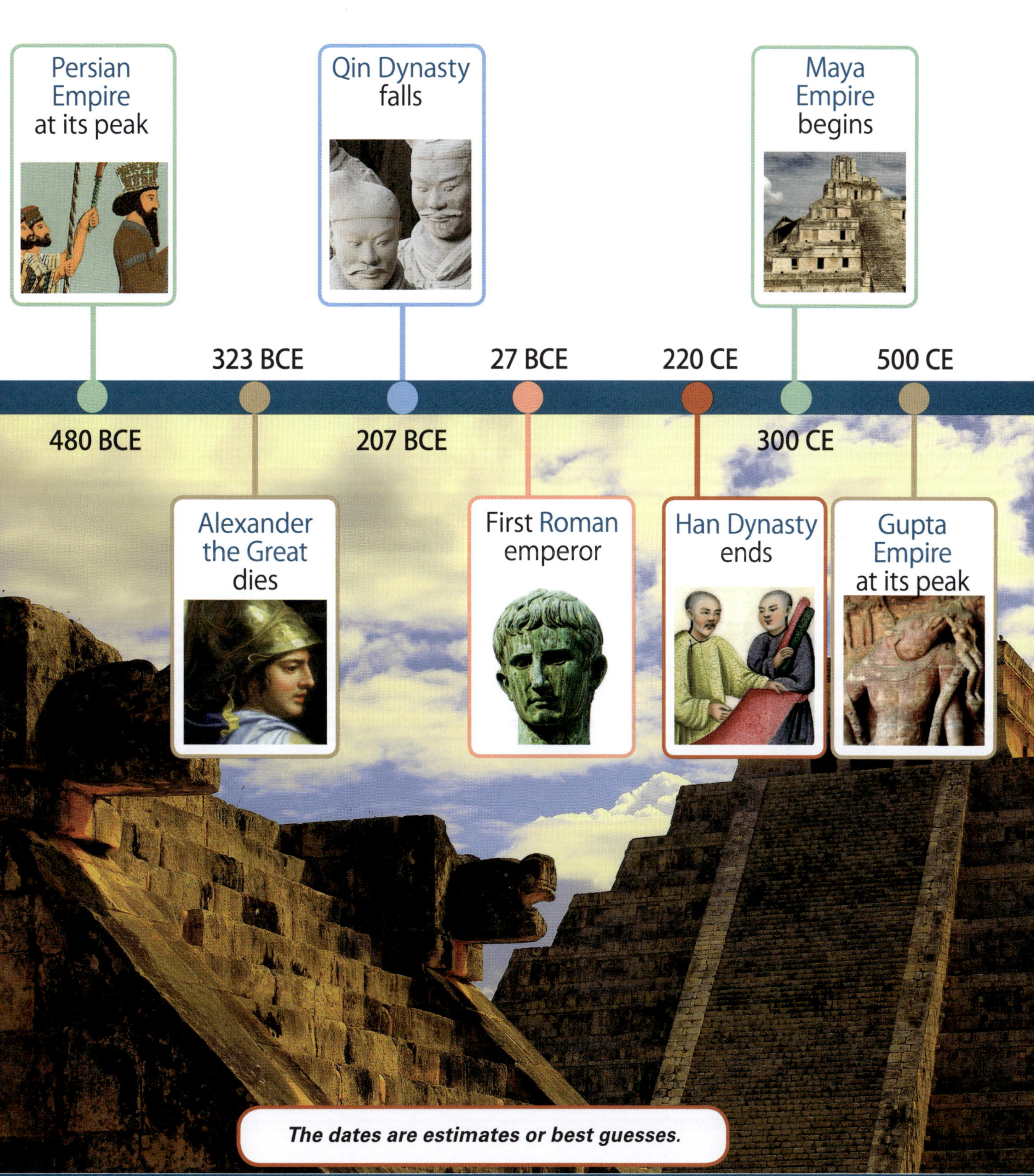

VOCABULARY

empire		a group of states or nations ruled by one powerful government
subject		a person controlled by an emperor or king
military		an army of trained soldiers
classical		judged over time to be important and high quality

Find the word!

An army of trained soldiers

__ __ __ __ __ __ __ __

VOCABULARY

century		a period of 100 years
democracy		a system of government where people vote for leaders
architecture		to design and construct buildings
tax		a payment from people to the government

A government where people vote

__ __ __ __ __ __ __ __ __

Classical Empires

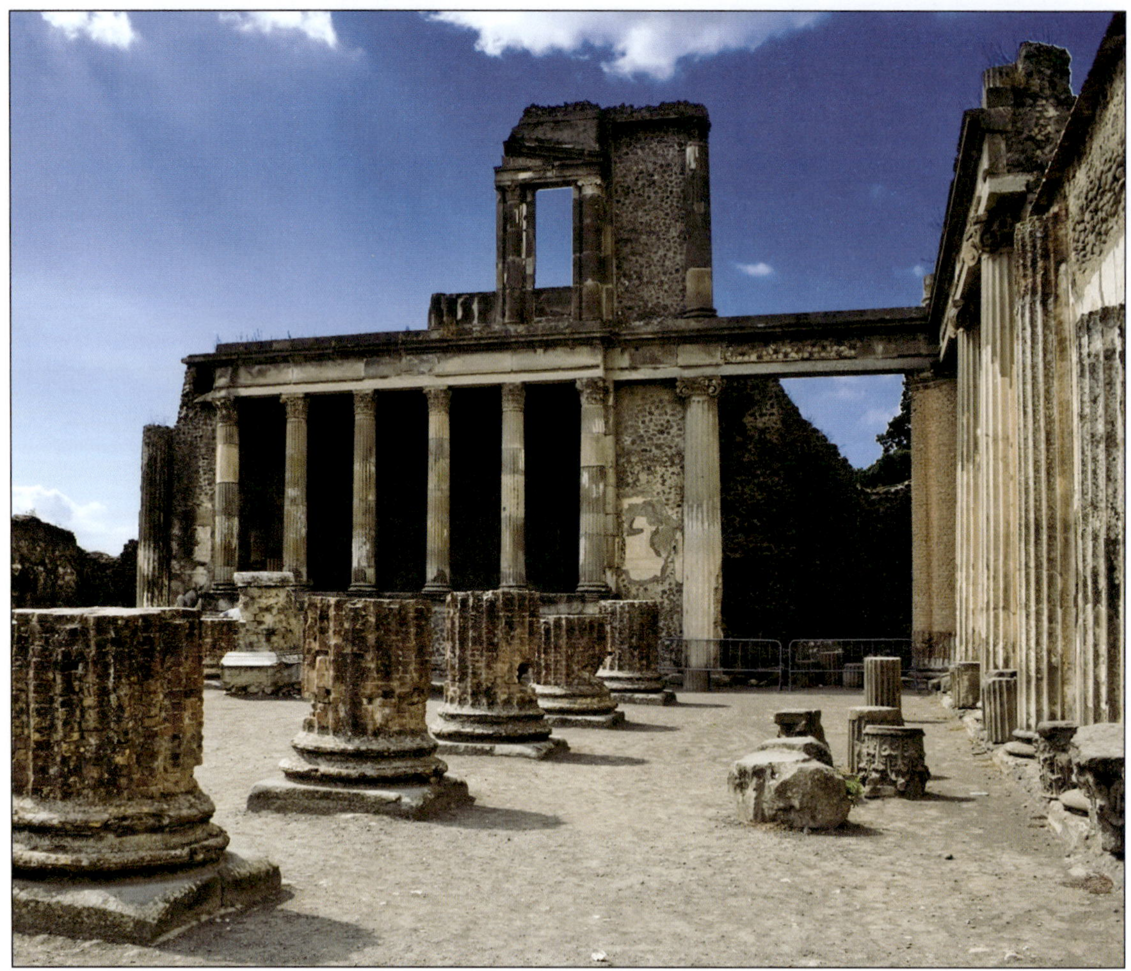

The **empires** in this era had several things in common. They ruled large areas of land. They had big cities plus vast farming areas. These empires had populations in the millions of people. **Subjects** were from different cultures and may have spoken a different language. Empires were difficult to manage. They needed complex governments that worked well.

Classical Empires			
Empire	**Page**	**Population**	**Year**
Persian	109	50 million	480 BCE
Han	115	60 million	2 CE
Roman	112	70 million	117 CE
Gupta	116	58 million	400 CE

These empires were often warlike. They had large and well-trained **militaries**. They controlled their subjects and defended their borders. Empires also used their militaries to conquer weaker nations. The people they conquered could be treated badly.

Many were killed or became slaves. But empires also brought wealth and new ideas to conquered lands.

Empires were often ruled by a single emperor.

More Trade

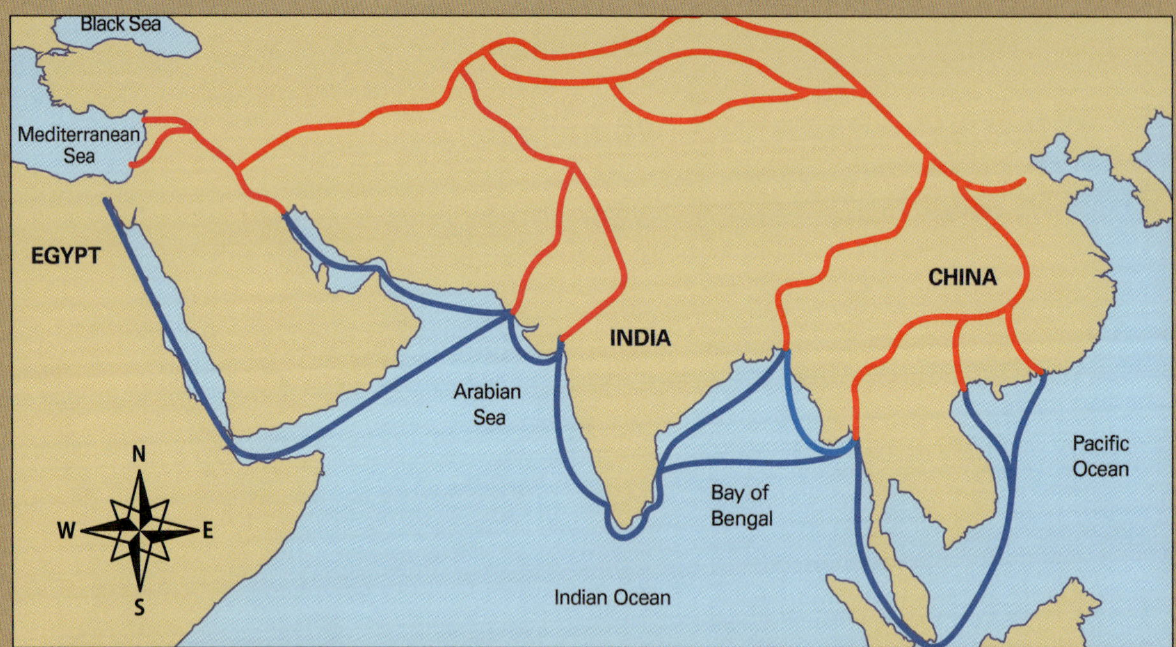

A trade is an exchange of goods. Trading was common in ancient cultures. They might trade grain for tin, or wine for pottery. The **classical** empires traveled long distances to trade. Rome traded gold for spice with India and silk with China. Mayan city-states traded goods like salt, jade, and cotton. Trade helped empires grow and prosper. Cultures also traded ideas. Religion, technology, and language were spread by trade.

Persian Empire

The Persian Empire was once the largest in the world. It stretched from the Indus Valley to southern Europe. By the fifth **century** BCE the empire included 50 million people. At the time, it had about 44 percent of the world's population. Later, it was invaded by Alexander the Great from Greece. Alexander's army defeated the Persians.

A painting of Darius, a great Persian king.

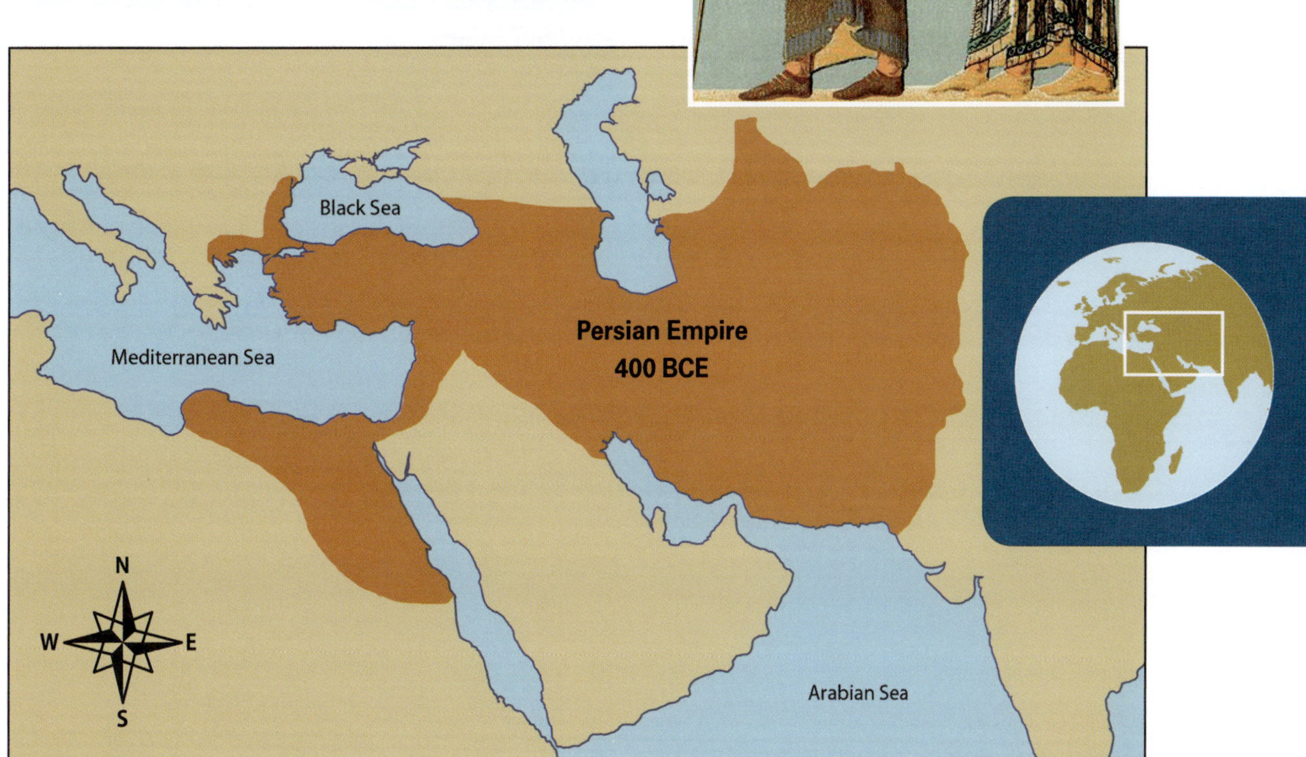

Greek Empire

A Greek statue of Alexander the Great from the second century BCE.

Classical Greece has a rich history. It's home to some of the first philosophers, like Plato. It was the first empire to try **democracy**. It was famous for important writers, scientists, and artists. It started the Olympics. Greece had powerful city-states in Athens and Sparta. Alexander the Great came from the northern part of Greece. He conquered the Classical Greek Empire.

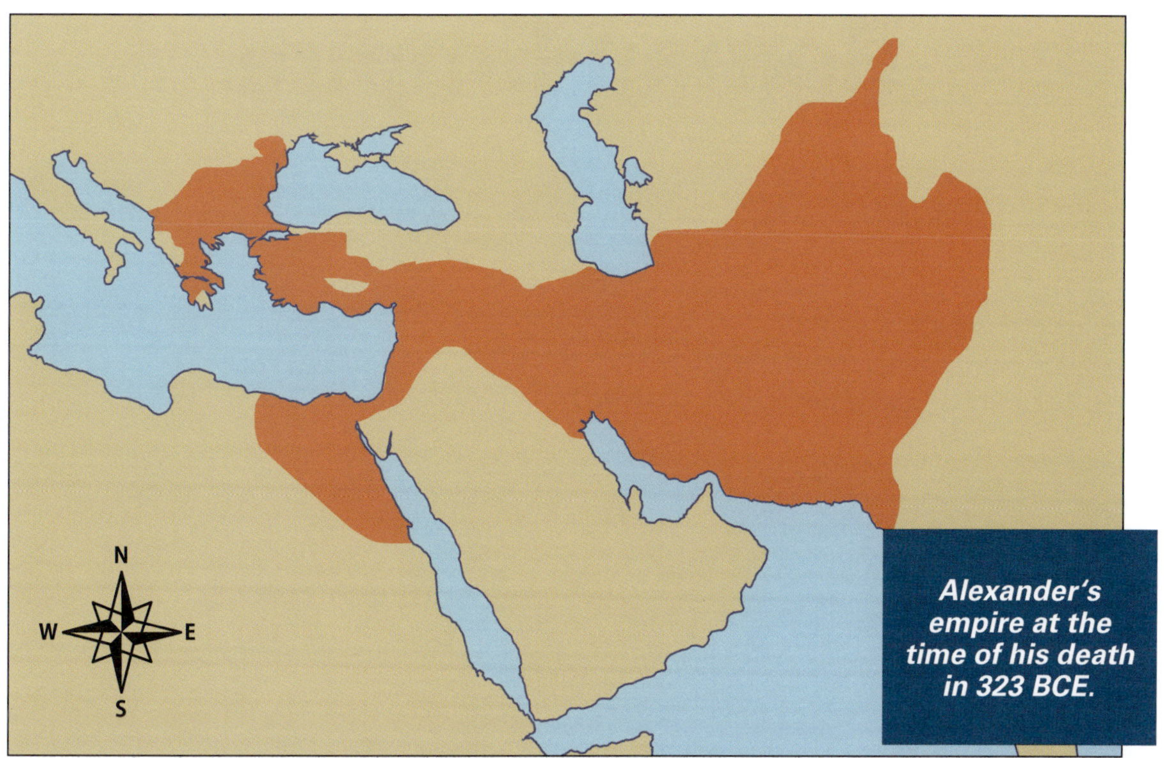

Alexander's empire at the time of his death in 323 BCE.

Alexander and his army then conquered land all the way to India. At the time it was the largest empire in the world. Alexander traveled with his military, but he never returned home. He died at age 32 in Babylon, in Mesopotamia. It was in 323 BCE. His generals divided the empire and ruled for many years. The Greek Empire was later conquered by the Roman Empire.

Roman Empire

A photograph of the Colosseum in Rome. It was built nearly 2000 years ago.

Rome grew in power as Greece was losing its influence. It went on to be an even more powerful empire than Greece. The Romans were good engineers and invented aqueducts to bring fresh water into Rome. Rome was also famous for its grand **architecture**, like the Colosseum. The Romans conquered much of Europe, including the Middle East and North Africa, and kept those territories for centuries before its decline.

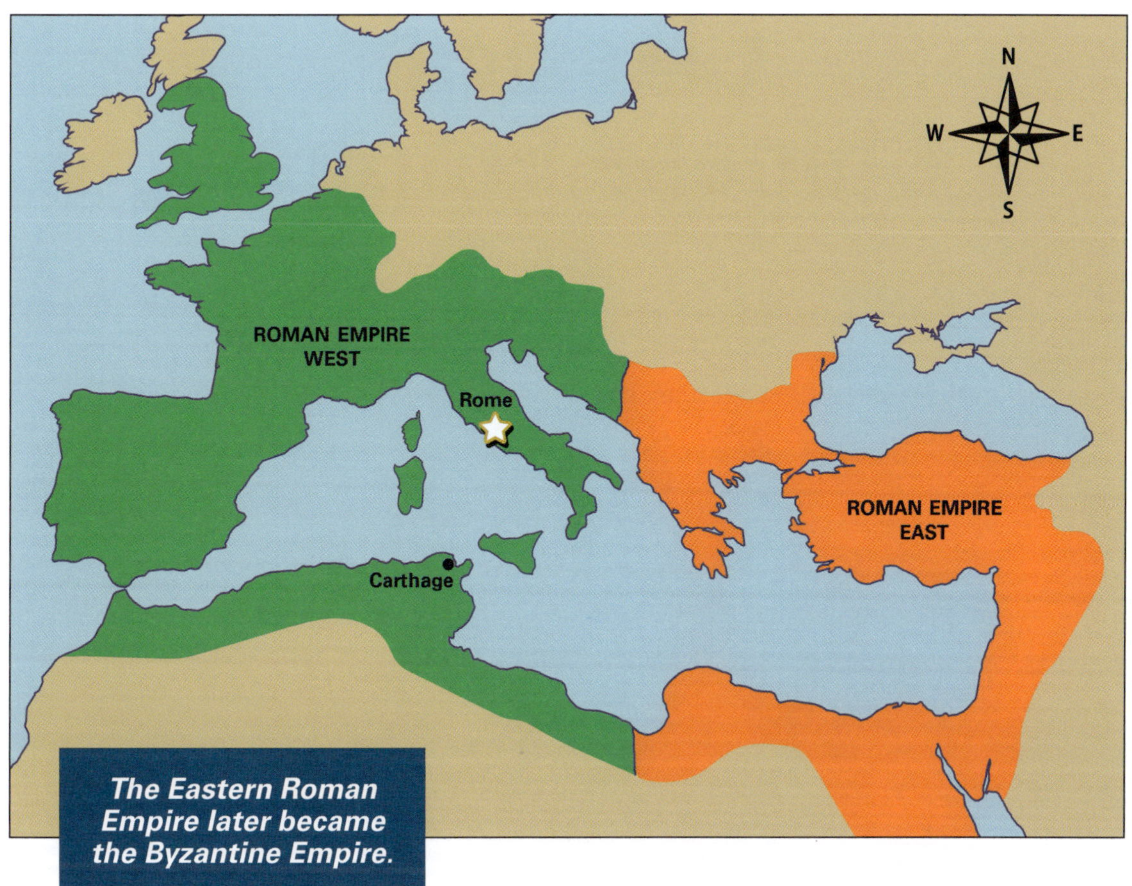

The Eastern Roman Empire later became the Byzantine Empire.

Rome grew by conquest. It fought many wars. Three wars were against Carthage of northern Africa. Rome eventually won and took over their vast territories. Rome's government was a republic. The senate was powerful. Because of civil wars it was taken over by emperors. Later, it divided into the two empires. The Western Empire fell to invaders in 476 CE. The Eastern Roman Empire continued for almost another thousand years.

Classical Chinese Empires

Terracotta or clay warriors from the Qin Dynasty.

In 221 BCE the Qin Dynasty united China, and it's remained one nation ever since. But the emperor was very harsh. He punished or killed those who disagreed with his rules. There were few freedoms and a lot of **taxes**. Shortly after he died his dynasty was overthrown. Recently, his tomb was discovered. It has thousands of life-sized clay statues of soldiers and horses. They were supposed to protect him in the afterlife.

Silk was traded to Rome and other empires.

The Han Dynasty followed the Qin. It lasted over 300 years. It kept many features of the Qin government but was not as harsh. The people prospered and the empire grew. They invented paper, the compass, and better sailing ships. They also traded silk goods with other empires by land and sea. But as the population grew, the people got poorer. The empire declined. Invaders from the north ended the Han Dynasty in 220 CE.

Silk comes from the cocoons of silk worms.

Classical Empires of India

An ancient Hindu site from the Gupta Empire.

The Mauryan Empire was in northern India. Its greatest leader was Ashoka. He was a warrior and conquered southern India. After a battle left many people killed, he gave up military conquest. He became a Buddhist and a kind leader. After Ashoka's death in 232 BCE, the Mauryan Empire began to decline. The Gupta Empire united India again about 500 years later. India was prosperous under Gupta rule. Learning, art, and religious expression flourished.

Maya Empire

The Maya Empire was in Central America. Their climate was warm and tropical. They invented a writing system and a calendar using hieroglyphs. They had vast trading networks and built grand buildings. Many Maya buildings still stand today. Classical Maya Empire flourished from 300 CE to 800 CE. It completely collapsed in 1500 CE because of Spanish invaders.

A Maya vessel with writing made in about 350 CE.

Rise and Fall of Classical Empires

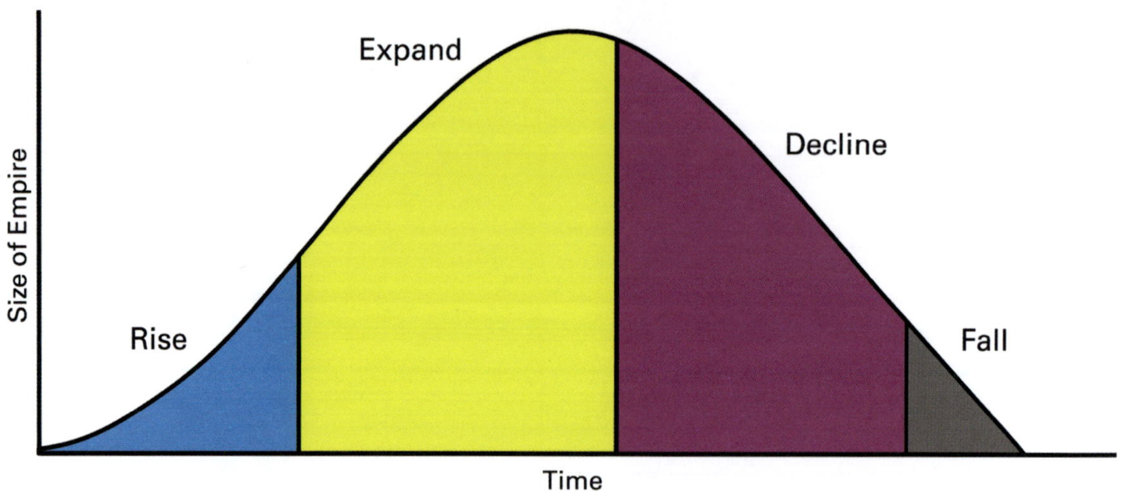

Classical empires flourished worldwide. They all ruled large areas and populations. They had writing systems and complex governments. They maintained trade networks. They used warfare and the military to conquer new territories. They had another thing in common—they all collapsed. All classical empires went through the same four stages. They rise, expand, decline, and fall.

QUIZ

Circle the correct answer.

1. ________ ruled large areas and populations.

Pyramids 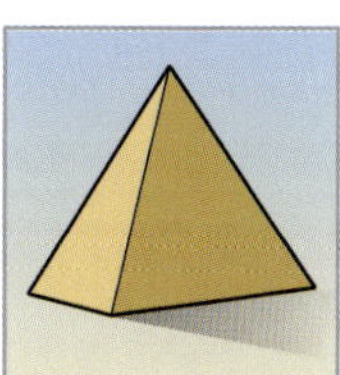

Writing 

Classical empires 

2. Classical empires conquered new lands with a ________.

military 

writing system 

religion 

3. Classical empires traveled long distances to ________.

oceans 

irrigate 

trade 

4. Classical empires made grand ________.

architecture 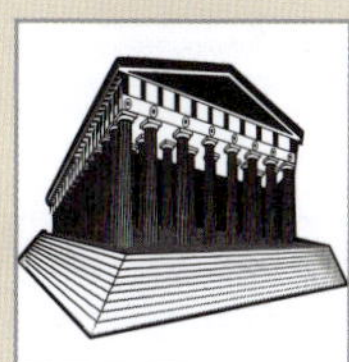

ice ages 

population 

5. A ________ is a period of 100 years.

military century 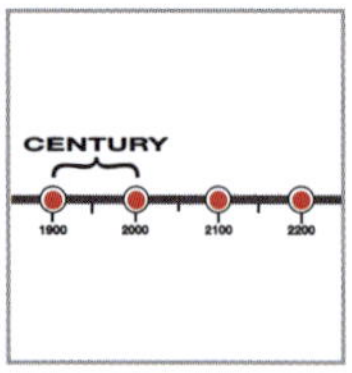 city-state

6. A government where people vote is a ________ .

country democracy  equator

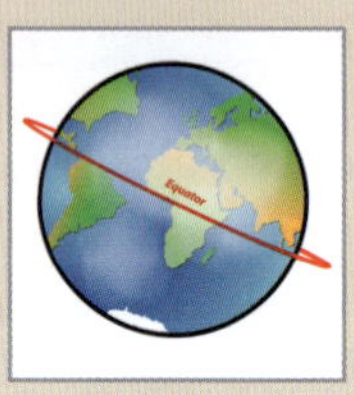

7. A ________ is a payment people make to the government.

trade slave  tax

Write About It

CHAPTER
8

Trade

A theme of history

Trade began during prehistoric times.

Trade can boost manufacturing.

Trade spreads ideas.

The slave trade created both wealth and misery.

Trade Timeline

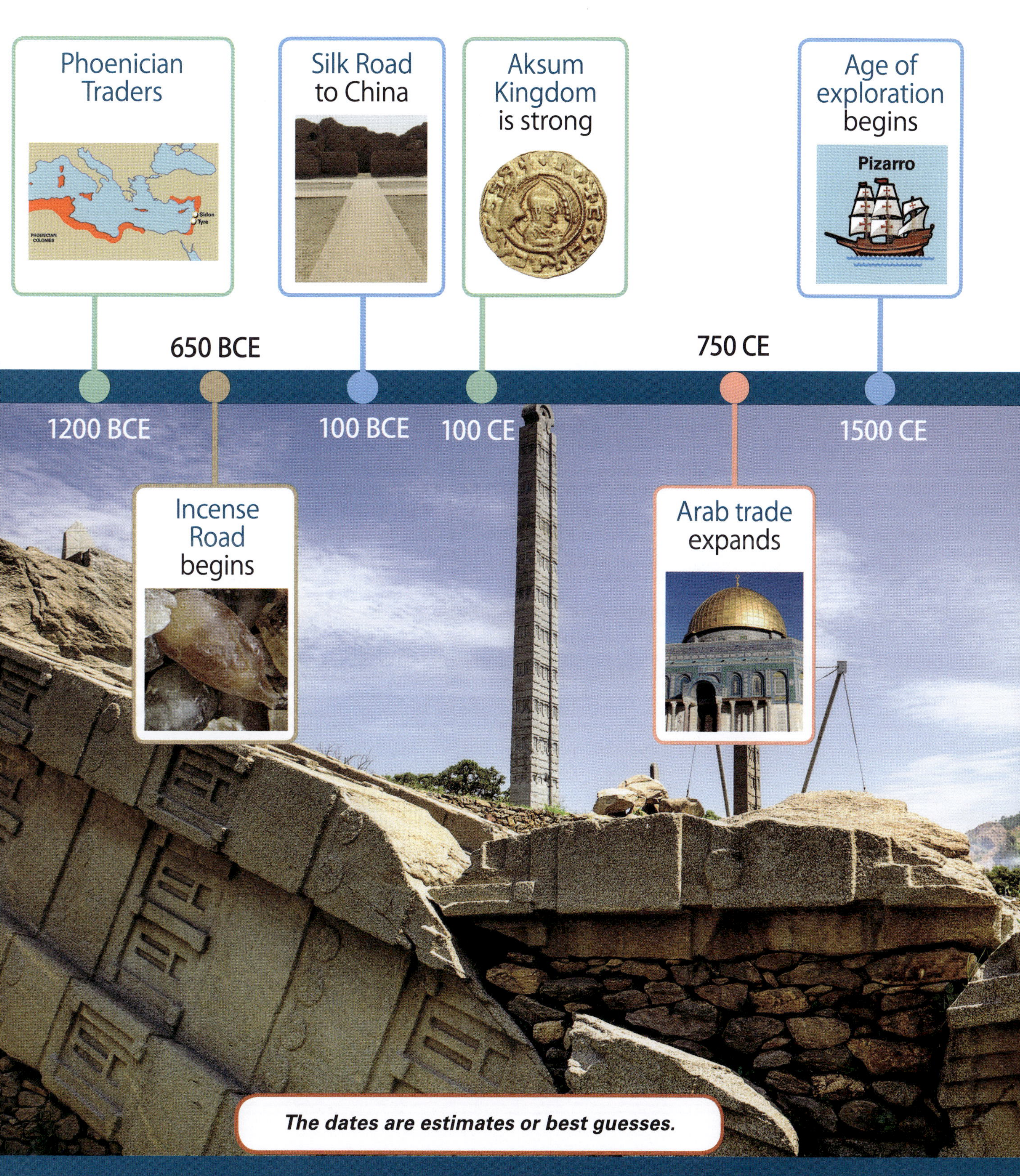

The dates are estimates or best guesses.

VOCABULARY

trade		to exchange goods or services
caravan		a group of merchants traveling together on land for safety
market		a place where goods are bought and sold
natural resource		a material provided by the earth that people use

A place to buy something

___ ___ ___ ___ ___ ___

VOCABULARY

manufacture		to produce a large number of items for use or trade
barter		to trade goods or services without using money
currency		money that's used in a culture
wealth		a lot of money or possessions

Find the word!

To make lots of something

___ ___ ___ ___ ___ ___ ___ ___ ___ ___ ___

Trade

Ancient trade map.

Trade is an important theme of history. But it wasn't invented like agriculture or writing. People always traded. Early cultures traded one thing for another thing, like salt for beads. Later cultures paid for traded goods with money. Even ancient cultures traded long distances. They often traveled by sea. It was faster and easier than over land. But they also traveled by **caravan**.

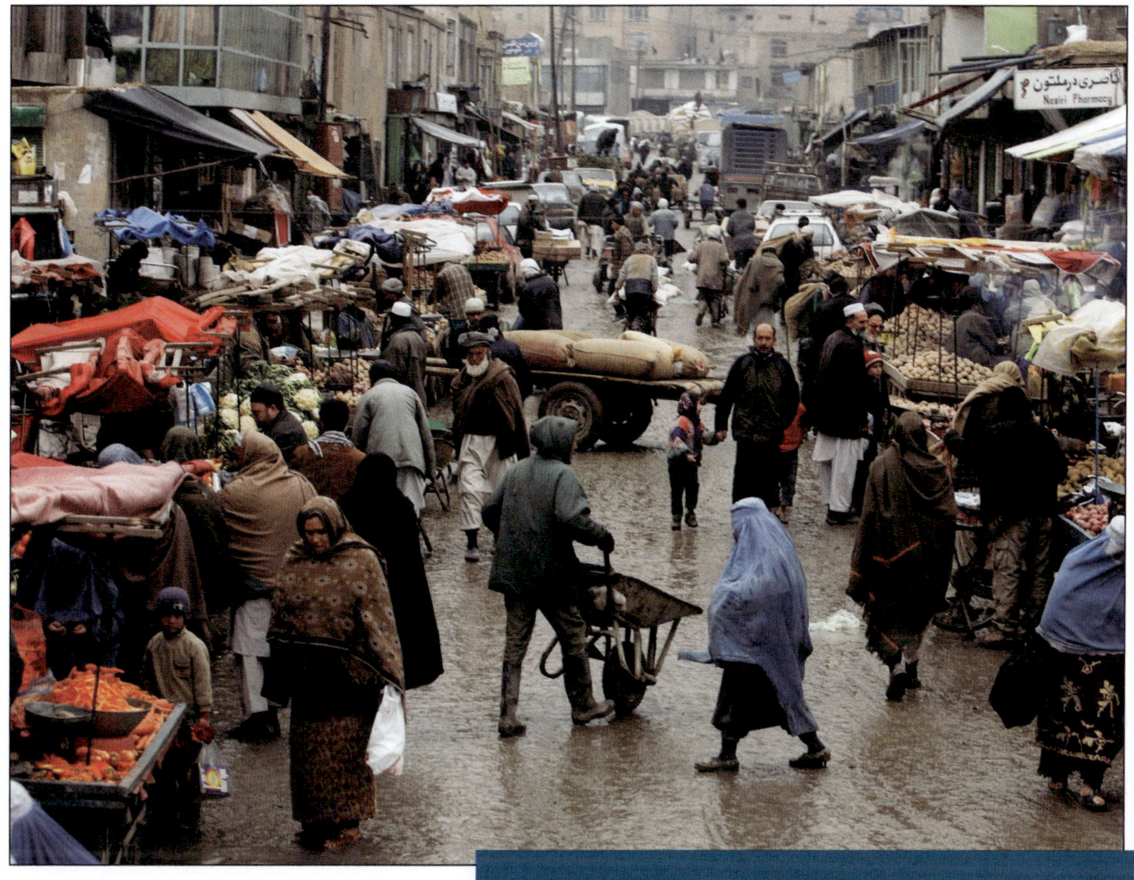

A market today showing a mix of cultures.

Trading usually took place in a **market**. People from different cultures would need to talk with each other. They needed to share a language. Greek became a common trading language in ancient times. Now it's English. Sharing a language helped spread ideas and customs. Religions spread through trade. So did disease. The bubonic plague was a terrible disease in the Middle Ages. It was brought to Europe by trading ships.

IN FOCUS

Manufacturing

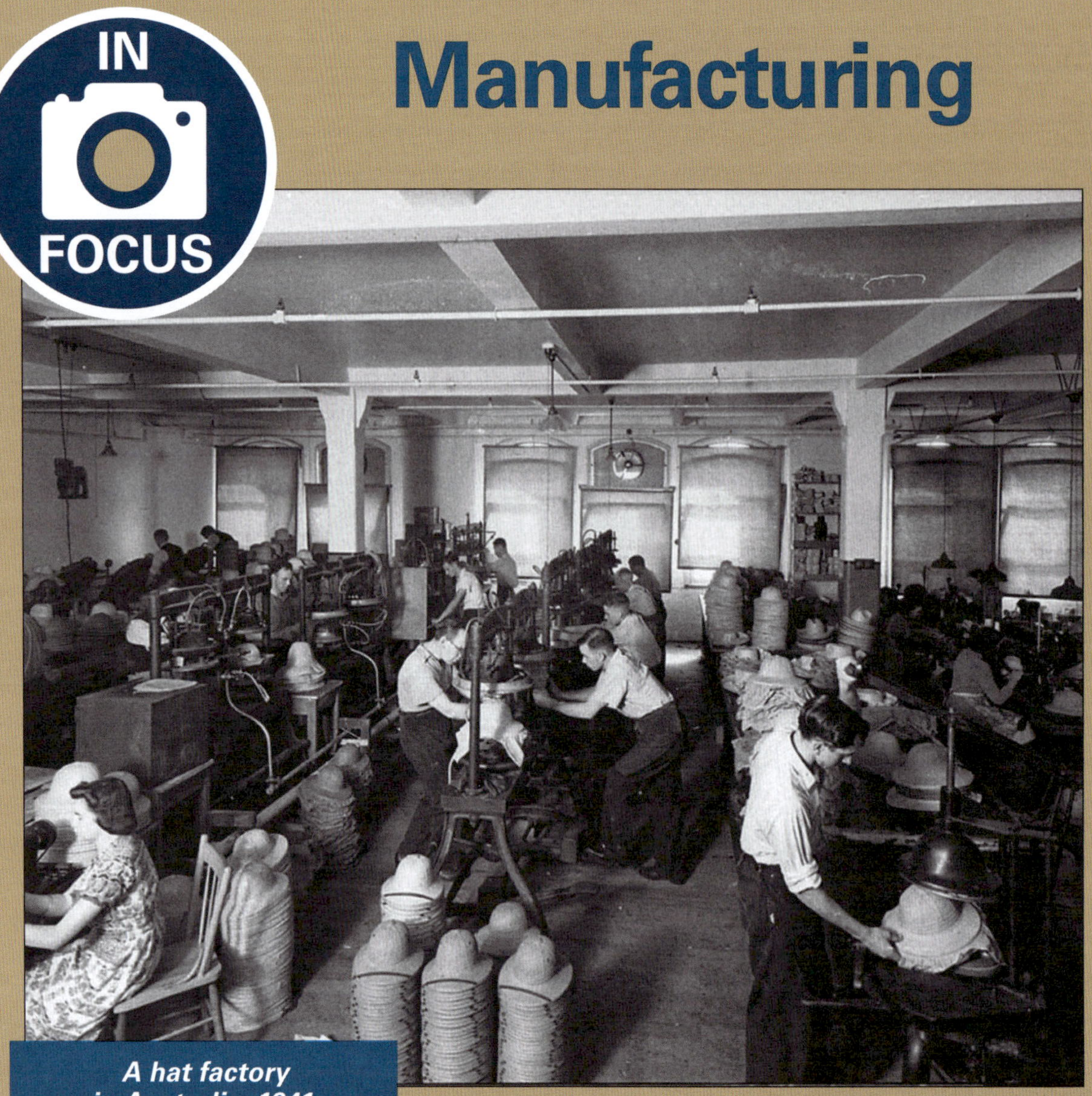

A hat factory in Australia, 1941.

To trade, a culture needs a product that another culture wants. Sometimes it's a **natural resource**. Gold, salt, copper, and oil are natural resources. A culture with few natural resources will have to **manufacture** a product to trade. Silk, pottery, steel, and computers are manufactured. Manufacturing products creates jobs. Early civilizations had artisans who made products. Later on, factories were common. Both helped the economy by creating jobs.

Obsidian

An ancient tool carved from an obsidian rock.

Obsidian is a natural resource. It's a rock that can be as sharp as glass, but stronger. It was in much demand in the ancient world. Obsidian was used to make spear and knife blades. It was later used for beautiful pottery and mirrors. It was an important resource all over the world. Historians believe obsidian was the first widely traded object.

A pile of obsidian rocks.

Phoenician Traders

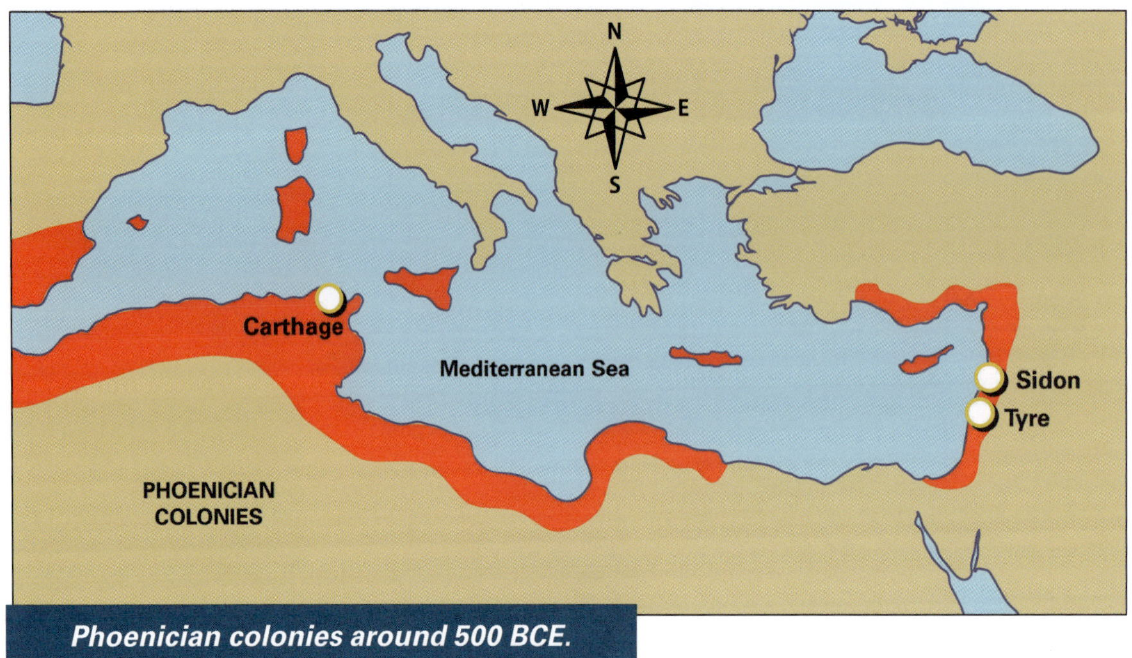

Phoenician colonies around 500 BCE.

Phoenicians were important ancient traders. They traded across the vast Mediterranean Sea. They built the best ships. They had a great product, mollusk, used to make purple dye. It became the color of royalty, especially for the Romans. The alphabet was brought to Europe by Phoenicians. They also founded Carthage. Carthage was a powerful culture that had wars with the Roman Republic.

A carving showing a Phoenician ship.

Silent Barter System

Traders used the silent **barter** system when language differences were a problem. It was called silent because they didn't talk to each other. They put goods at a given spot. Their trading partners did the same. If the trade worked for both partners, they exchanged the goods. Traders in Africa used this system to trade gold for salt.

A map showing salt for gold trade routes in Africa.

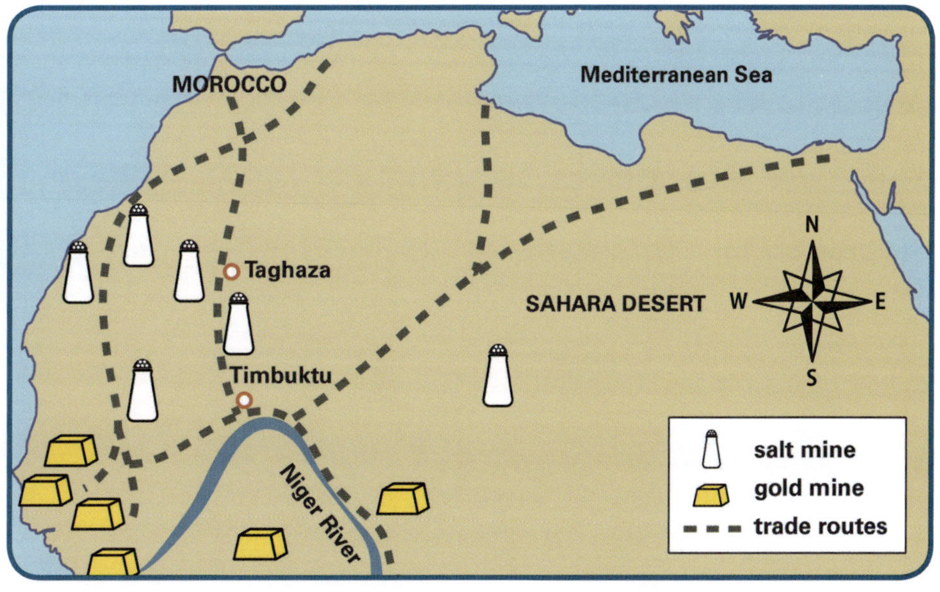

Incense Road

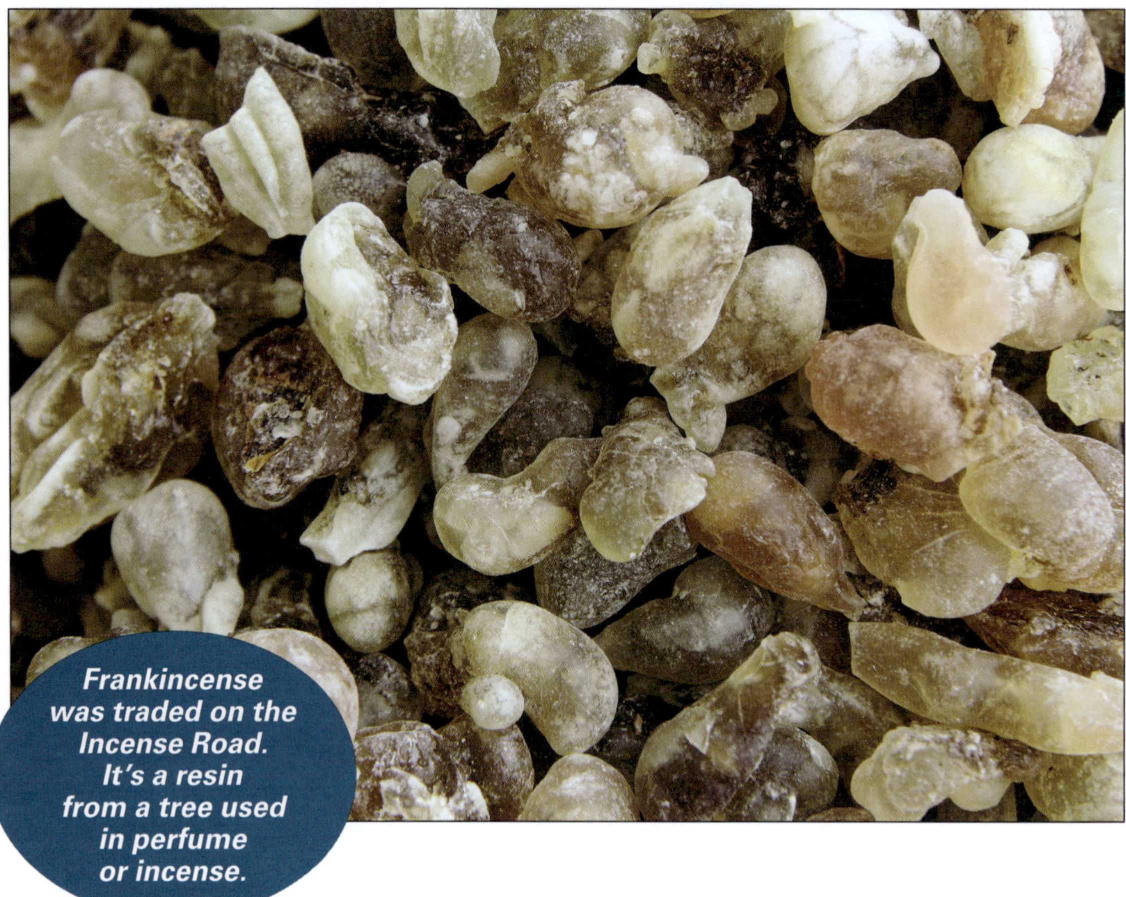

Frankincense was traded on the Incense Road. It's a resin from a tree used in perfume or incense.

The Incense Road was a successful trade route for almost 800 years. Traders carried products like spices and incense from the Arabian Peninsula to the Mediterranean Sea. It was a long and dangerous route over land and sea. The products were lightweight to make the trip easier. The Incense Road lasted from about 650 BCE to 150 CE.

Silk Road

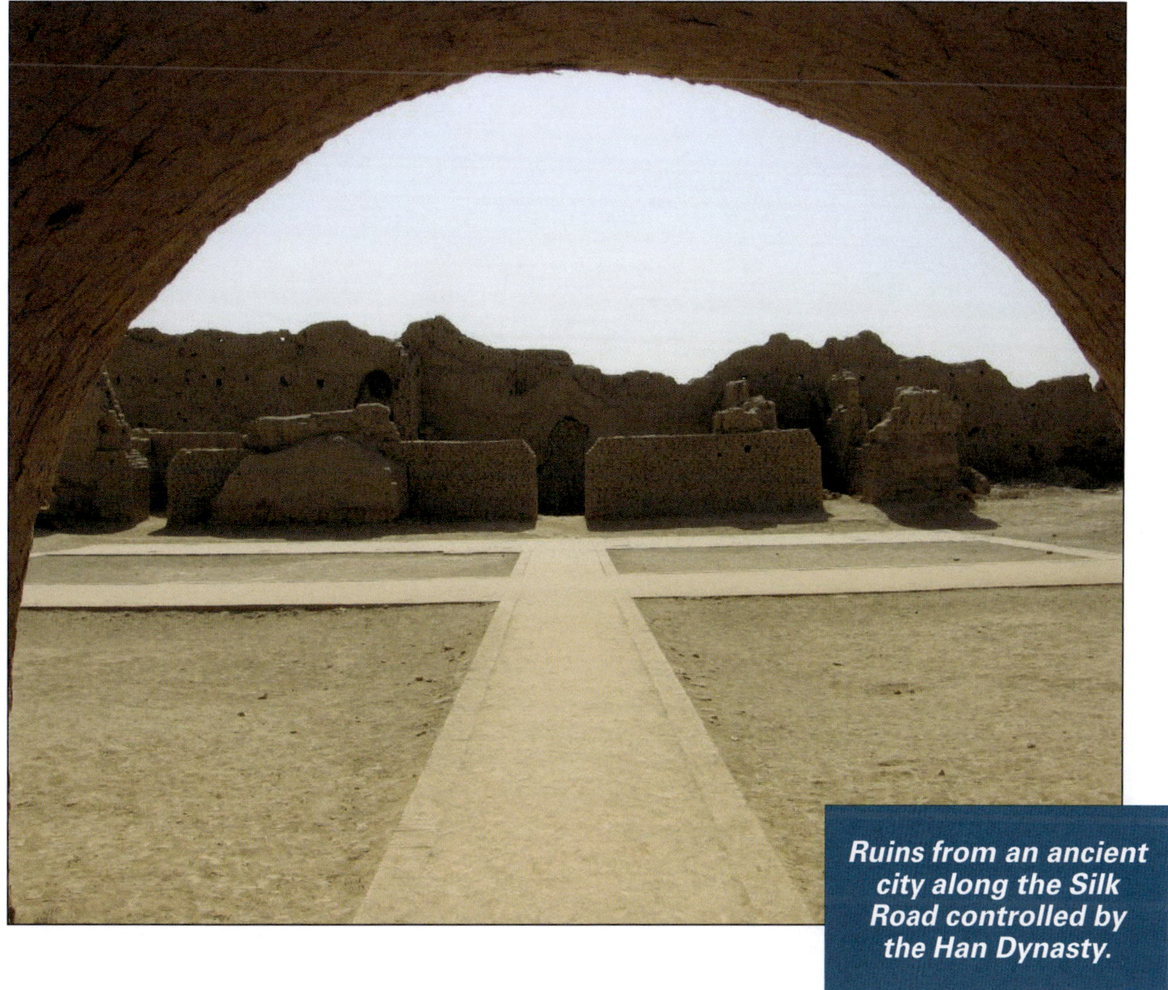

Ruins from an ancient city along the Silk Road controlled by the Han Dynasty.

The Silk Road started during the Han Dynasty in China. Other empires had great demand for Chinese silk. The Silk Road was 4000 miles long. It went through many states and cultures along the way. Marco Polo traveled the Silk Road beginning in 1271 CE. He traveled between Europe and China and wrote about his adventures. He introduced many Europeans to the wonders of China.

Kingdom of Aksum

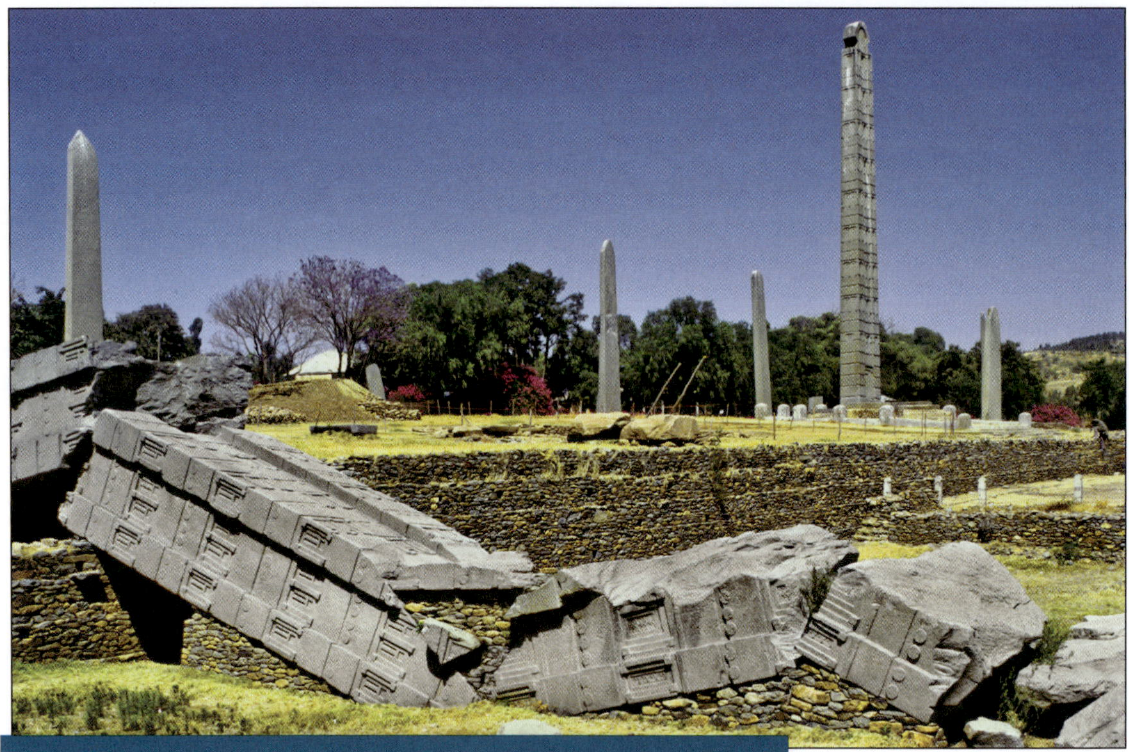

Aksum is known for its large steles or stone columns.

The Kingdom of Aksum was a powerful trading empire. It was located in northeast Africa along the Red Sea. From 100 CE to 500 CE it controlled much of the trade between India and the Roman Empire. It created its own **currency**. Historians can trace the kings of Aksum by examining their coins. Historians also study the large columns the Aksumites carved from stone.

Coins from Aksum, circa 410 CE

Arab Traders

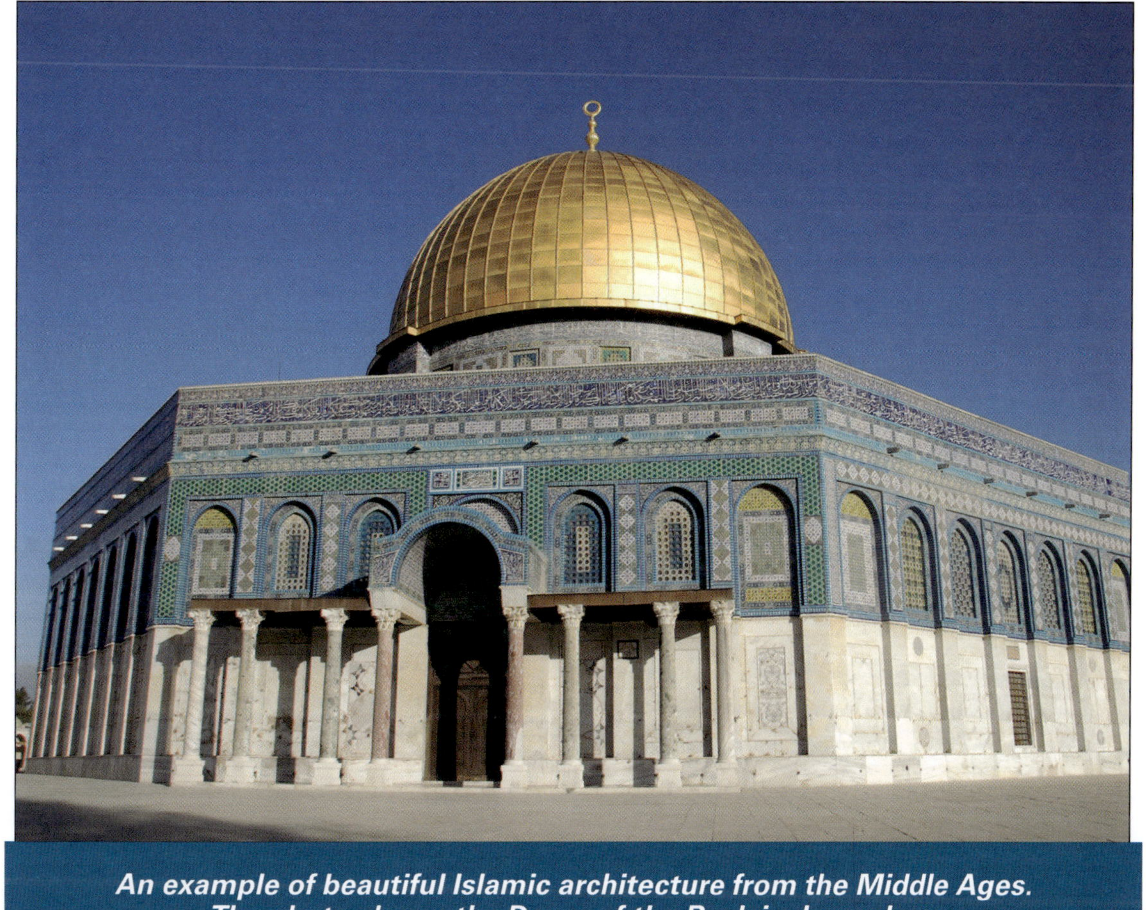

An example of beautiful Islamic architecture from the Middle Ages. The photo shows the Dome of the Rock in Jerusalem.

Arab nations built a strong trading network during the Middle Ages. The Arab traders brought goods from Africa and Asia to Europe. The Arab nations were Islamic. Trading helped spread the religion of Islam. It also created **wealth**. The Arab nations created wonderful art and architecture. They are also known for advancing science and medicine. They introduced Arabic numerals to Europe. That's the number system we use today.

Trade and Exploration

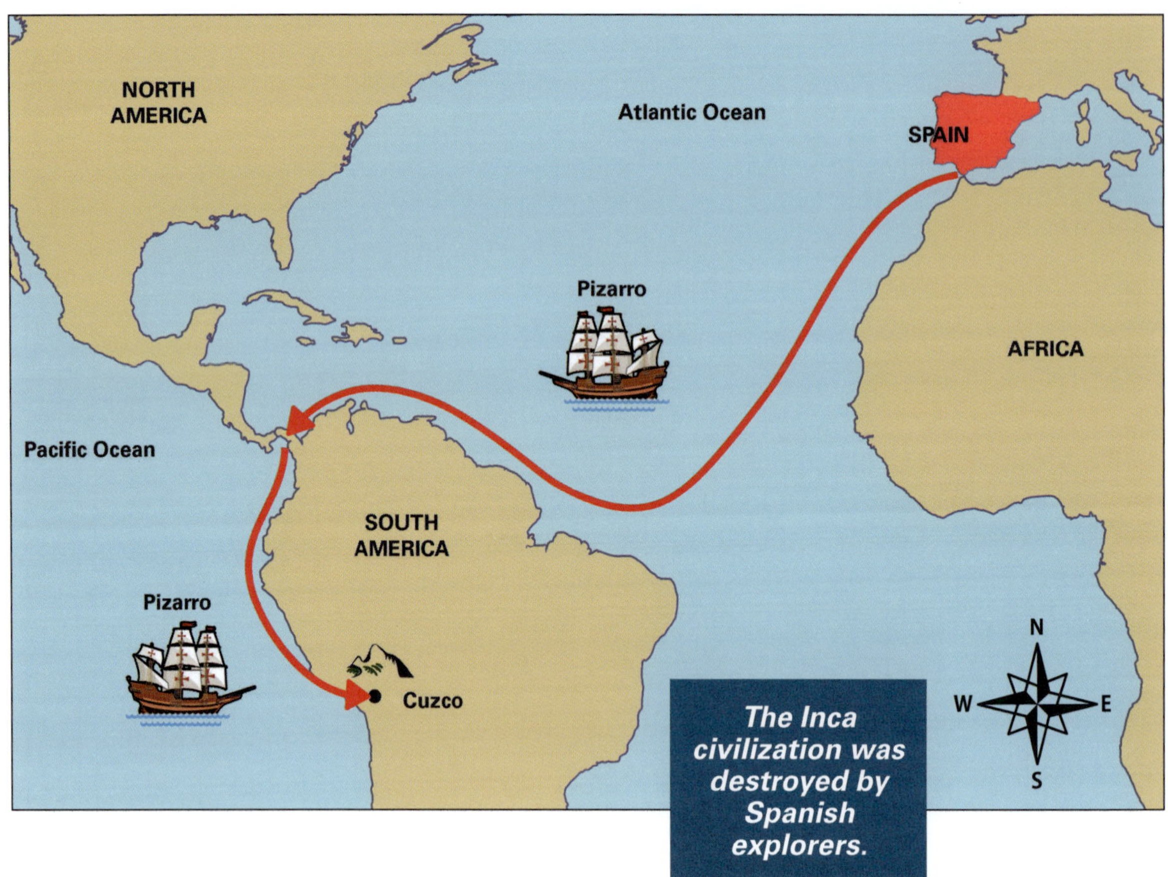

The Age of Exploration began around 1500 CE. Europeans sailed the world to expand trade routes. They found new lands, including the Americas. They met cultures unknown to them. The Incas and Aztecs were large civilizations with much wealth. The Spanish didn't trade with them. The Spanish just took their gold and silver and destroyed their cultures. Trade can turn into conquest.

Atlantic Slave Trade

A drawing showing the loading of slaves on a ship for trade.

Europeans set up colonies in the Americas. They grew valuable crops like sugar and tobacco. But they needed a lot of workers. So the Atlantic slave trade began. European ships brought captured Africans to the Americas as slaves. About 11 million slaves were traded between 1550 and 1800. It brought wealth to the traders but misery to the slaves.

E-commerce

You can buy and sell products from all over the world through e-commerce.

The invention of the Internet led to a new way of trading. E-commerce is a virtual marketplace. You don't visit a real market or store. You look at web pages on your computer. You can buy and sell products from all over the world without leaving your home. Trade between nations is still important today. But the Internet lets you become a global trader too.

QUIZ

Circle the correct answer.

1. Trade began during ______.

documents

prehistoric times

the Roman Empire

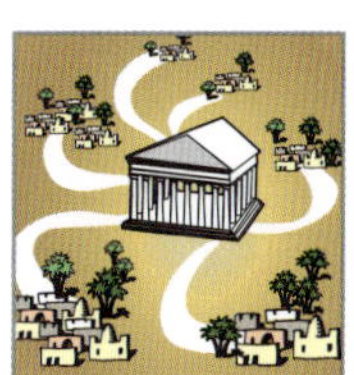

2. Producing a large number of the same item is ______.

military

manufacturing

social class

3. Ideas like religion and technology are often spread by ______.

trade

protein

archaeologists

4. The slave trade created misery for the ______.

archaeologists

market

slaves

5. Money used in a culture is their ______.

currency natural resource religion

6. Travelers along the Incense Road crossed the desert by ______.

empire cavalry caravan

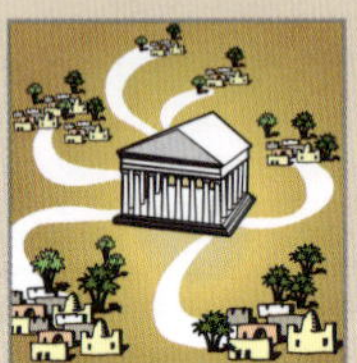

7. Exchanging goods without money is to ______.

barter century writing

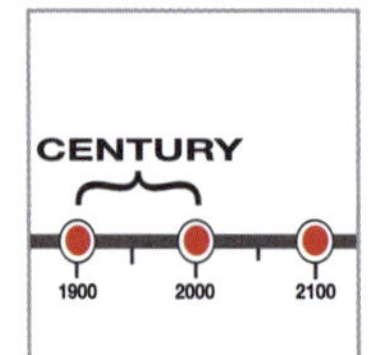

Write About It

CHAPTER 9

Middle Ages

An era of history 500 to 1450

The Roman Empire fell and its territory divided into smaller states.

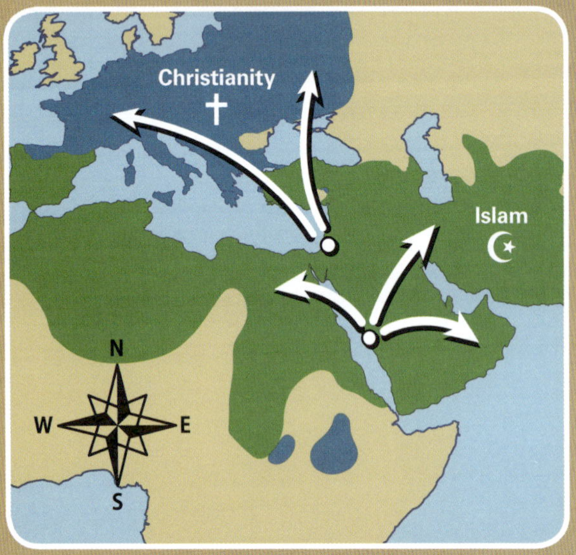

Religions expanded into new lands.

The bubonic plague spread death through Asia and Europe.

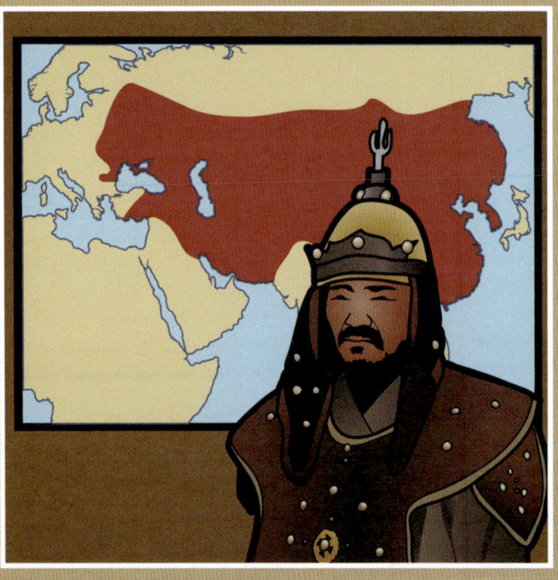

Mongol Empire became a superpower.

Middle Ages Timeline

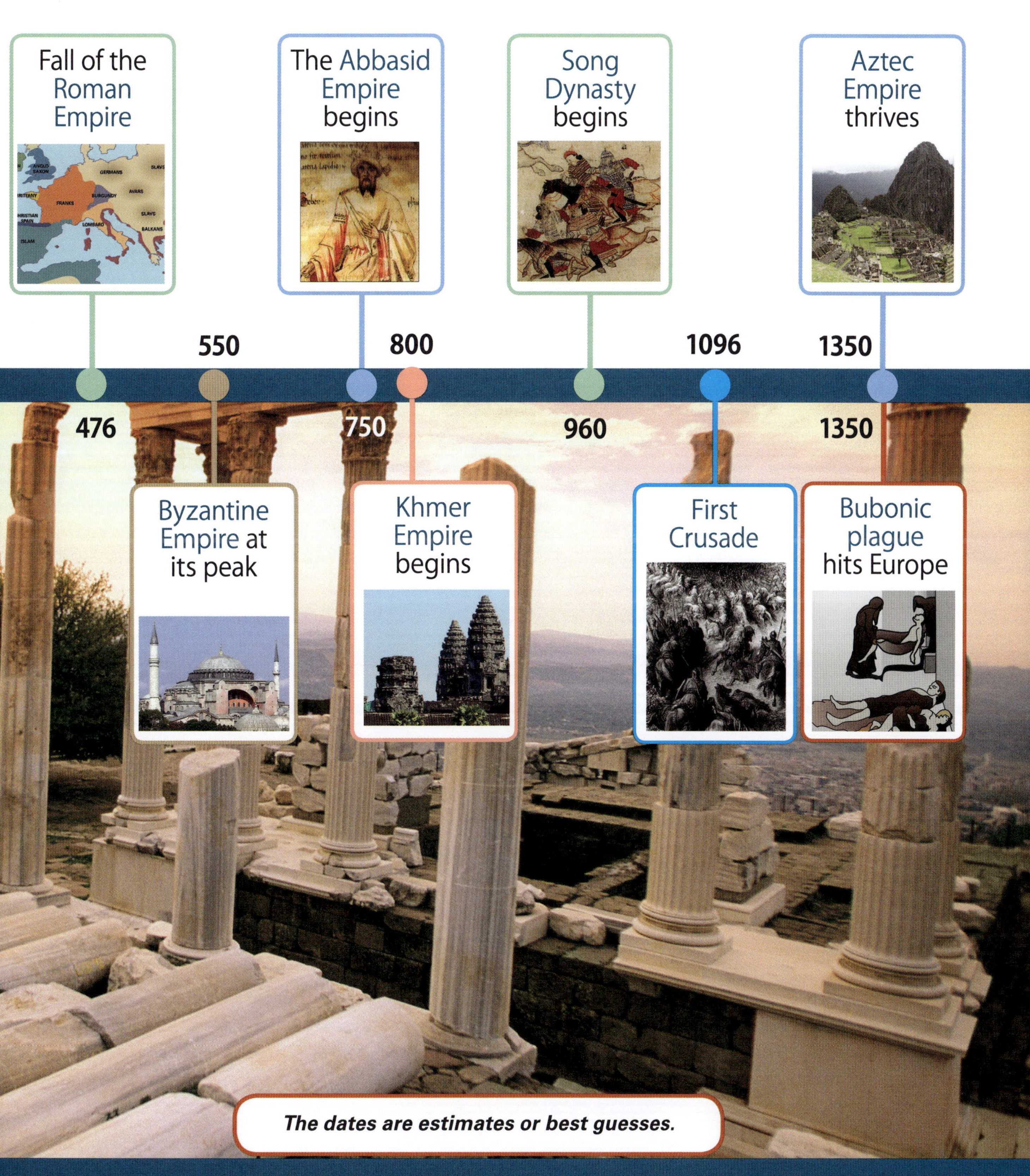

Fall of the Roman Empire
476
Byzantine Empire at its peak
550
The Abbasid Empire begins
750
Khmer Empire begins
800
Song Dynasty begins
960
First Crusade
1096
Aztec Empire thrives
1350
Bubonic plague hits Europe
1350
The dates are estimates or best guesses.

VOCABULARY

feudalism		a social system that ranks people by power and status
Christianity		a major religion based upon the teachings of Jesus Christ
Islam		a major religion based upon the teachings of Muhammad
Crusades		wars for control of the Holy Land

A social system that ranks people

___ ___ ___ ___ ___ ___ ___ ___ ___

VOCABULARY

dynasty	 a line of rulers from one family
medieval	 relating to the Middle Ages
cavalry	 soldiers who fought on horseback
plague	 a terrible disease that spreads

Find the word!

Soldiers on horseback

__ __ __ __ __ __ __

Middle Ages

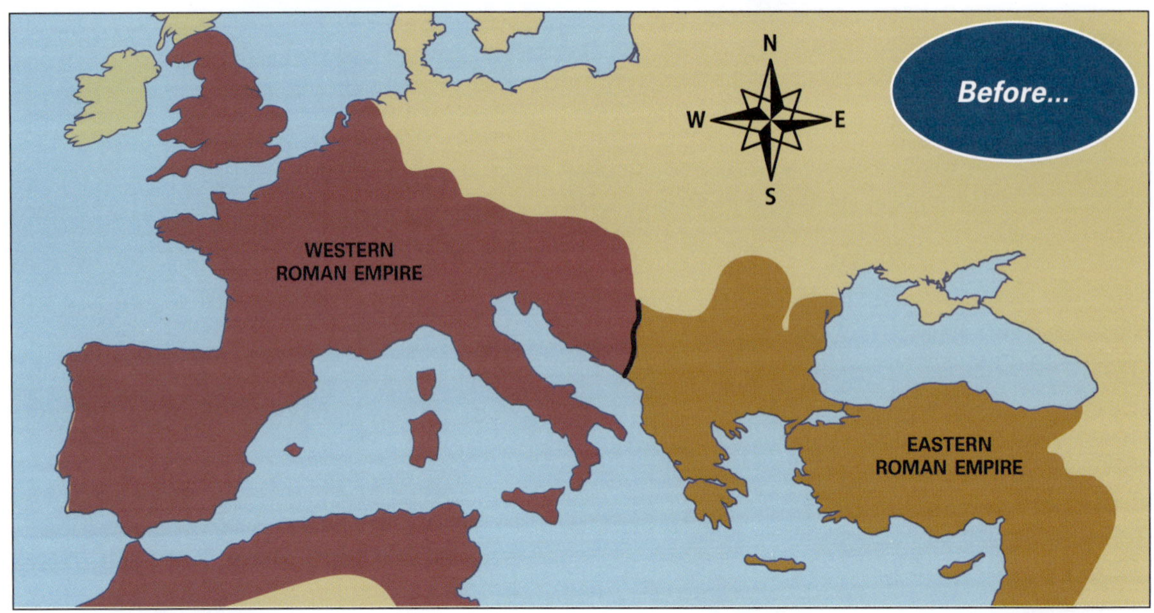

This era begins with the fall of the Western Roman Empire. That vast territory was divided into smaller states. **Feudalism** became an important economic system in Europe. States were run by royalty, like kings and queens. A few rich nobles were landowners. Knights were soldiers who protected the nobles. But most people were very poor and life was hard.

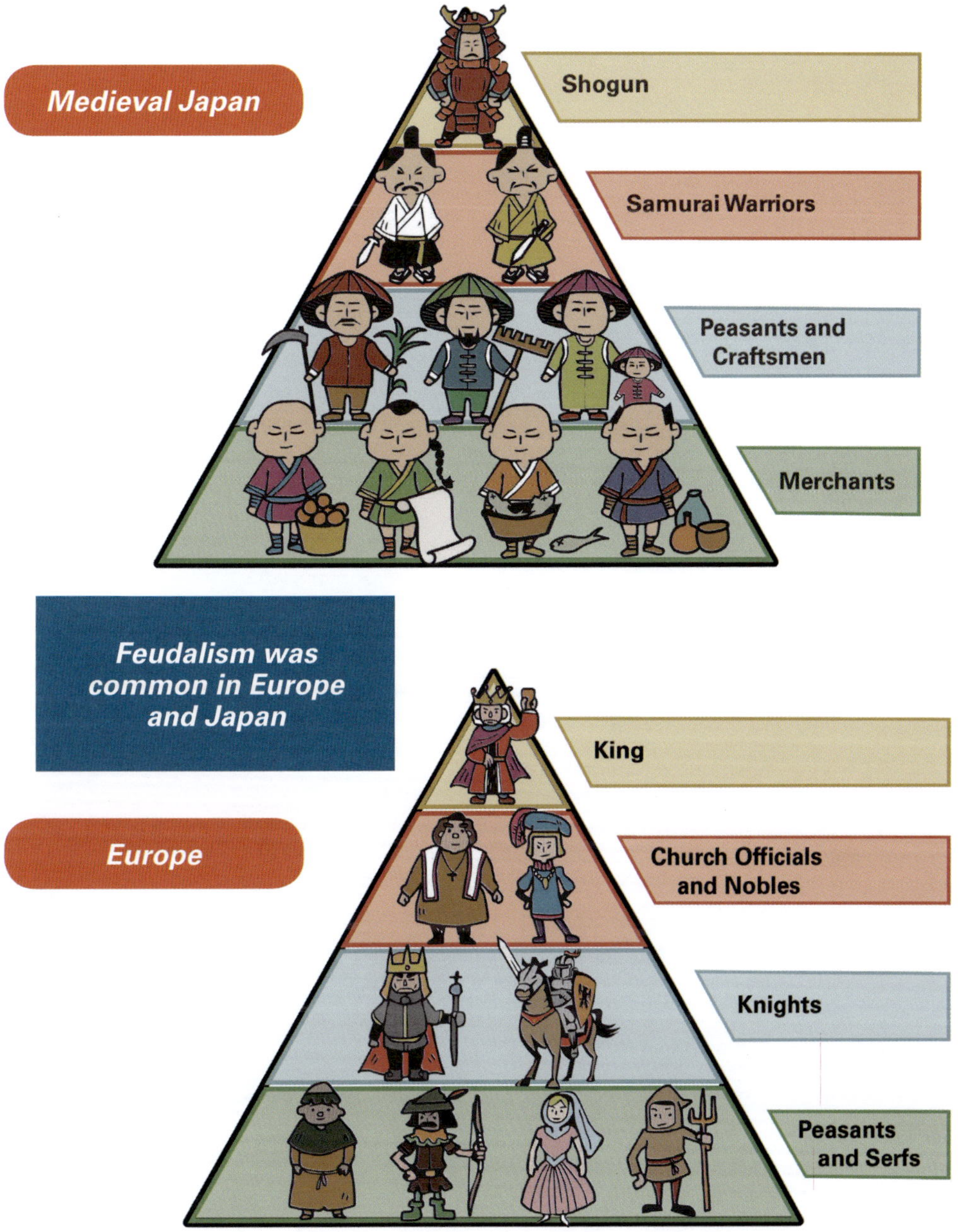

Many cultures around the world advanced during this era. The Arab states became powerful and wealthy. China and India had thriving civilizations. The Inca and Aztec cultures grew in the Americas. But they had no contact with the rest of the world. New empires also developed in Africa. Near the end of this era the Mongol Empire became a superpower.

Religion

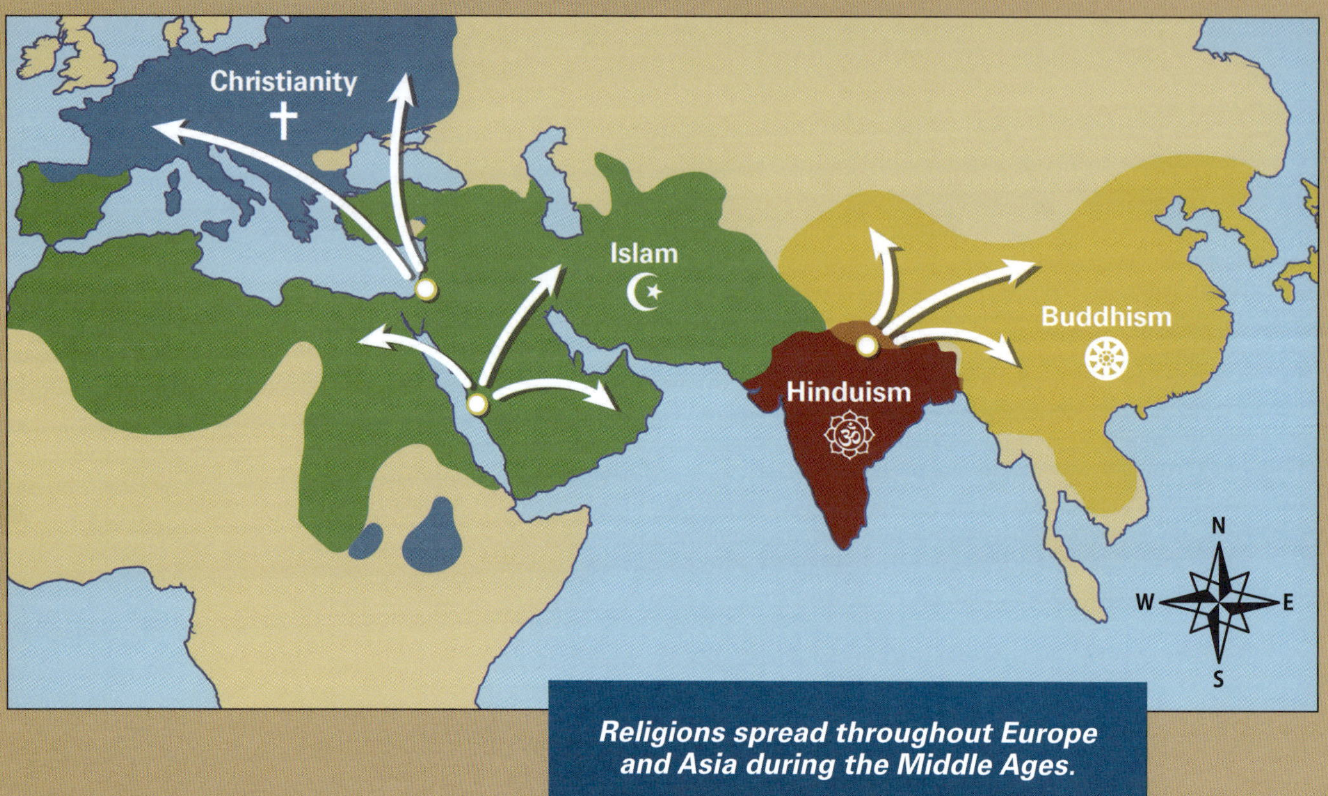

Religions spread throughout Europe and Asia during the Middle Ages.

Religions spread throughout Europe and Asia during the Middle Ages. In this era, the role of religion was front and center. Governments and religions joined together. Many key events were influenced by religion. **Christianity** spread throughout Europe. **Islam** became the primary religion in the Middle East. And the Buddhist religion reached new territories in Asia. At times the Christian and Islamic states were at peace. But there were also long periods of war and conflict.

Byzantine Empire

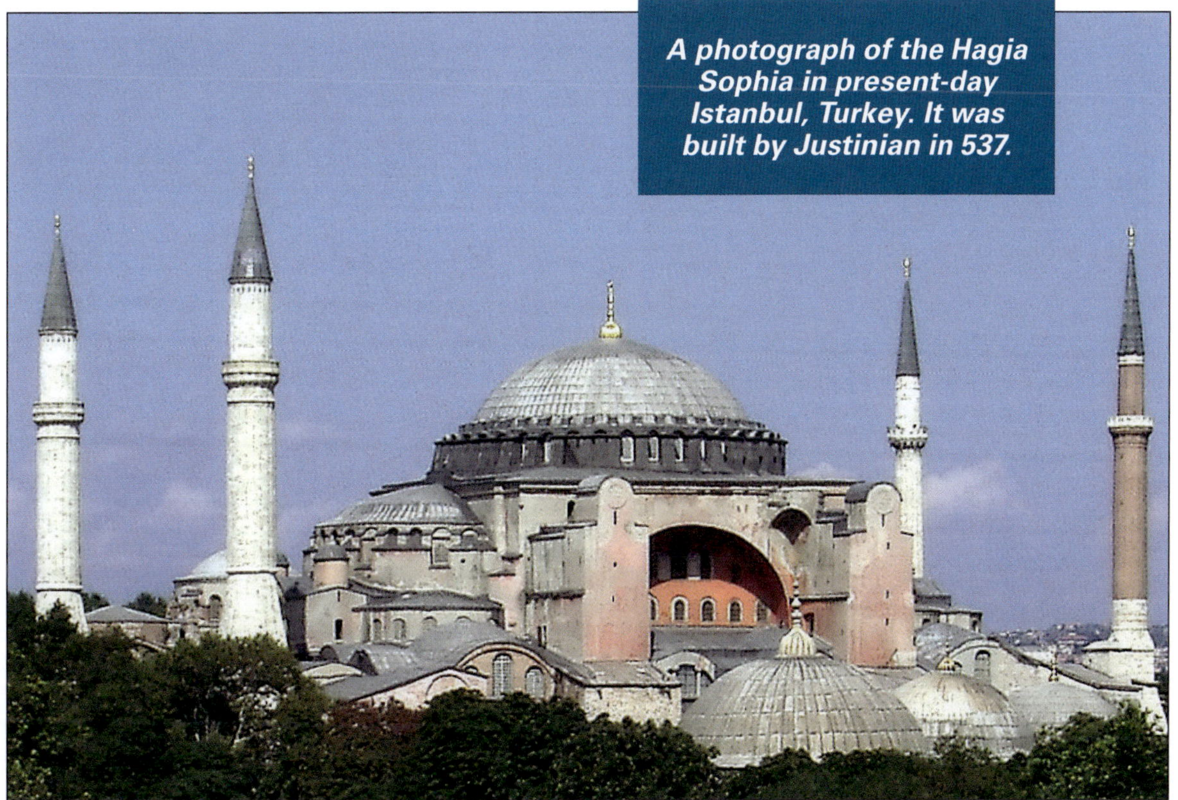
A photograph of the Hagia Sophia in present-day Istanbul, Turkey. It was built by Justinian in 537.

The Byzantine Empire began as the Eastern Roman Empire. Constantinople was its capital. It grew to its biggest under Emperor Justinian around 550. The Byzantine Empire was a Christian state that split from the Roman Catholic Church. The Byzantine Eastern Orthodox Church is common today in eastern Europe and Russia. Later, it lost territory to Islamic states. The Byzantine Empire fell to the Ottoman Empire in 1453.

Abbasid Empire

A painting of Jabir ibn Hayyan, known as the father of chemistry.

The Abbasid Empire began by overthrowing the Umayyads in 750. Both empires were Islamic. The Abbasid family believed they were more closely related to Muhammad, the founder of Islam. The empire grew very large. But Abbasidians didn't rule the states in the empire. They gave religious leadership from the capital in Baghdad. Science and philosophy flourished during this time. The Abbasid Empire ended when the Mongols sacked Baghdad in 1258.

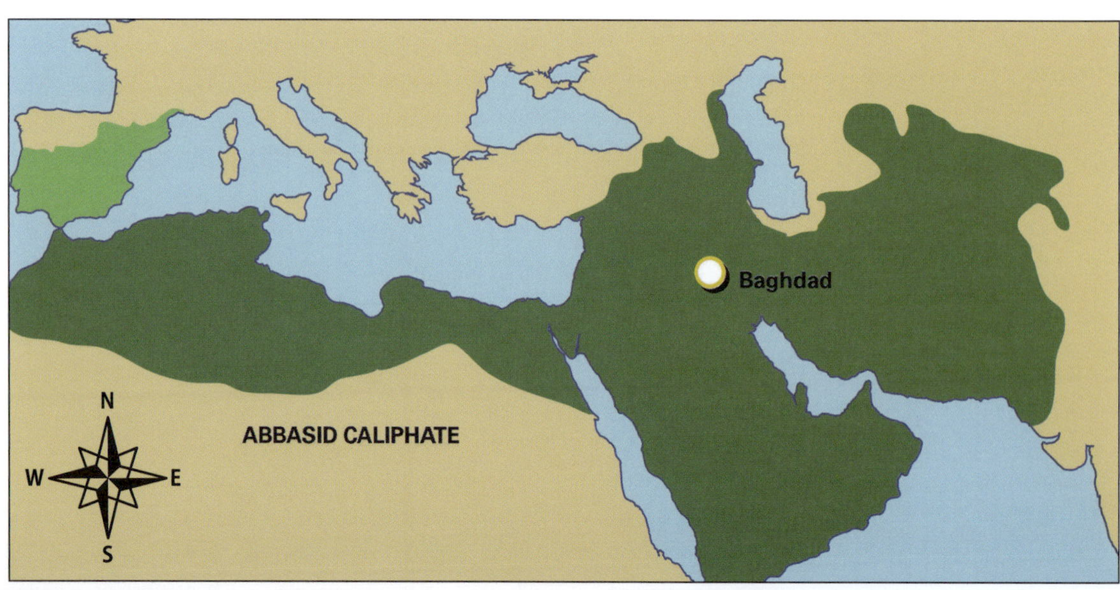

The Crusades

Drawing of a major battle during a crusade.

European Christians wanted to take back their Holy Land from Islamic rule. The first **crusade** began in 1095. Armies of Christians traveled to Palestine to wage war. The last crusade was in 1487. Jews, Christians, and Muslims were killed in large numbers. In the end, Islam continued to rule Palestine until modern times.

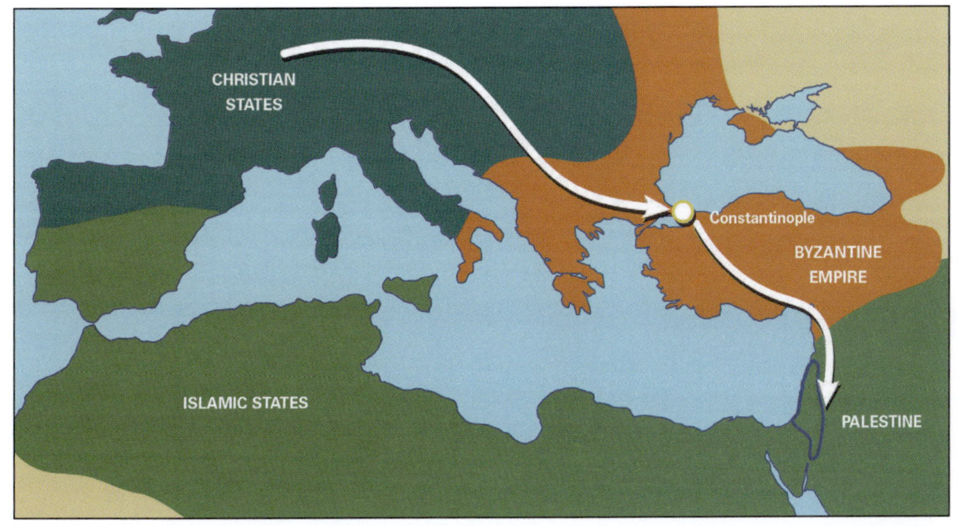

Tang and Song Dynasties

The Tang **Dynasty** took control in 618. The Tang united China and gained new territories. They expanded trade routes and accepted Buddhism. The Song Dynasty rule began in 960. The Song lost some territory. But China became the most advanced and populous culture in the world. The Chinese had many important inventions, like gunpowder and paper. Their population grew to over 100 million people.

Medieval Japan

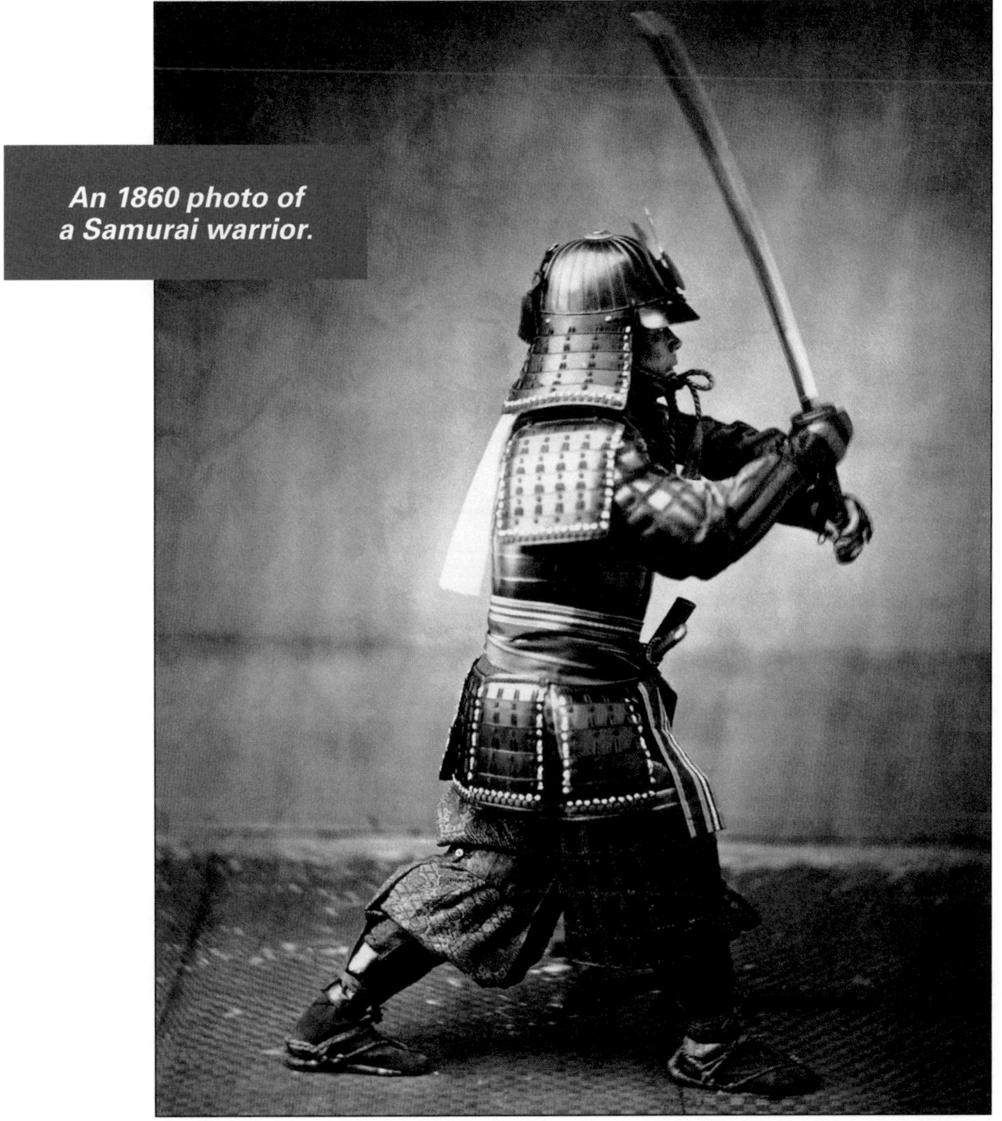

An 1860 photo of a Samurai warrior.

Japan is an island nation. Geography protects Japan from invaders. But they were influenced by others. Their writing system came from China, and Buddhism came from Korea. Japan developed a feudal system different than the one in Europe. Warfare was common in **medieval** Japan. Top military leaders became very powerful, as did Samurai warriors. Japan didn't have contact with Europeans until 1542.

Mongol Empire

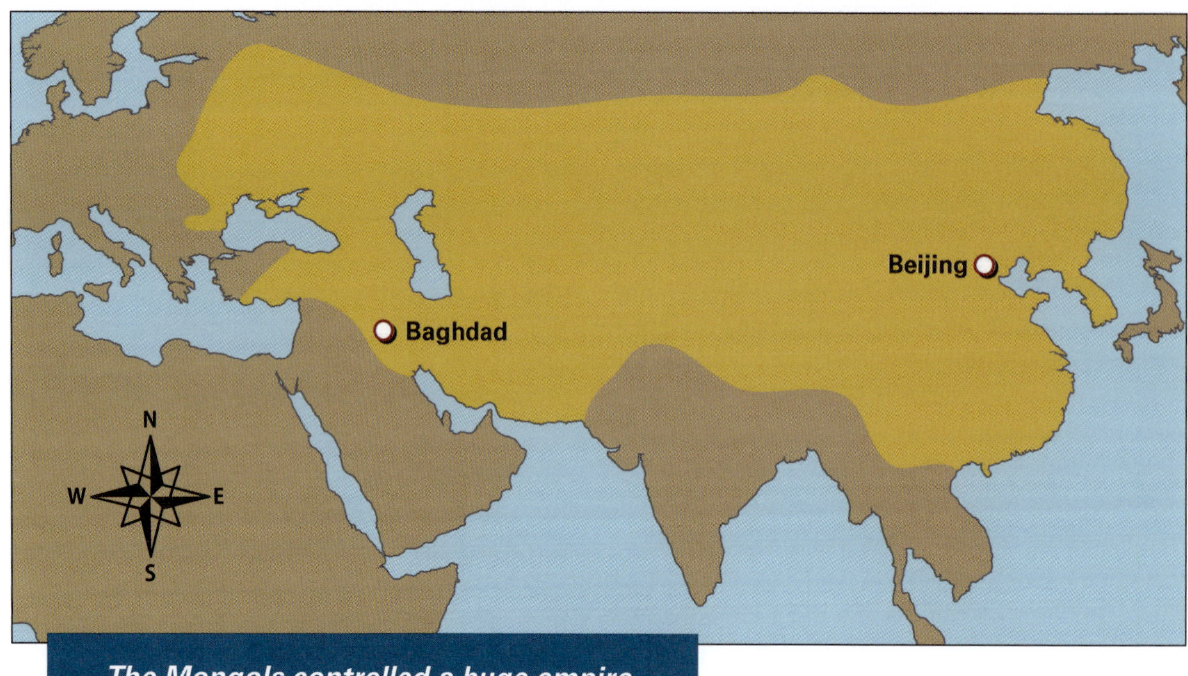

The Mongols controlled a huge empire.

The Mongols were nomads from Mongolia. They were great on horseback and were fearsome warriors. They united for conquest under Genghis Khan. The empire grew rapidly because of their huge and powerful **cavalry**. In warfare they were ruthless. Once a territory was conquered they were more humane. They protected trade routes like the Silk Road. People could travel safely. After Genghis Khan died, his relatives fought for control of the empire.

Genghis Khan conquered China.

Kublai Khan was the grandson of Genghis Khan. He took control in 1260. He became the first invader to conquer all of China. He started the Yuan Dynasty. Its capital was in present-day Beijing. The Mongols now ruled the largest empire in the history of the world. It soon was divided into four parts. Then the Yuan Dynasty was conquered by the Ming Dynasty in 1368. That ended the Mongol Empire.

Khmer Empire

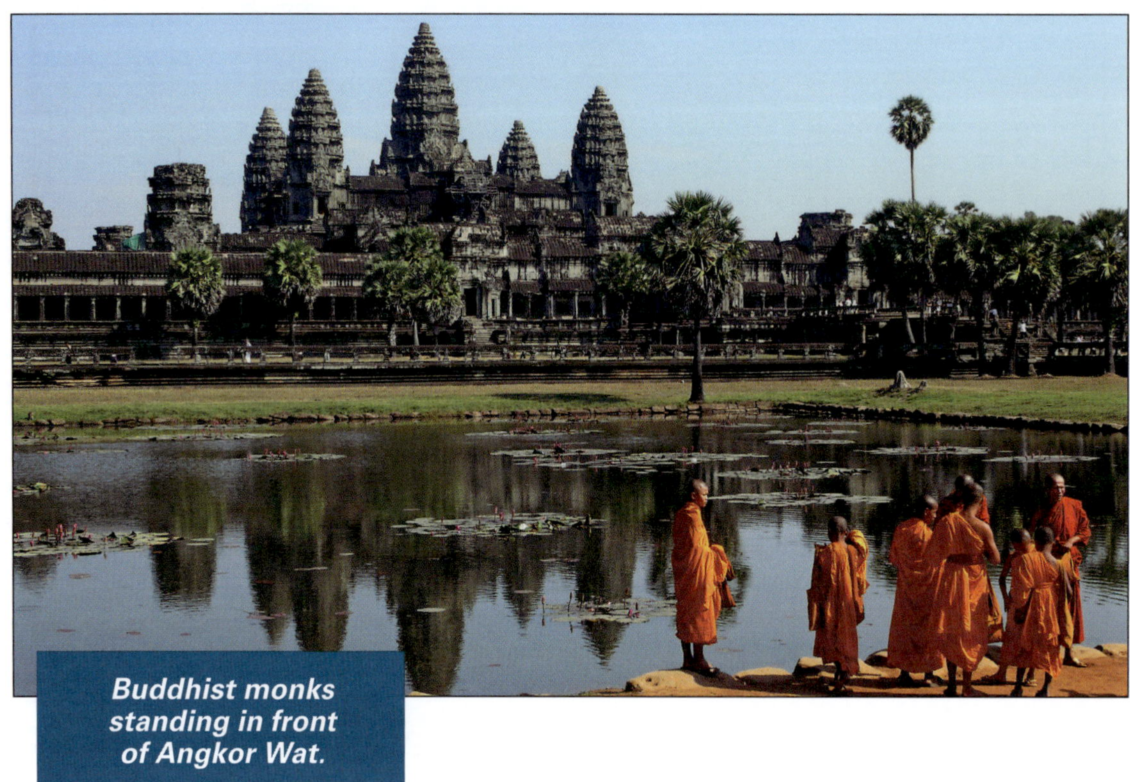

Buddhist monks standing in front of Angkor Wat.

The Khmer Empire ruled much of southeast Asia during the Middle Ages. They had a long history of trade with India. The Hindu and Buddhist religions and their writing system came from India. They also traded with China. The Khmer Empire had contact with the Tang, Song, and Yuan Dynasties. Angkor was the capital. At its peak, it may have been the largest city in the world.

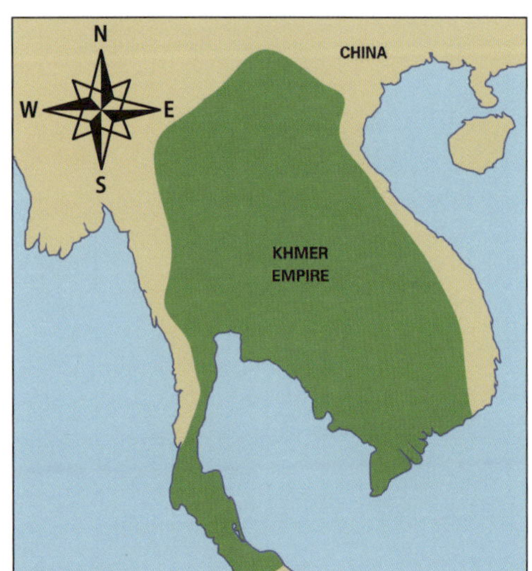

Aztec and Inca Empires

Machu Picchu was built for an Inca emperor.

The Aztecs lived in central Mexico. Tenochtitlan was their capital. It was built on an island in Lake Texcoco. It grew into a huge city of about 250,000 people. The Aztecs were warlike. They practiced human sacrifices to a sun god. The Inca Empire began in the Andes Mountains of South America. Their empire grew to stretch over a thousand miles. They built a great road network. Both the Inca and Aztec Empires were destroyed by the Spanish.

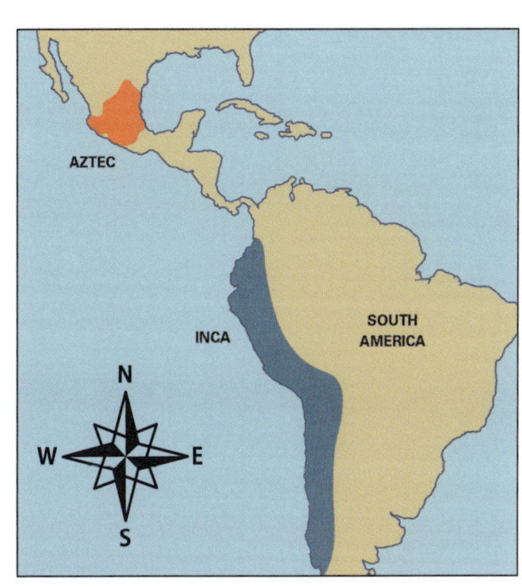

Black Death

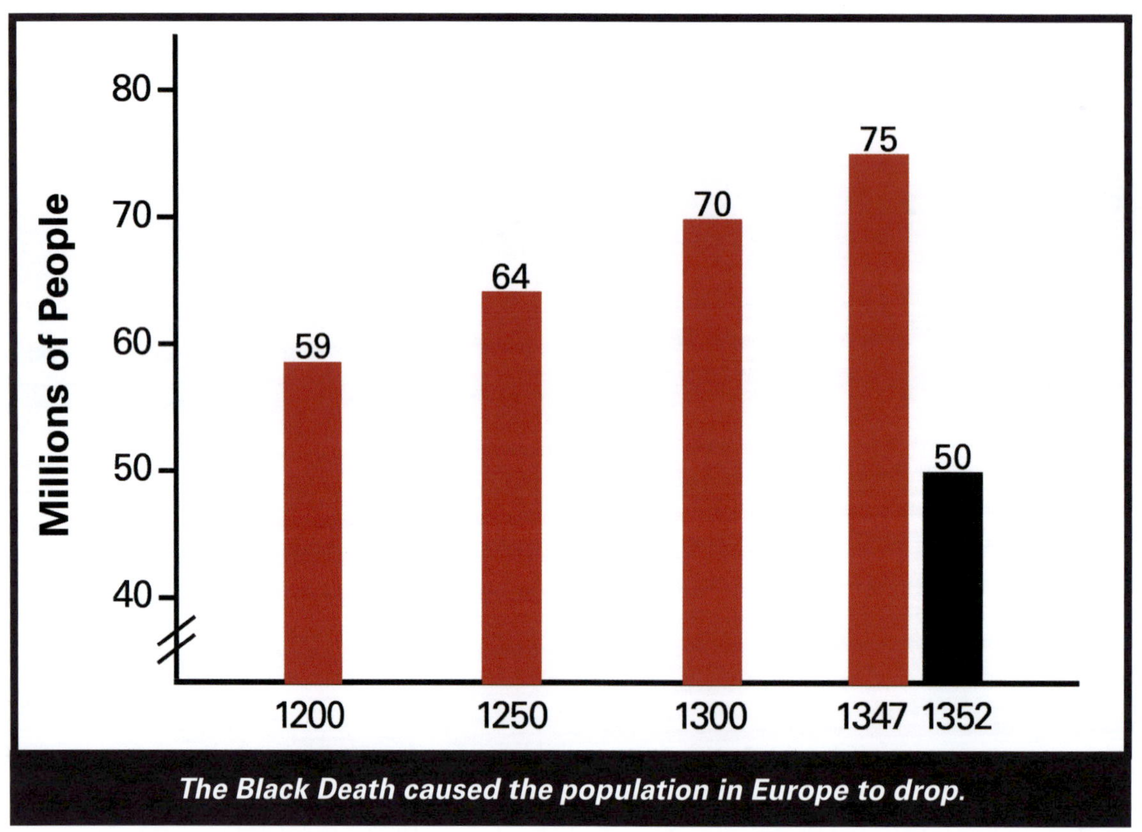

The Black Death caused the population in Europe to drop.

During the Middle Ages the bubonic plague spread through Asia and Europe. This **plague** was called the Black Death. We know today that it was spread to people by fleas that lived on rats. Sick people also spread the disease. It struck Europe in 1347. Within five years 20 million people died. The Black Death also came back to Europe from time to time. It was greatly feared. The people had no idea then what caused the disease.

The plague was spread by fleas on rats.

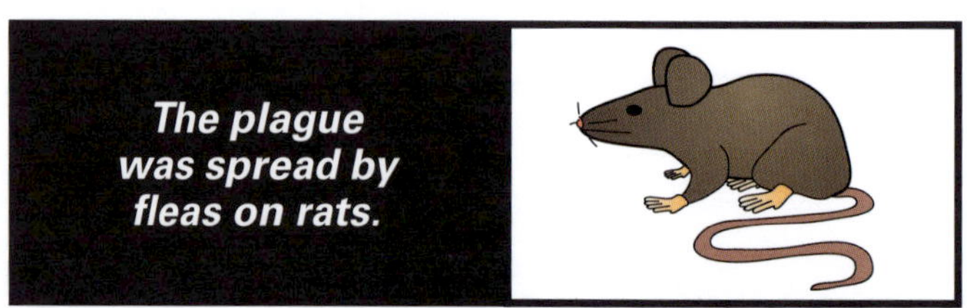

QUIZ

Circle the correct answer.

1. The Middle Ages began when the ______ Empire fell.

Roman | Christian | African

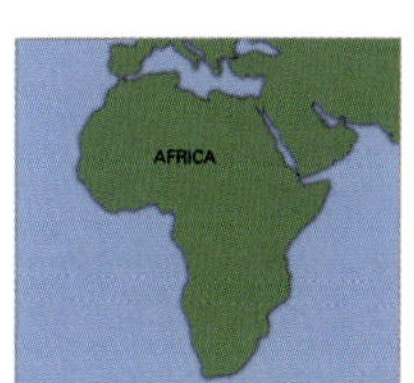

2. ______ expanded into new lands during the Middle Ages.

Democracy | Fertile | Religions

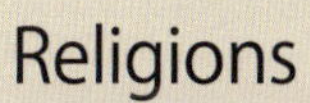

3. ______ is a social system that ranks people by class.

Feudalism | Currency | Medieval

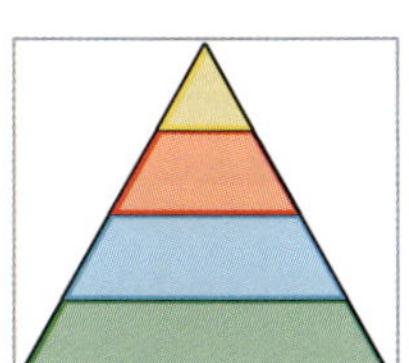

4. The ______ became a superpower during the Middle Ages.

Crusades | Mongol Empire | equator

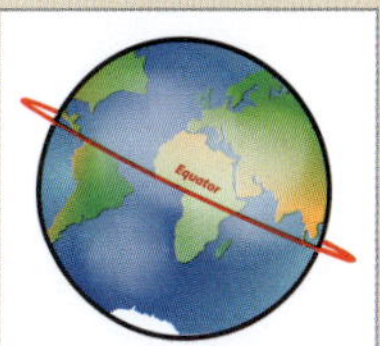

5. The ______ were wars to take control of the Holy Land.

medieval taxes Crusades

6. A ______ is a line of rulers from one family.

dynasty pyramid city-state

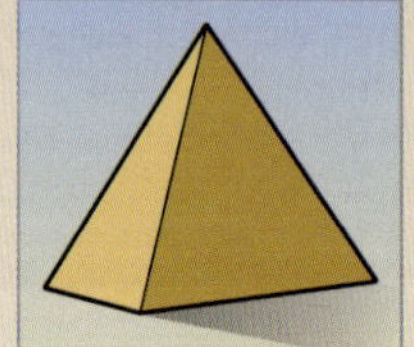

7. The ______ was a terrible disease in Europe.

bronze plague government

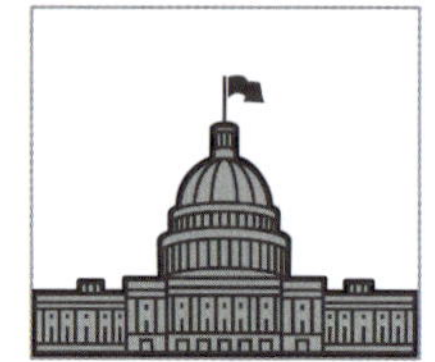

Write About It

CHAPTER
10

Religion

A theme of history

Religion began in prehistoric times.

A religion can have branches or division.

Religion helps cultures share beliefs and rituals.

Religious differences have led to wars.

Timeline

Founding of the major religions

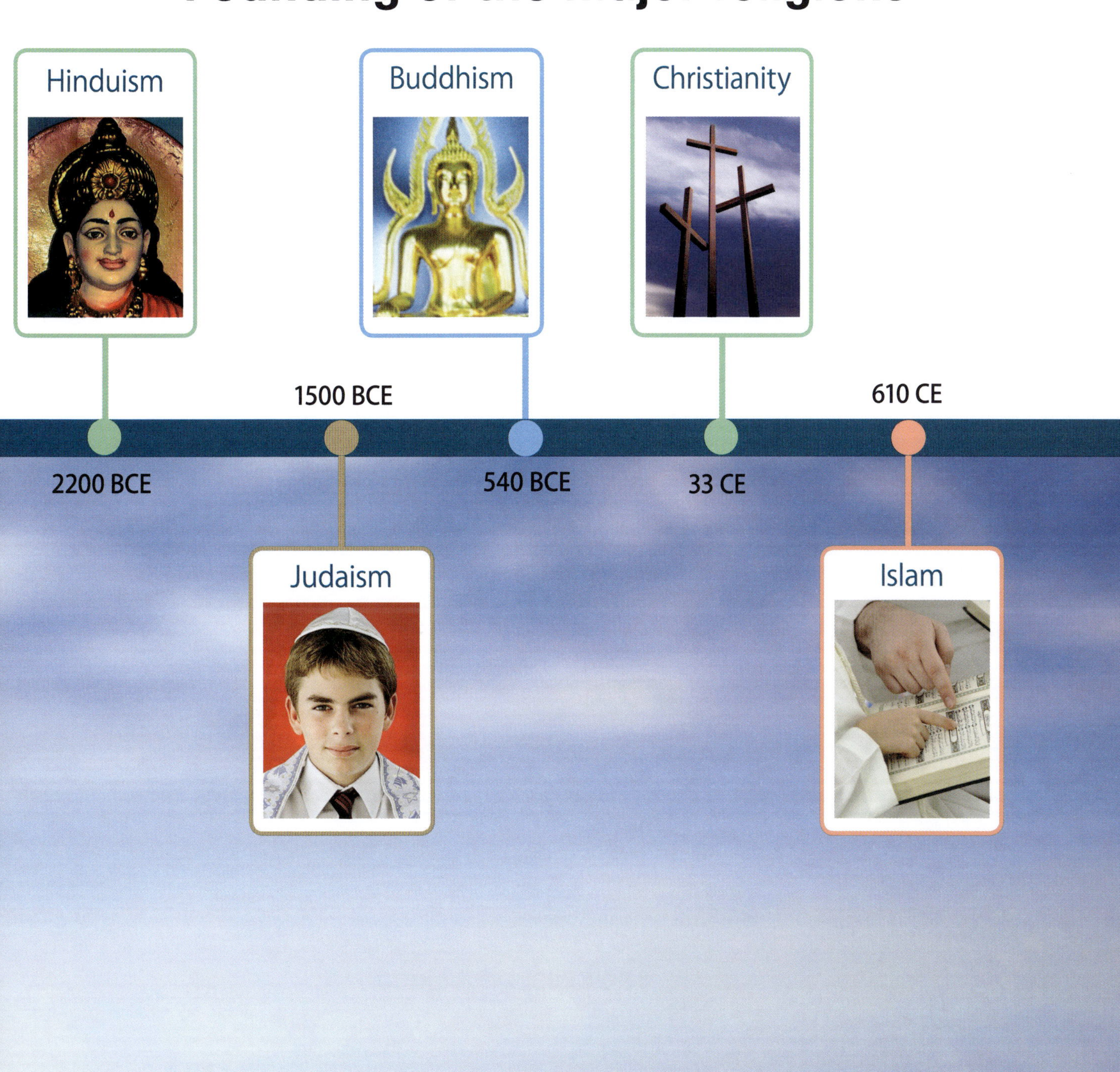

The dates are estimates or best guesses.

VOCABULARY

religion		a set of beliefs that include a higher power like god
ritual		a religious ceremony
monotheism		the belief that there's only one god
reincarnation		the belief that your spirit will live again after you die

Find the word!

The belief in one god

__ __ __ __ __ __ __ __ __ __

VOCABULARY

The Holocaust	mass killing of Jews and others during WWII
pope	the head of the Roman Catholic Church
Reformation	a reform movement that led to the Protestant religion
Muslim	a follower of Islam

The head of the Roman Catholic Church

___ ___ ___ ___

Religion

Islam

Christianity

Judaism

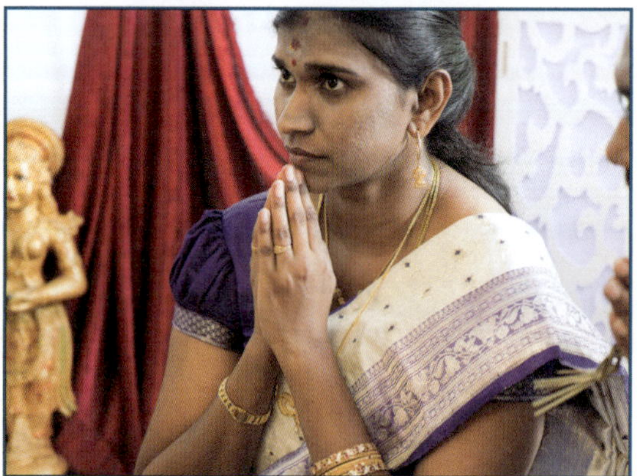

Hinduism

Buddhism

Religion has been around since prehistoric times. Religion is a set of beliefs. Followers accept the beliefs as truth. These often include rules given by a god or gods. Religion can give people a purpose and a shared sense of right and wrong. Religious **rituals** and holidays can bind people together. But different religions can have very different ideas.

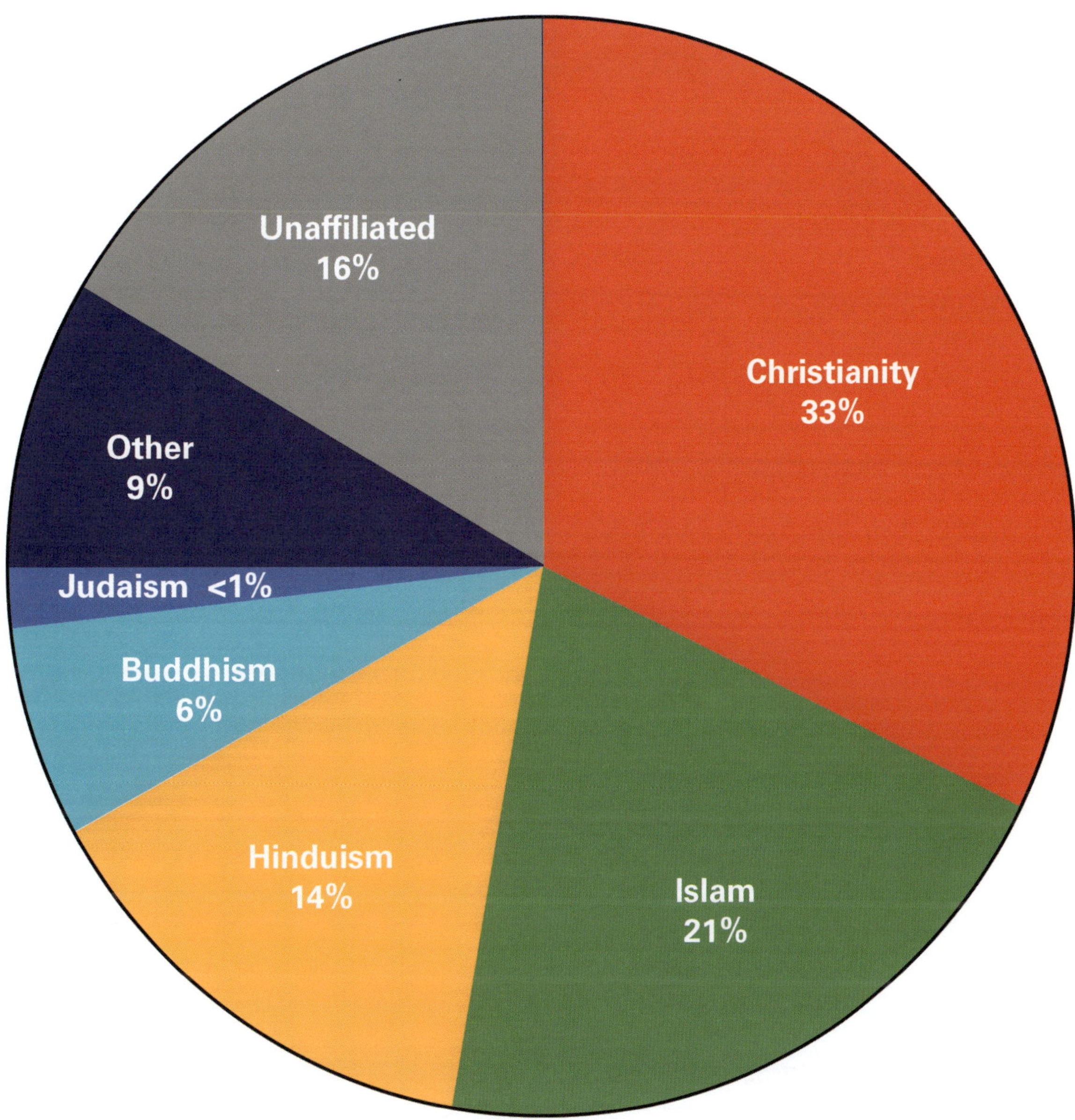

Many wars have been fought over religion. Governments have been created and destroyed by religious leaders. Throughout history, people have been punished or killed because of their beliefs. But sharing a religion has also brought cultures together. And moral codes have brought peace and safety to many people. Religion has been an important theme in world history.

Shared Beliefs

RELIGION	ORIGIN	SCRIPTURE	MONOTHEISTIC	RELIGIOUS LEADER
Judaism	Middle East	Torah	Yes	Abraham
Christianity	Middle East	Bible	Yes	Jesus
Islam	Middle East	Qur'an	Yes	Muhammad
Buddhism	India	Tipitaka	Yes and No	Buddha
Hinduism	India	Vedas	No	?

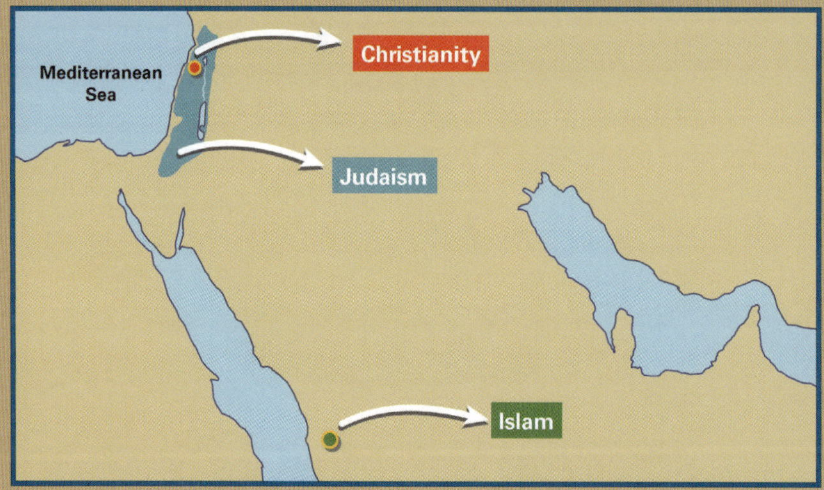

Followers of a religion have much in common, but different religions have similarities too. **Monotheism** is the foundation of Judaism, Christianity, and Islam. Each has a sacred text. The Christian Bible includes the Old Testament from Judaism. And Jesus and Abraham are mentioned in the Islamic Qur'an. Both Hinduism and Buddhism began in India. And all religions have rules for right and wrong behavior.

Hinduism

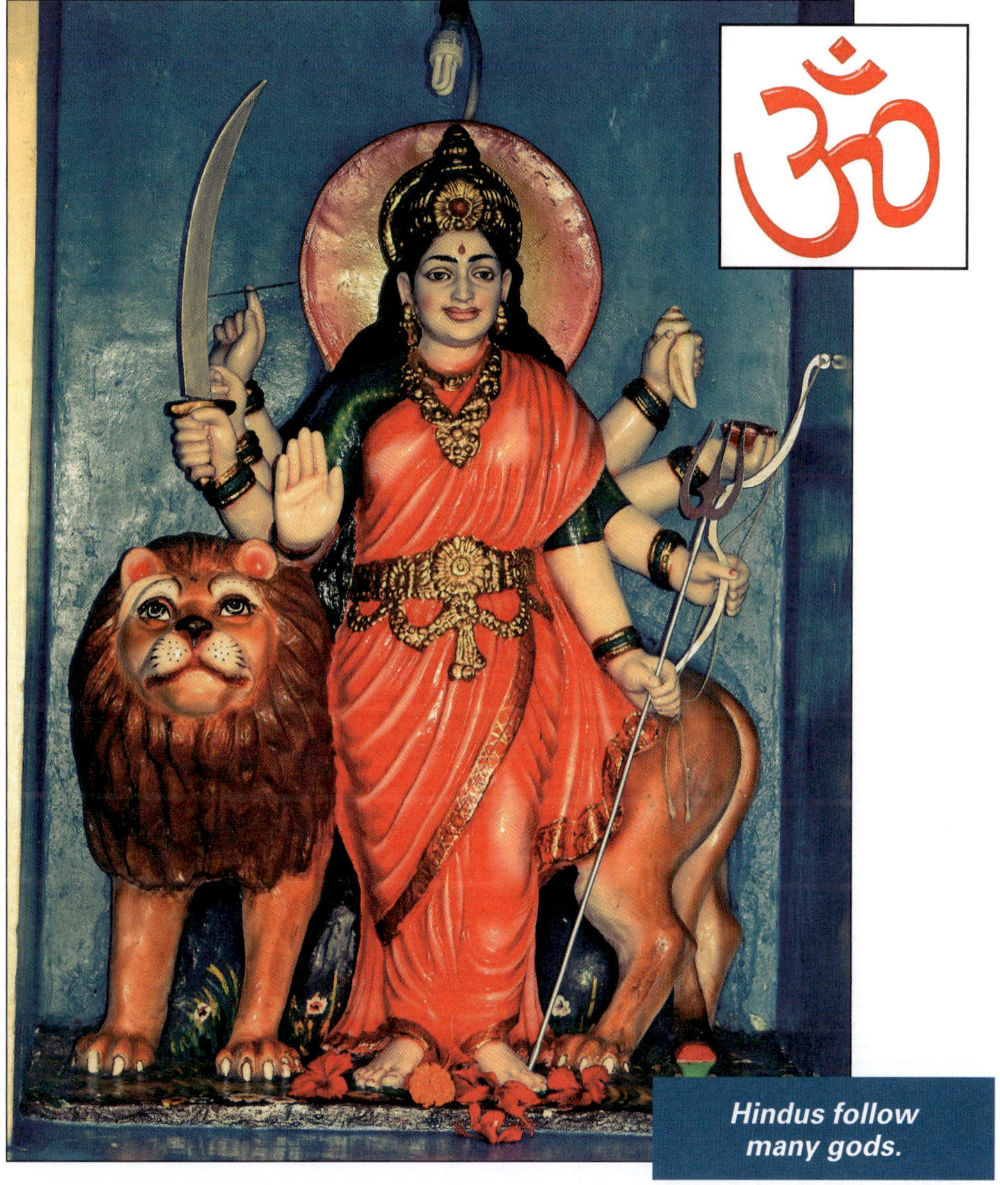

Hindus follow many gods.

Hinduism is a very old religion. It doesn't have a prophet or a single god. Common beliefs include karma and **reincarnation**. Karma means that your current life is affected by a previous life. Hinduism is the most common religion in India. Hindu beliefs contributed to the caste system of India. People were born into a caste and stayed there no matter what. India is changing that system today.

Judaism

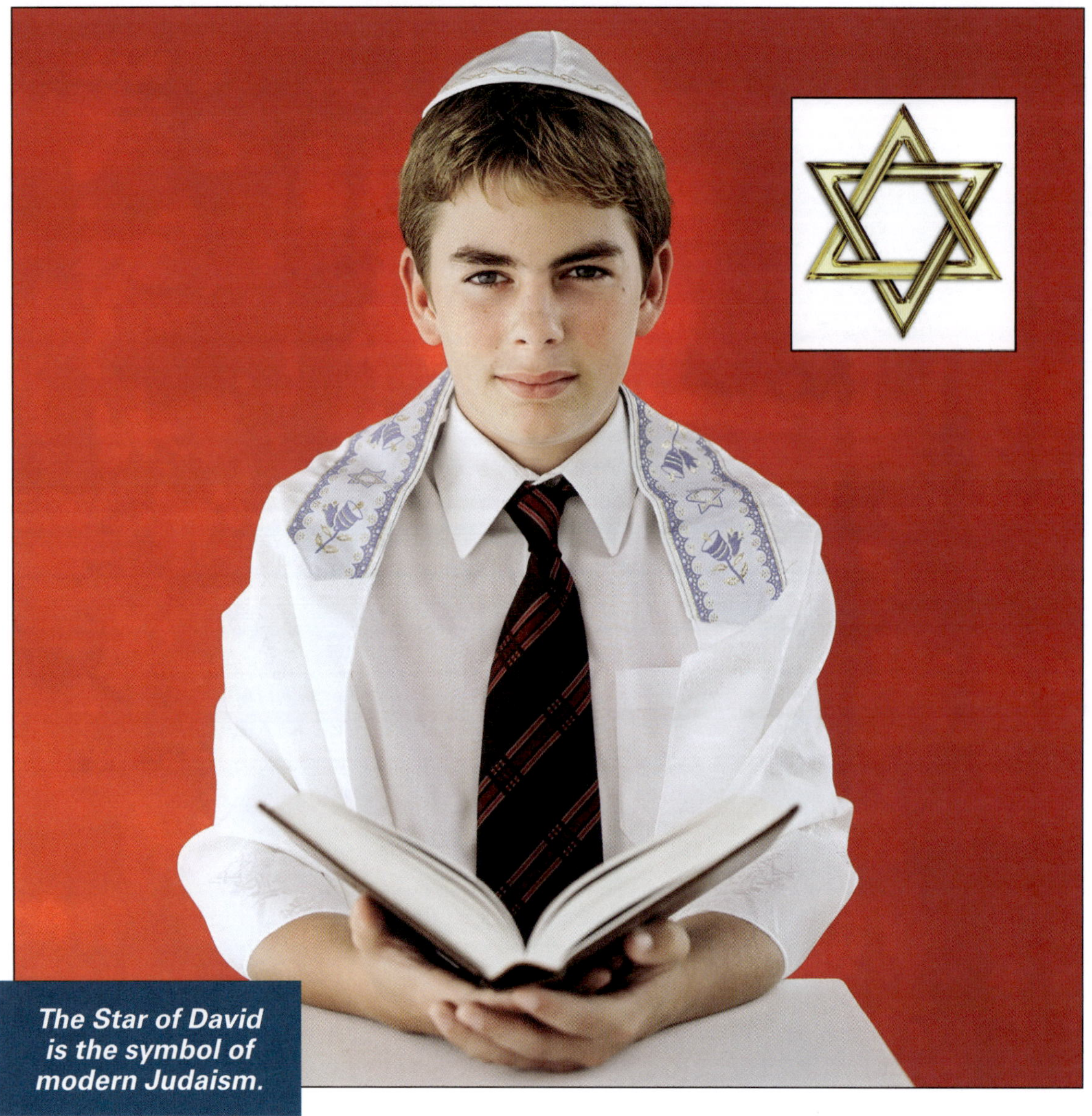

The Star of David is the symbol of modern Judaism.

Judaism was the first major religion to believe in one god. The Torah is their sacred text. Today it has different branches, like Orthodox and Reform. Judaism began in ancient times when Abraham led the Hebrews out of Mesopotamia to Canaan. That became their promised land. But they were driven away from there many times by Christian and Islamic forces.

Map of Israel.

They moved to other communities in Europe and the Middle East. Many Jews kept their traditions alive. But since they were different, the Jews were often badly treated. At times, Jewish communities had to move to stay safe. Today the nation of Israel is a Jewish state. It began in 1948, following **The Holocaust** of the Second World War. Israel now contains areas of their ancient promised land.

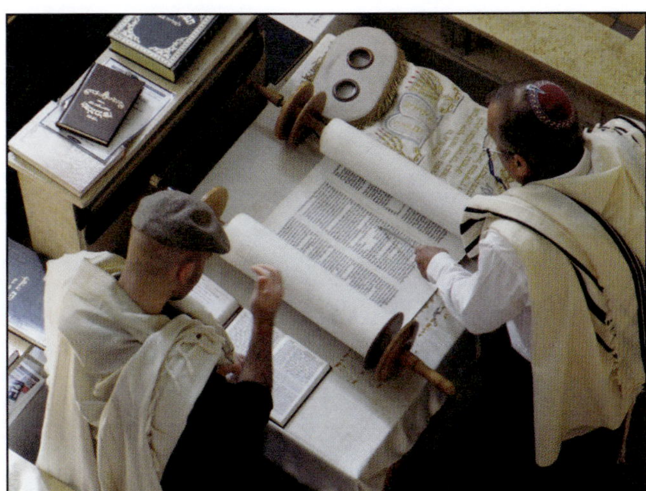

Reading from the Torah Scroll is a Jewish tradition.

Christianity

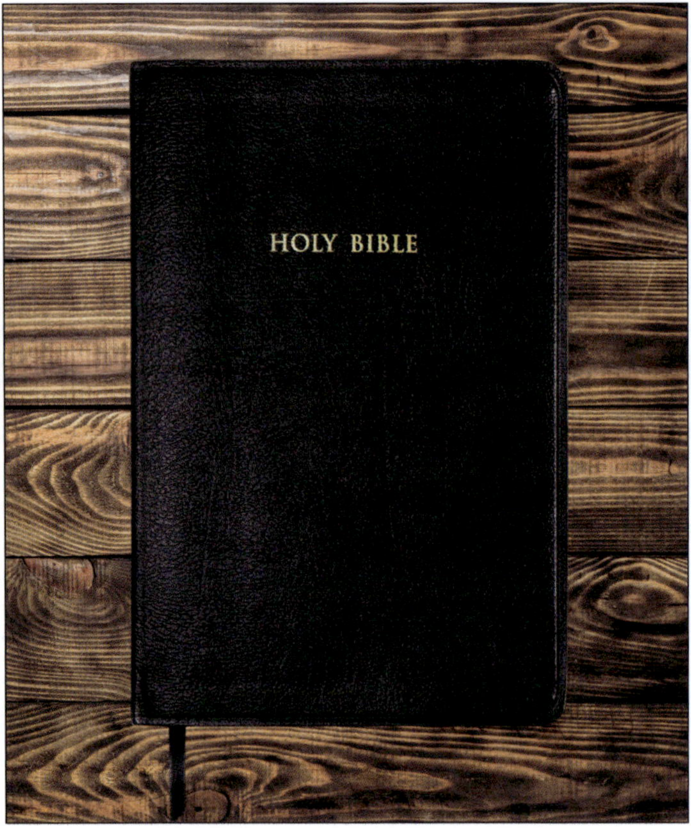

The Bible is the sacred text of Christians.

Christianity is based on the life and teachings of Jesus Christ. It began when Jesus died in about 33 CE. Christians believe he's the son of God. The Roman Empire ruled the Holy Land during that time. It was against Christianity for centuries. That changed in 313 when the Roman Emperor Constantine became a Christian. Christianity expanded into Europe during the Middle Ages.

The cross is a symbol of Christianity.

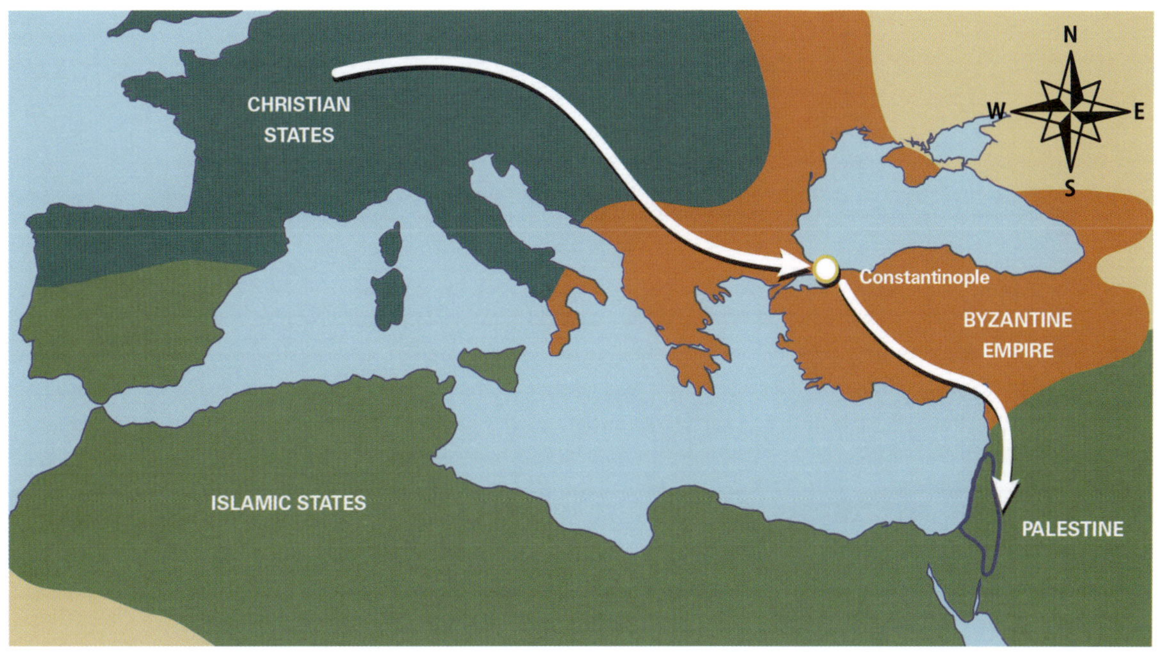

The **Crusades** caused conflict between European Christians and those in the Byzantine Empire. Christianity split into two churches—the Roman Catholic and Eastern Orthodox. The **pope** remained the head of the Catholic Church. He lost control of some European churches during the **Reformation**. Protestant became a branch of Christianity. During the Age of Exploration, Christianity spread around the world.

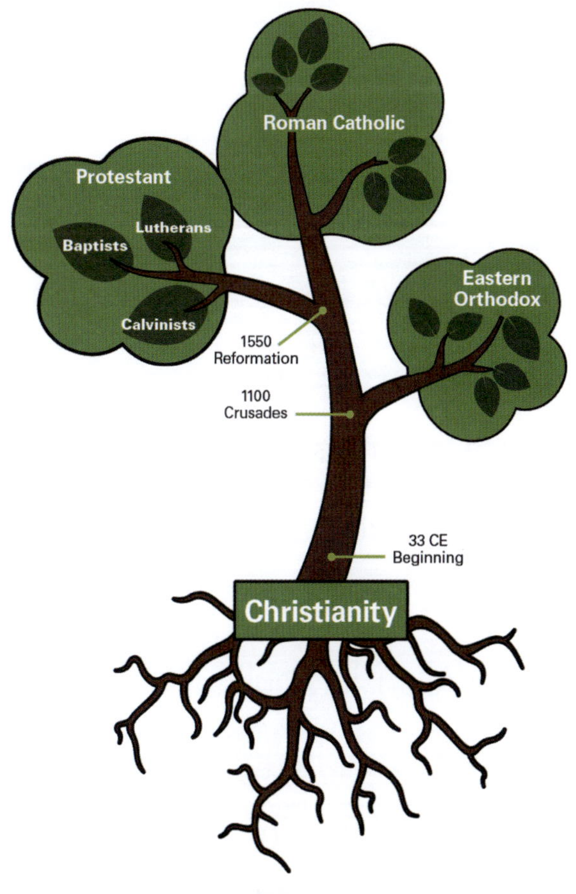

Islam

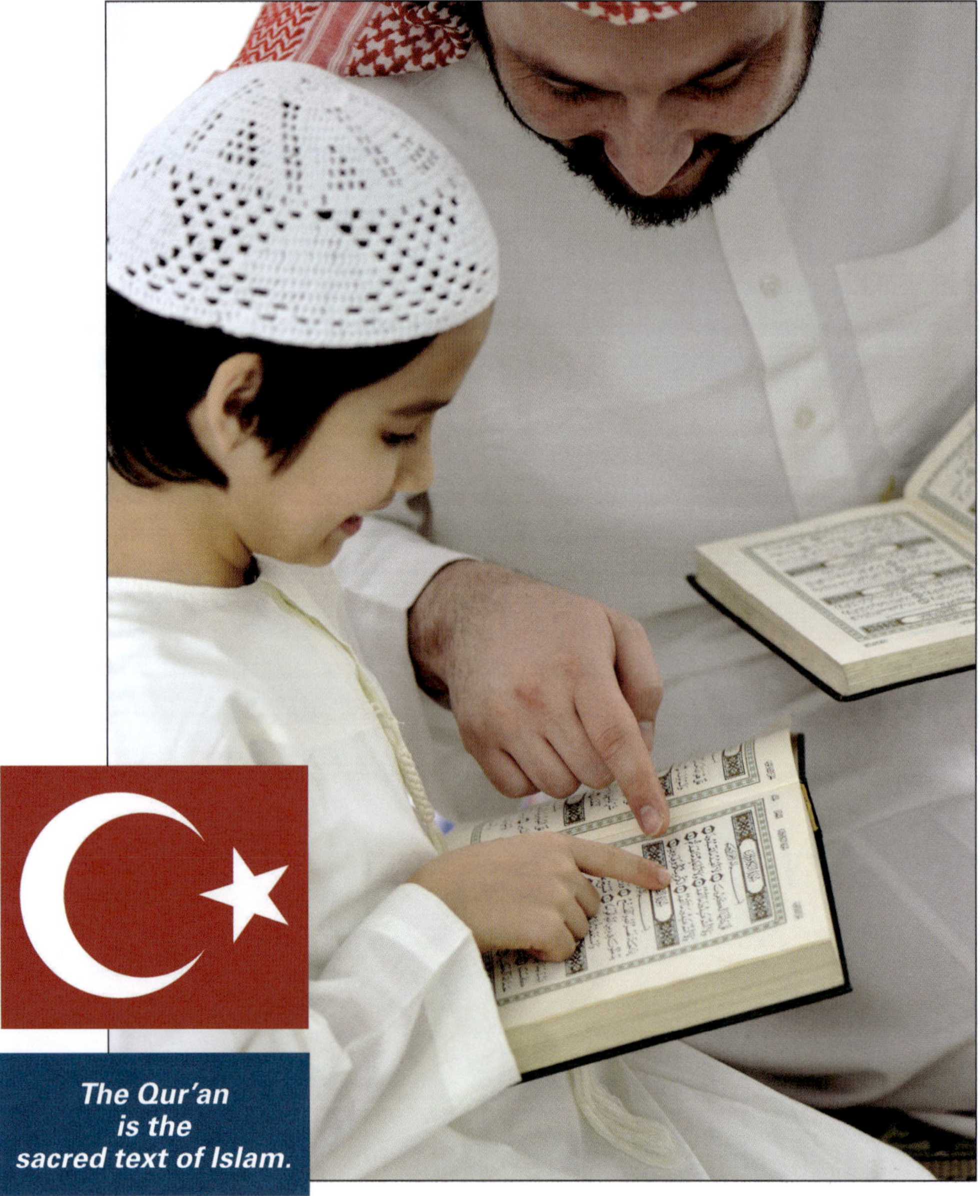

The Qur'an is the sacred text of Islam.

Islam is a monotheistic religion. **Muslims** follow the teachings of Muhammad. They believe he is the last and true prophet of God, or Allah. Islam began in 610 when Muhammad received a revelation from Allah. It is built upon the five pillars of faith, prayer, giving, fasting, and pilgrimage. Islam believes Abraham and Jesus are earlier prophets of Allah.

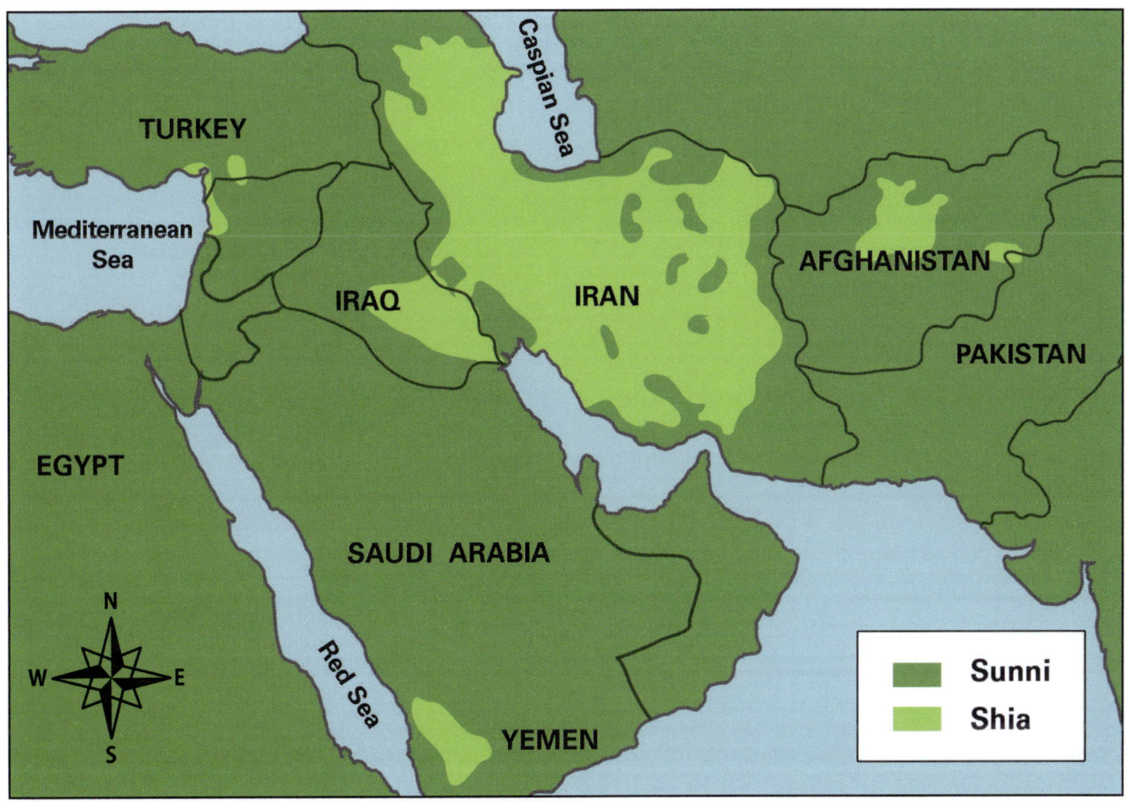

Islam expanded quickly. It became the religion of great empires, like Abbasid and Ottoman. Within Islam there are two main branches—the Sunni and Shia. The split happened soon after Islam began. Most Muslims are Sunni. The two branches have had periods of peace and war. Today most Shia Muslims live in or around Iran.

A photograph of the Hajj, the Islam pilgrimage to Mecca.

Buddhism

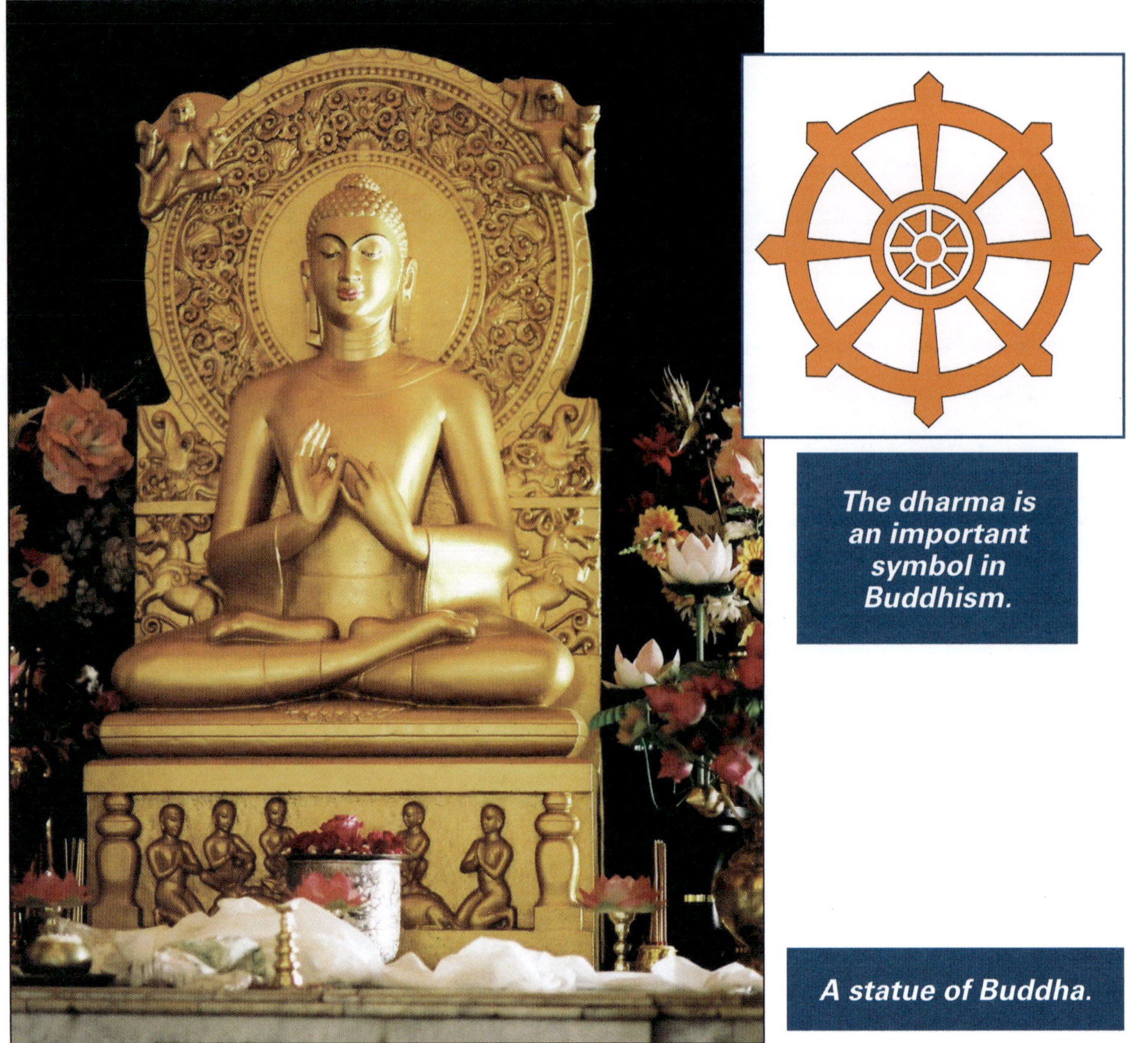

The dharma is an important symbol in Buddhism.

A statue of Buddha.

Buddhism is based upon the life and teachings of Siddhartha Gautama. He became the Buddha after he was enlightened in about 580 BCE. Buddha means Enlightened One. Buddhists believe in a cycle of reincarnation until you attain enlightenment or nirvana. Buddhism began in India. Over time it spread through Asia. It reached China in about 150 CE and Japan around 550 CE. Today it's the main religion in Southeast Asia.

QUIZ

Circle the correct answer.

1. Religion began in ________.

oceans | prehistoric times | medieval era

2. Religion is a shared set of beliefs and ________.

archaeology | timelines | rituals

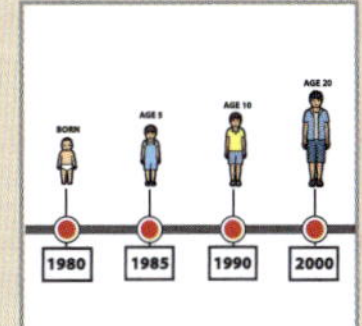

3. Religious differences have led to ________.

wars | cultivation | alphabet

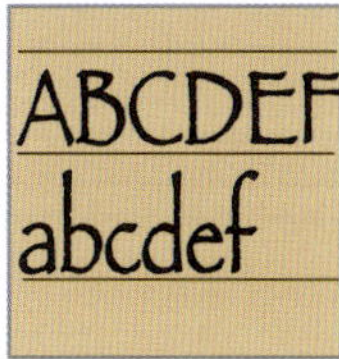

4. ________ helps some people find peace and serenity.

Plague | Iron | Religion

5. The ______ is head of the Catholic Church.

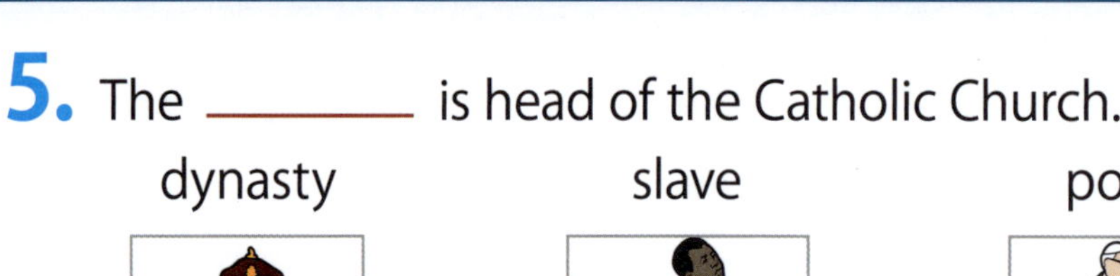

dynasty | slave | pope

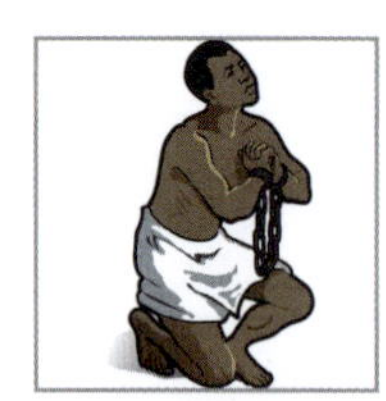

6. A ______ is a follower of Islam.

cuneiform | Muslim | ocean

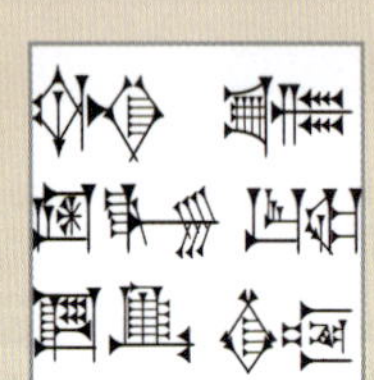

7. The belief that there's only one god is ______.

monotheism | government | military

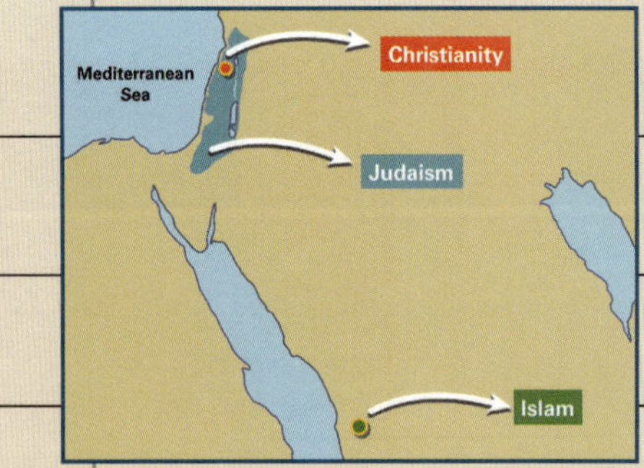

Write About It

CHAPTER 11

Early Modern

An era of history 1450 to 1800

The Age of Exploration led to voyages to the New World.

Colonization led to global empires.

The Enlightenment led to discoveries in science.

The Industrial Revolution led to new machines and factories.

Early Modern Timeline

1450-1800

The dates are estimates or best guesses.

VOCABULARY

New World	North and South America and nearby islands
nationalism	patriotic feelings for your country
Renaissance	a rebirth of art and culture
Age of Enlightenment	an era when people began to use reason and science to understand the world

Strong feelings for your country

___ ___ ___ ___ ___ ___ ___ ___ ___ ___ ___

VOCABULARY

monarchy		a government run by a king, queen, or other royalty
Age of Exploration		an era when sea voyages sailed to new lands
colonization		having settlements away from your homeland
Industrial Revolution		rapid development of new machines and factories

Government run by a king

___ ___ ___ ___ ___ ___ ___ ___

Early Modern Era

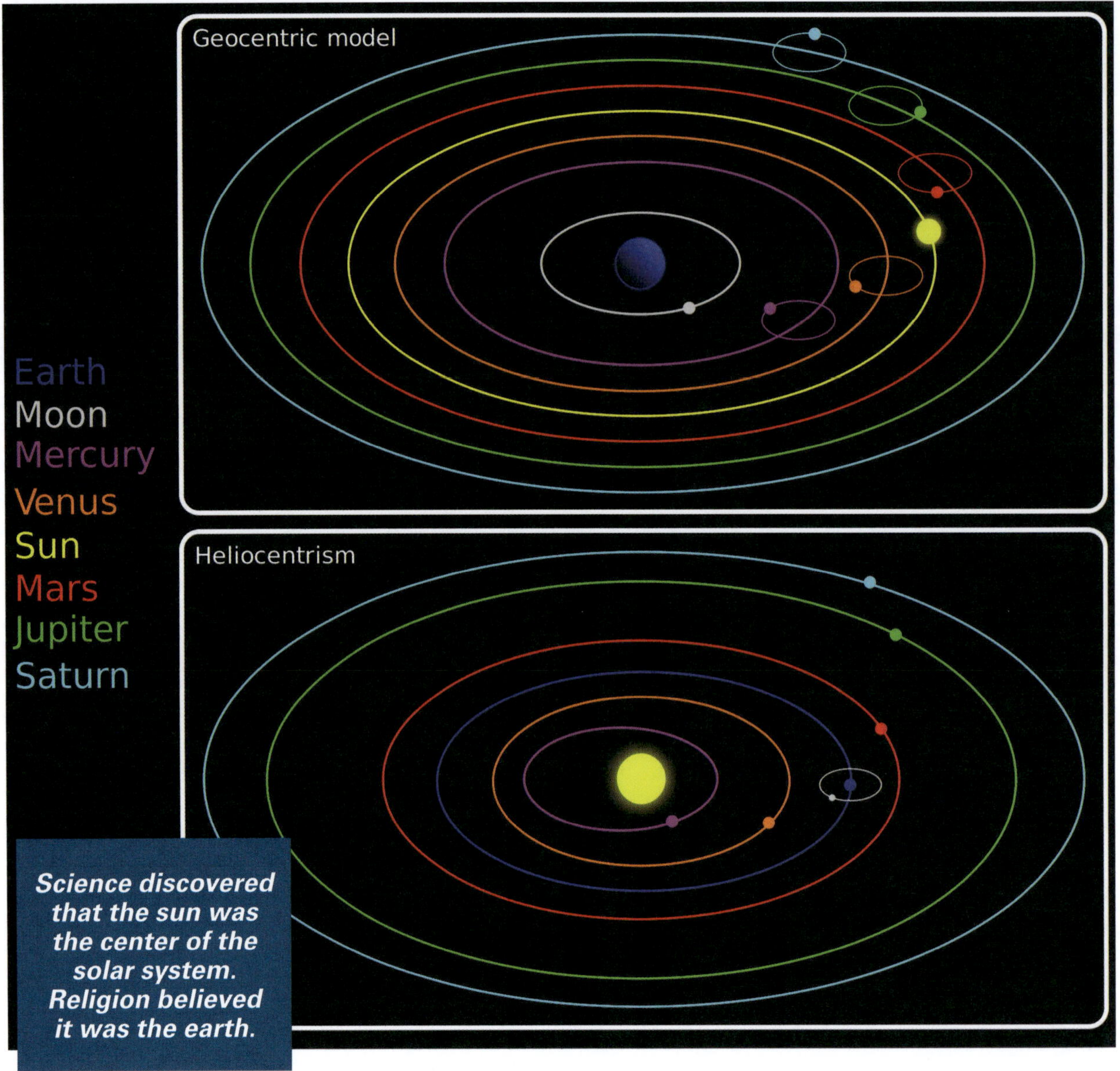

Science discovered that the sun was the center of the solar system. Religion believed it was the earth.

This era begins with growth in art, science, and global exploration. Art in Europe and China flourished and is still appreciated today. Science slowly replaced religion as the best way to explain the natural world. European explorers sailed to the **New World**. Then European nations claimed vast areas of land. They destroyed many native cultures in the process.

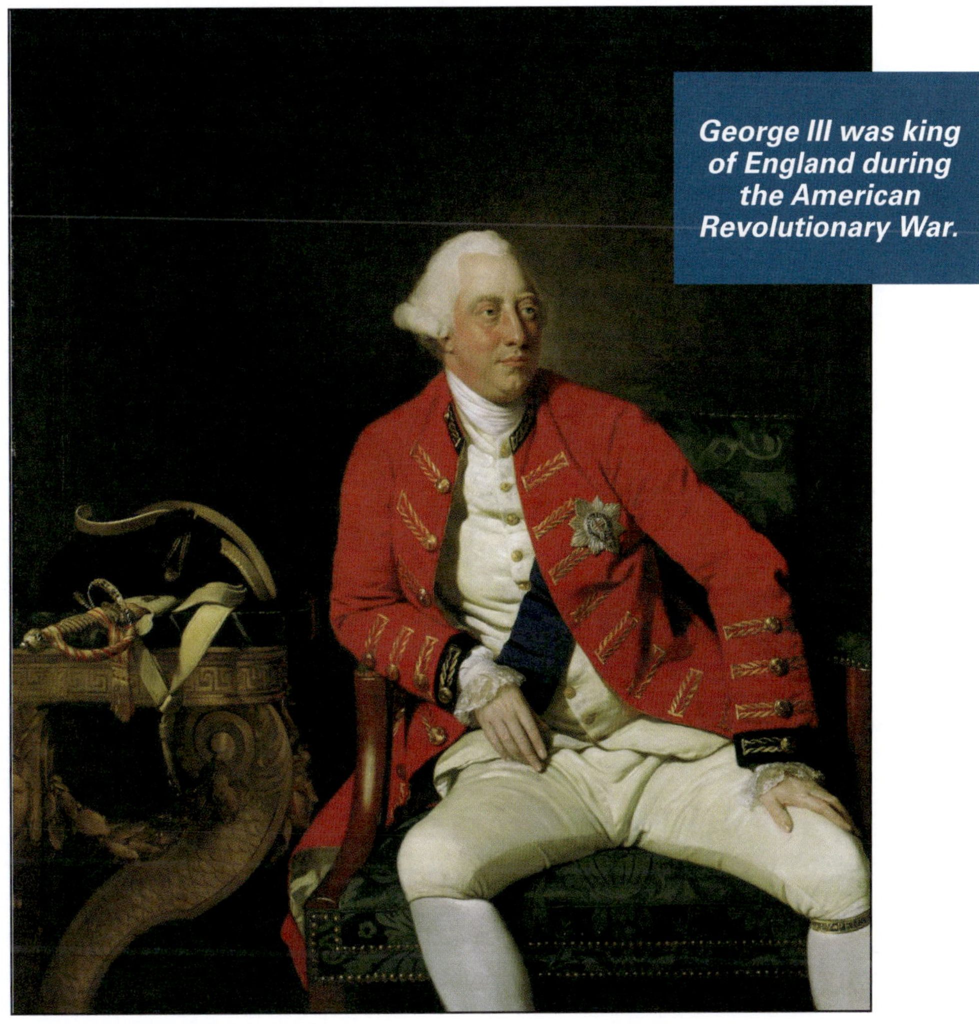
George III was king of England during the American Revolutionary War.

The Ottoman Empire controlled the Middle East. Kings ruled much of Europe. Religious differences led to wars. The Ming Dynasty brought prosperity to China. When it declined, China became isolated. European nations founded colonies. A global trading network created great wealth. But the colonies grew stronger too. This era ends with America winning the Revolutionary War against England.

Road to Independence

The Loyalists were people in America who supported King George III.

PATRIOTS	LOYALISTS
Did not like the king. 	Liked the king. 
Believed the king did not have the right to tax. 	Believed the king had the right to tax. 
Fought for freedom. 	Fought for the king of England. 
Helped to make a new country. 	Moved away from the United States. 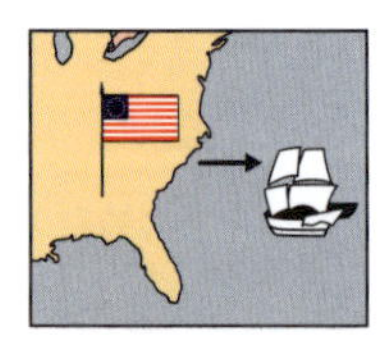

England established the Jamestown colony in America in 1607. Many more people came to America. But the colonists wanted freedom. **Nationalism** became a common belief. In 1783, America became the first nation to fight and win a revolution against a colonial empire. In the next century, many South American nations followed a similar road to independence.

Renaissance

A Michelangelo mural on the Sistine Chapel ceiling in Rome, painted between 1534-1541.

The Mona Lisa by Leonardo da Vinci, painted around 1503.

The plague swept through Europe near the end of the Middle Ages. The population in Italy decreased a lot. Afterward, a rebirth began in the Italian city of Florence. It was called the **Renaissance**. People again studied the work of Classical Greeks. The Renaissance spread throughout Europe. Beautiful art was created with an emphasis on the human form. This art is still appreciated today.

Reformation

A portrait of Martin Luther, who started the Protestant Reformation in 1517.

The Reformation was a protest against the Roman Catholic Church in Europe. The protesters wanted reforms so they started the Protestant Church. The Catholics and Protestants fought for many years. The Thirty Year's War, 1618-1648, was especially brutal. But in the end, people could choose what church to belong to. The pope remained the religious leader of Catholics but not Protestants.

Age of Enlightenment

Name	Picture	Years	Description
Francis Bacon		1561–1626	Used the Scientific Method
William Shakespeare		1564–1616	Wrote famous plays like Romeo and Juliet
Galileo Galilei		1564–1642	Astronomer who discovered the moons of Jupiter
Song Yingxing		1587–1666	Wrote an encyclopedia in Chinese
Sir Isaac Newton		1642–1726	Explained the laws of gravity
Benjamin Franklin		1706–1790	A Founding Father of America
Wolfgang Amadeus Mozart		1756–1791	Musical genius

The Catholic Church was all-powerful in Europe until the Reformation. Afterward, people could use reason rather than religion to understand how nature works. Science, art, and music flourished. The **Age of Enlightenment** began. Discoveries in science changed the world. New forms of government were studied that influenced the Founding Fathers of the United States.

Age of Exploration

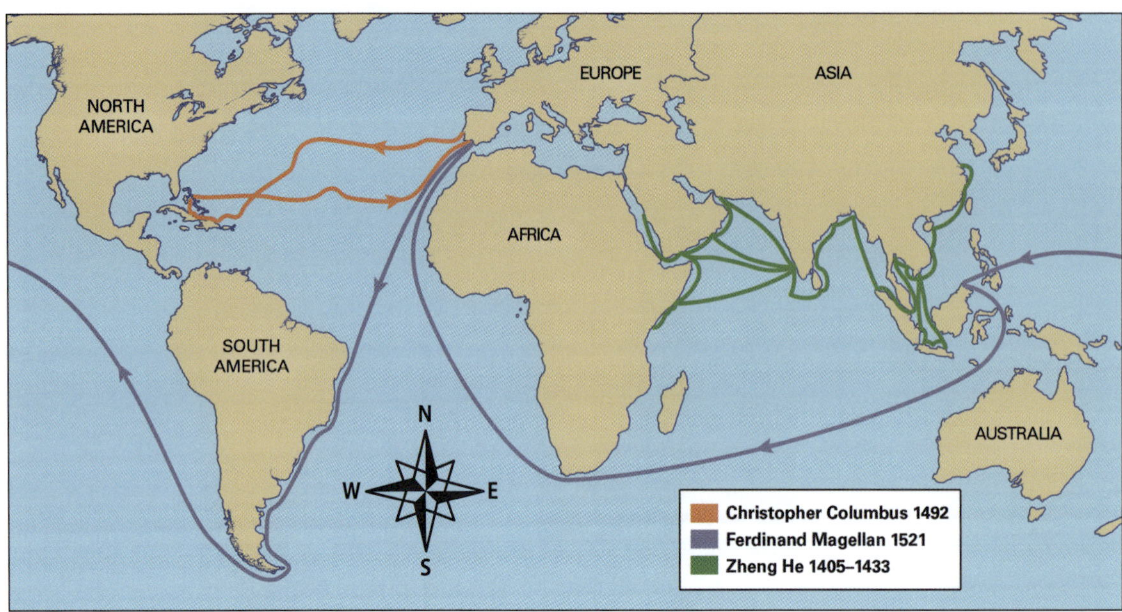

The European **monarchies** wanted new trade routes to Asia. They paid for sea voyages to find them. But in 1492 Christopher Columbus sailed to America instead. The **Age of Exploration** began. Soon, many new lands were reached. Explorers sailed and mapped much of the unknown world. They also spread Christianity, making it the world's largest religion.

Zheng He from China explored new lands before Christopher Columbus.

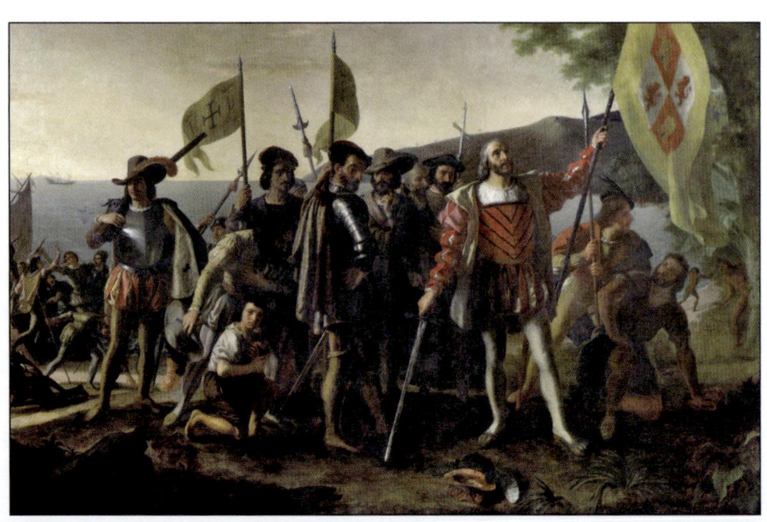

A painting showing the landing of Christopher Columbus in the New World.

Land Claims

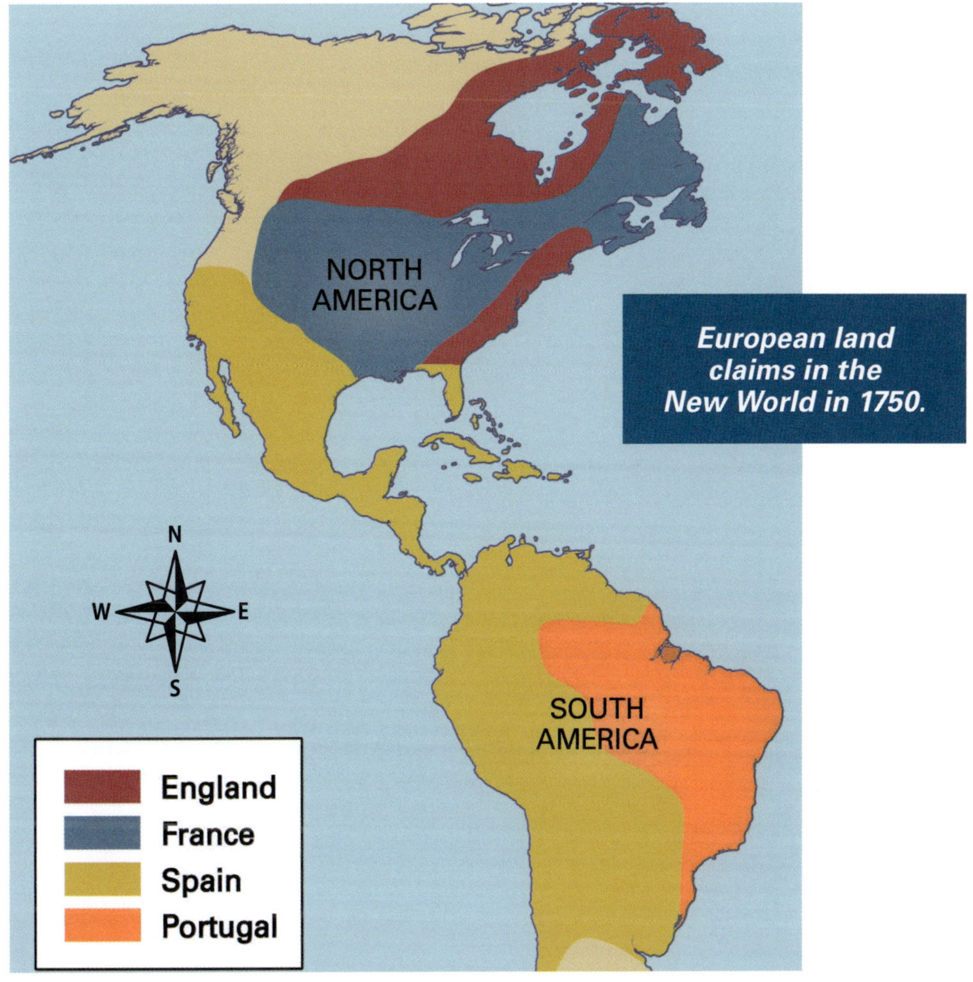

European land claims in the New World in 1750.

The Europeans claimed vast areas of the new land for themselves. They took natural resources, like gold. They set up colonies to grow crops and imported slaves to work the fields. **Colonization** led to great wealth. European nations like Spain and England were the first to rule global empires. But the native people suffered greatly. Many died from unfamiliar diseases. Conquest and slavery also took their toll.

Russian Empire

Russia is still the largest country in the world.

Russia became independent of the Mongols in 1485. Czars then ruled Russia as absolute monarchs. They quickly expanded their territory, but it remained isolated. Czar Peter the Great changed that. He westernized Russia by adopting European ideas and culture. He built St. Petersburg, a magnificent capital. Later, Catherine the Great helped make Russia a major European power. Czars continued to rule Russia until the 1900s.

A painting of Catherine the Great.

A Golden Age of China

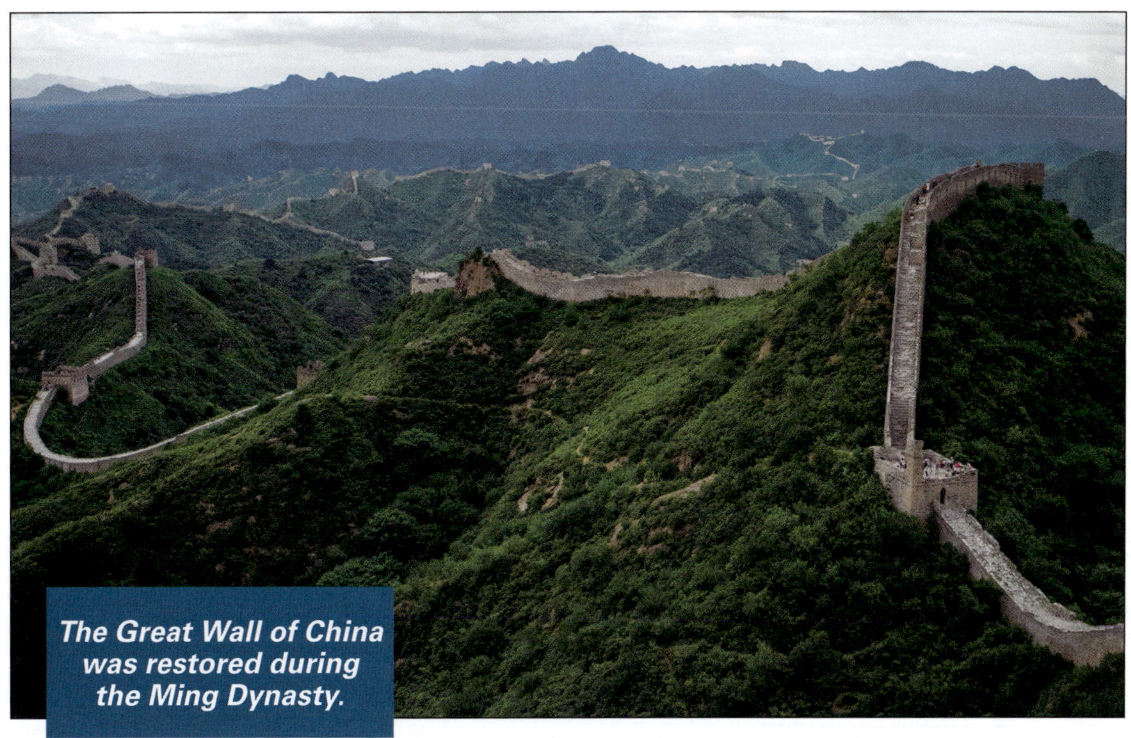

The Great Wall of China was restored during the Ming Dynasty.

The Mongol-run Yuan Dynasty was overthrown by the Ming in 1368. China was again ruled by the Chinese. The Ming Dynasty built a thriving society. They maintained an efficient government and school system. They expanded agriculture and food distribution. They sent the largest ships in the world on voyages of exploration and trade. The Ming Dynasty ended in 1644. The Manchu people from China's north started the Qing Dynasty.

A photograph of the Forbidden City in present-day Beijing.

Islamic Empires

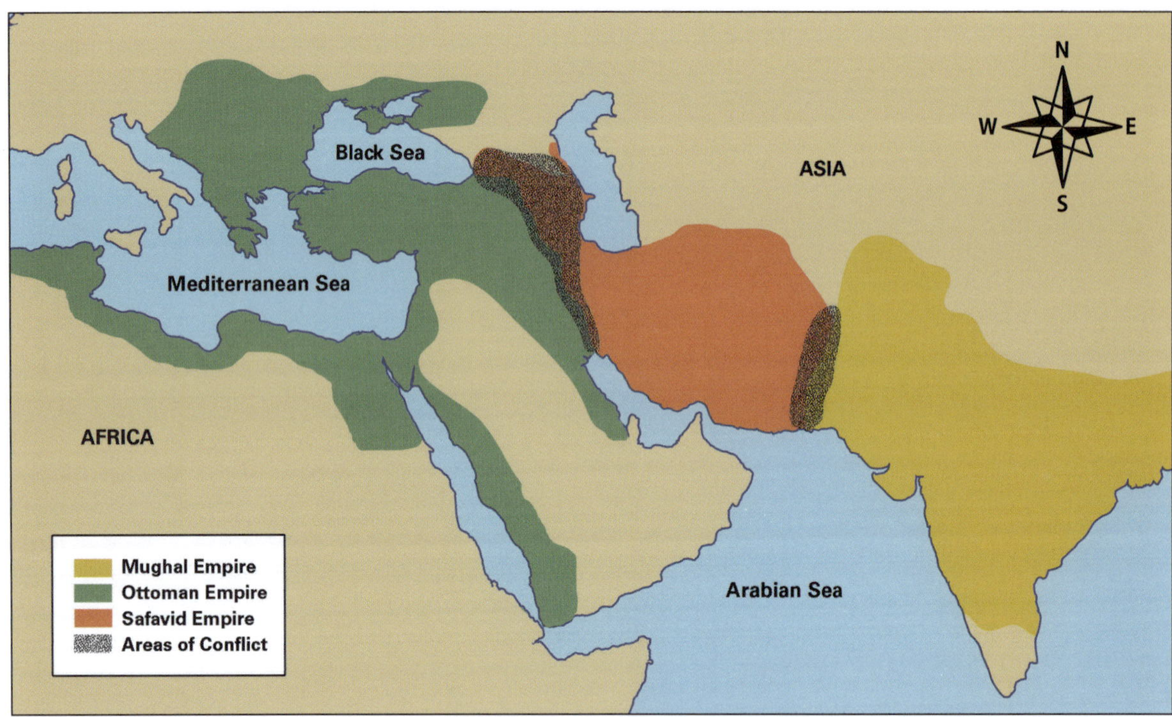

Three Islamic Empires ruled during this era. They are sometimes called the gunpowder empires because they successfully used modern firearms to gain control of their lands. The Ottoman Empire was the largest and most powerful. In 1453 they conquered Constantinople, which is now called Istanbul. That ended the Byzantine Empire. The Ottoman Empire lasted for nearly 500 years.

The Taj Mahal in India. The Mughals created splendid architecture.

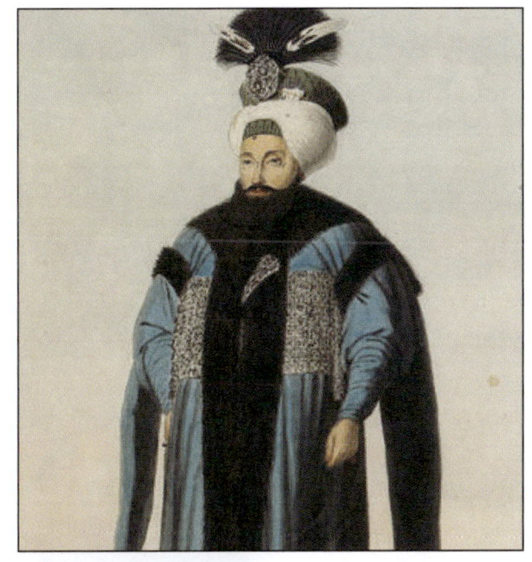

An Ottoman sultan. They were Sunni.

A Safavid shah. They were Shia.

A Mughal emperor. They were Sunni.

The Safavids took control of Persia in the early 1500s. They followed the Shia branch of Islam and made it their state religion. The Ottomans were Sunni and were often at war with the Safavids. Much of the Safavids' territory is still Shia today. The Mughals invaded India from the north. Over time they controlled most of the country. At first, war with Hindus and Buddhists was common. Later, Mughal rule became more peaceful.

Industrial Revolution

Iron making was important during the Industrial Revolution.

The **Industrial Revolution** began in England around 1750. People created new machines. Many were used in manufacturing. Many people left farming to work in factories, like cotton mills. This increased the population of cities. Inventions like the steam engine helped many industries. That led to other inventions, like the railroad. Soon the Industrial Revolution spread around the world.

England imported cotton for their cotton mills.

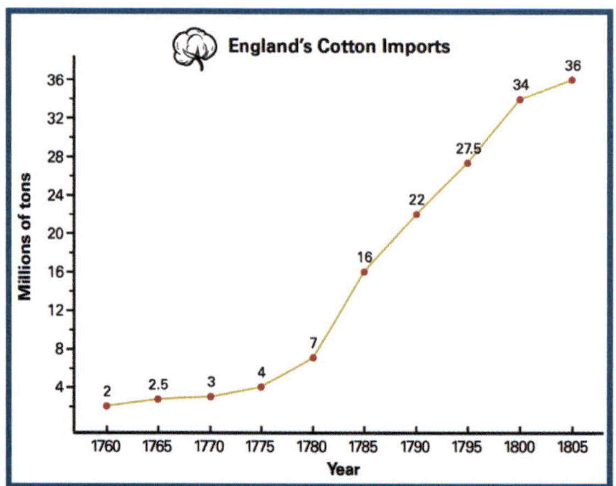

QUIZ

Circle the correct answer.

1. The New World was discovered during the ______.

century | Age of Exploration | Ice Age

2. ______ is having settlements away from your homeland.

Colonization | Renaissance | Monarchy

3. The ______ led to discoveries in science.

tax | Neanderthals | Age of Enlightenment

4. The ______ led to new machines and factories.

feudalism | plague | Industrial Revolution

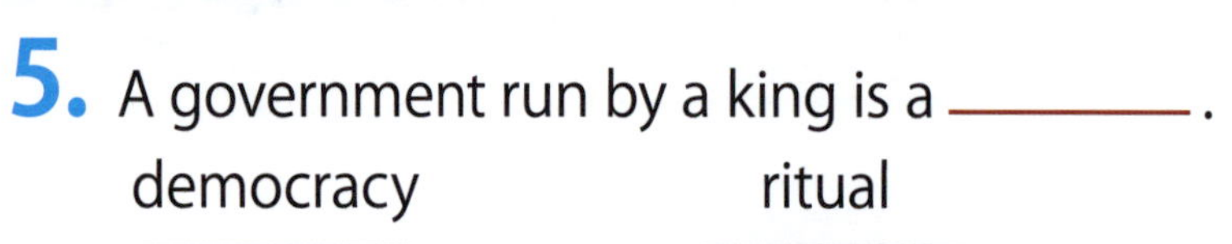

5. A government run by a king is a ______.

democracy	ritual	monarchy

6. Patriotic feelings for your country is ______.

classical	fertile	nationalism

7. The ______ was a rebirth of art and culture.

Crusades	manufacture	Renaissance
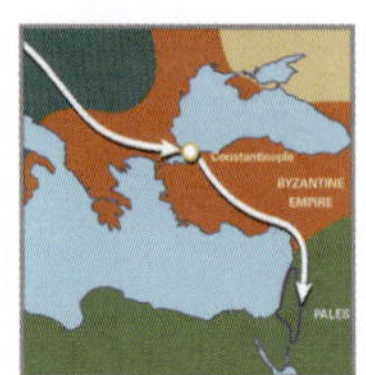		

Write About It

CHAPTER
12

War

A theme of history

War has existed since prehistoric times.

Revolutionary wars have toppled governments.

Advances in weapons led to more war casualties.

Terrorism is a threat today.

War Timeline

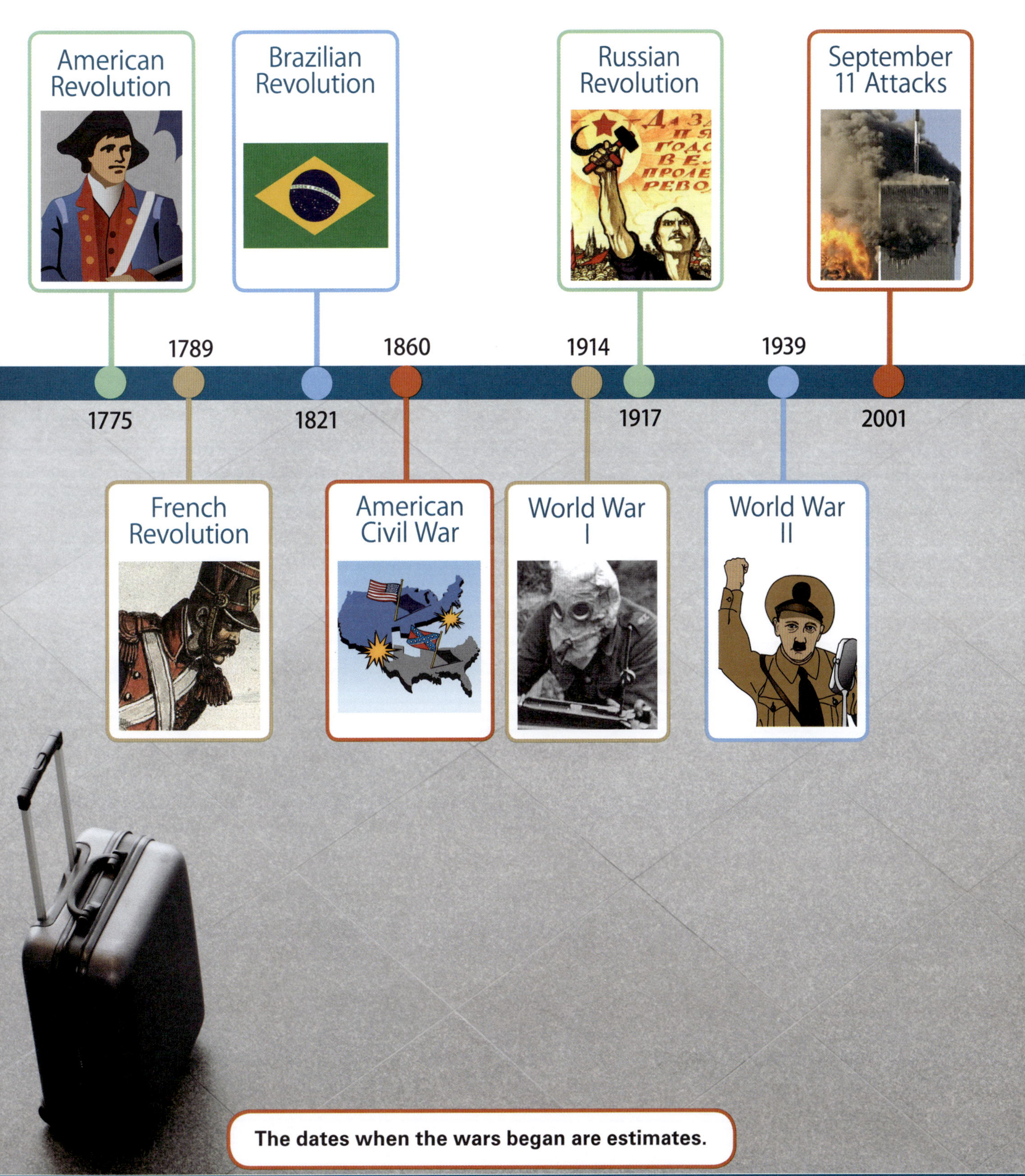

The dates when the wars began are estimates.

VOCABULARY

casualty	a person injured or killed in a war
independence	self-rule
aristocracy	a wealthy class in a society, often related to royalty
refugee	a person displaced by war

A person who had to move because of war

___ ___ ___ ___ ___ ___ ___

VOCABULARY

genocide		trying to kill everyone of a group, like a race or religion
nuclear weapon		a bomb or missile that uses nuclear energy to make an enormous explosion
civilian		a person not in the military
cyberwarfare		a nation attacking a computer network of another nation

A bomb or missile that makes an enormous explosion

___ ___ ___ ___ ___ ___ ___

___ ___ ___ ___ ___ ___

War

A battle scene by Jean-Henri Marlet, painted in 1819.

Wars are destructive, and they have always been with us, from early human history until now. Early wars only involved small groups of people. Wars caused more damage when civilizations developed militaries. A large military can conquer much land, killing many people along the way. The Mongol Conquests was the deadliest war of its time because of the vast territory conquered.

TYPES OF WAR	
Revolutionary War	people revolt to change government
Civil War	people in the same nation fight each other
Chemical Warfare	nations use chemicals, like poison gas
World War	including many powerful nations in two or more continents
Nuclear War	nations use nuclear weapons, like an atomic bomb
Cyberwarfare	nations attack computer networks

Technology also led to more **casualties**. Early wars were fought with spears and clubs. Gunpowder made more powerful weapons, like rifles and cannons. The deadliest war was World War II. It was fought over a huge area and included modern weapons, like jets. Today's technology is very advanced. But recent wars have had less casualties because they covered less area.

An 1862 photograph from the American Civil War.

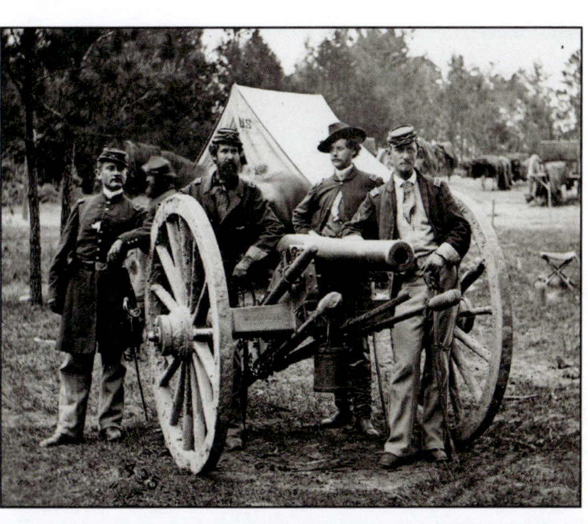

Revolutionary War

WARS OF INDEPENDENCE			
Nation	**Ruler**	**Year Began**	**Nation Flag**
America	England	1775	
Mexico	Spain	1810	
Argentina	Spain	1816	
Columbia	Spain	1819	
Brazil	Portugal	1821	

A revolutionary war happens in nations with serious government problems. The people revolt to change how their nation is run. The American Revolutionary War was against a colonial power. America didn't want to remain a colony of England. Later, other nations fought for their **independence**. Brazil revolted against Portugal. Mexico and many South American nations gained independence from Spain.

GOVERNMENTS CHANGE			
Nation	**Years at War**	**Old Government**	**New Government**
France	1789-1799	Monarchy	Democracy
Russia	1917-1921	Monarchy	Communism
China	1912-1949	Military Ruler	Communism
Iran	1978-1979	Monarchy	Islamic Republic

People can overthrow their own government too. The French Revolution overthrew the ruling **aristocracy** during times of economic hardship. It started a democracy that later became a model for Europe. The Russian and Chinese Revolutions happened during a period of war. Both revolutions led to communist governments. The Iranian Revolution overthrew a monarchy to become an Islamic Republic.

A poster from 1922 celebrating the Russian Revolution.

Civil War

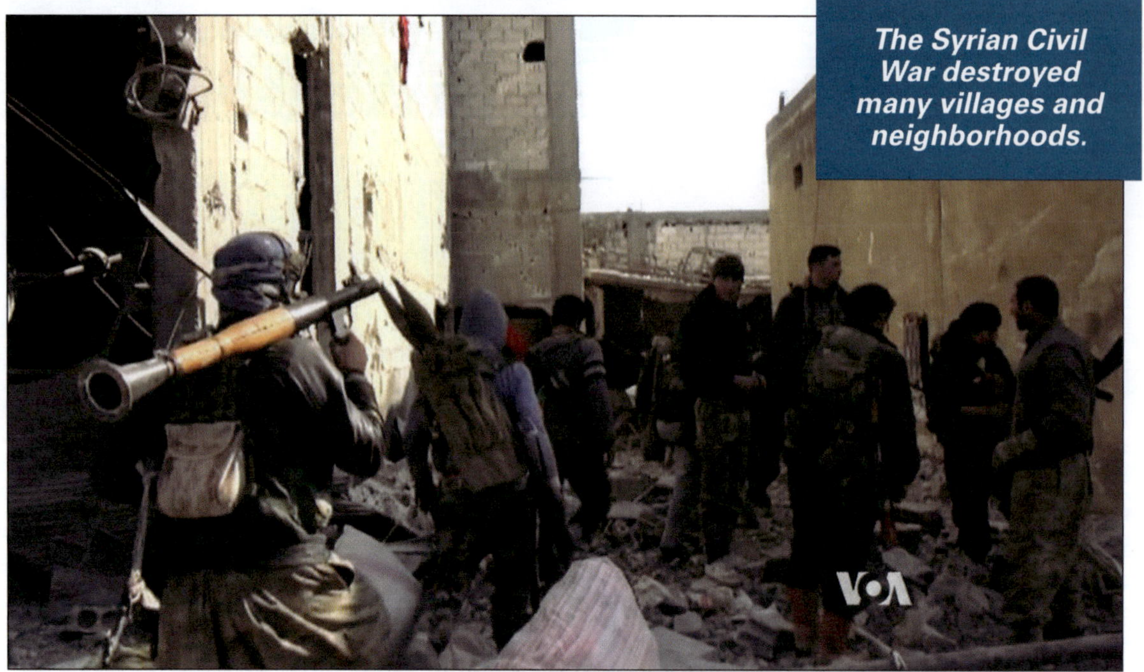

The Syrian Civil War destroyed many villages and neighborhoods.

Civil wars are fought between people of the same country. They can be especially brutal. Like a revolution, there's no foreign invaders. Battles can appear anywhere, and you're fighting against people like you. Civil wars have occurred throughout history. Our Civil War was by far the deadliest war in America's history. A recent civil war was fought in Syria. It resulted in over one million **refugees**.

Genocide

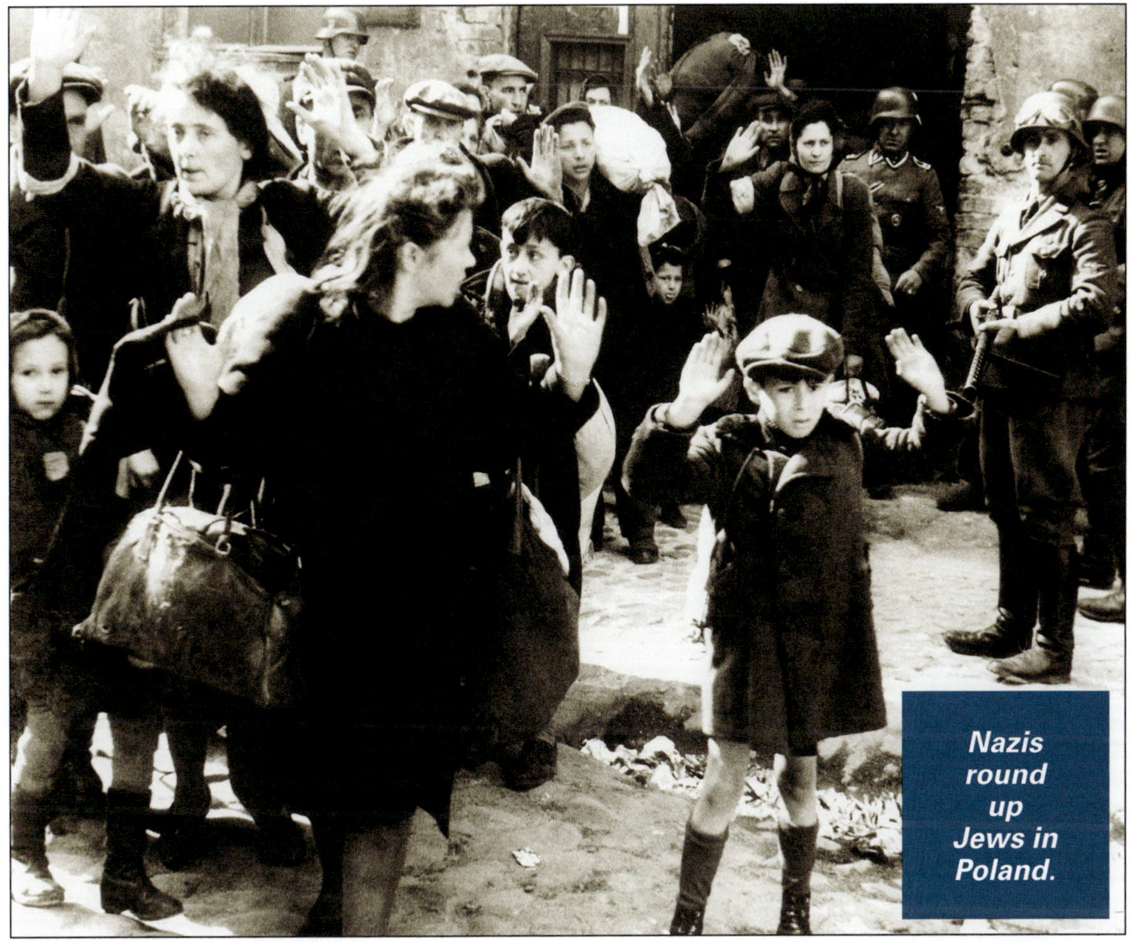

Nazis round up Jews in Poland.

Genocide has happened numerous times. Many innocent people have been killed because of their religion or race. The Holocaust was especially terrible. During World War II, Nazi Germany tried to kill all the Jews in Europe. They even created poison gas chambers to kill more efficiently. Six million Jews died. But can it still happen? In 2016, a Serbian leader was convicted of genocide for killing thousands of Muslims.

World Wars

World War I was the first war to use poison gas and airplanes in battle.

A world war has many nations fighting each other. The war includes battles on more than one continent. Two great conflicts of the 20th century were World War I and World War II. There were two sides to each war. Powerful nations aligned against each other. World War I was fought mostly in Europe. But there were battles in the Middle East and Asia too.

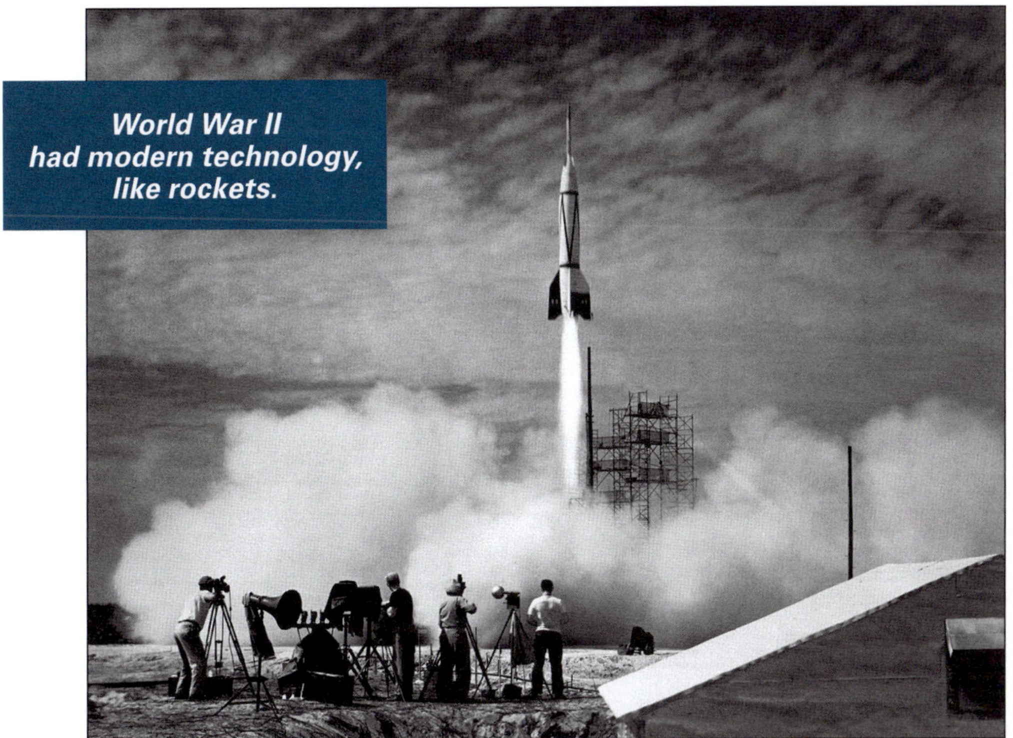

World War II had modern technology, like rockets.

World War II had the most casualties of any war in history. It truly was worldwide. Germany and Japan fought against the Allies of the United States, Great Britain, and Russia. The Allies won. It was the only war to use a **nuclear weapon**, the atomic bomb. The United States dropped the bomb on Japan. It ended the war. This weapon was so destructive, it hasn't been used again.

A photograph taken in 1945 from an airplane shortly after the United States dropped a nuclear weapon on Japan.

Terrorism

A photograph of the Twin Towers in New York after terrorists flew airplanes into them.

Terrorists are small groups fighting a more powerful enemy. They commit acts of violence against **civilians** to get their goals known. They want to make people afraid. They attack nonmilitary targets. Terrorism has been around for a long time. One example was during the French Revolution. It was called the Reign of Terror. In the United States a terrorist group attacked victims in America. It was called the Ku Klux Klan.

The Ku Klux Klan was a terrorist group because it killed innocent people, especially blacks.

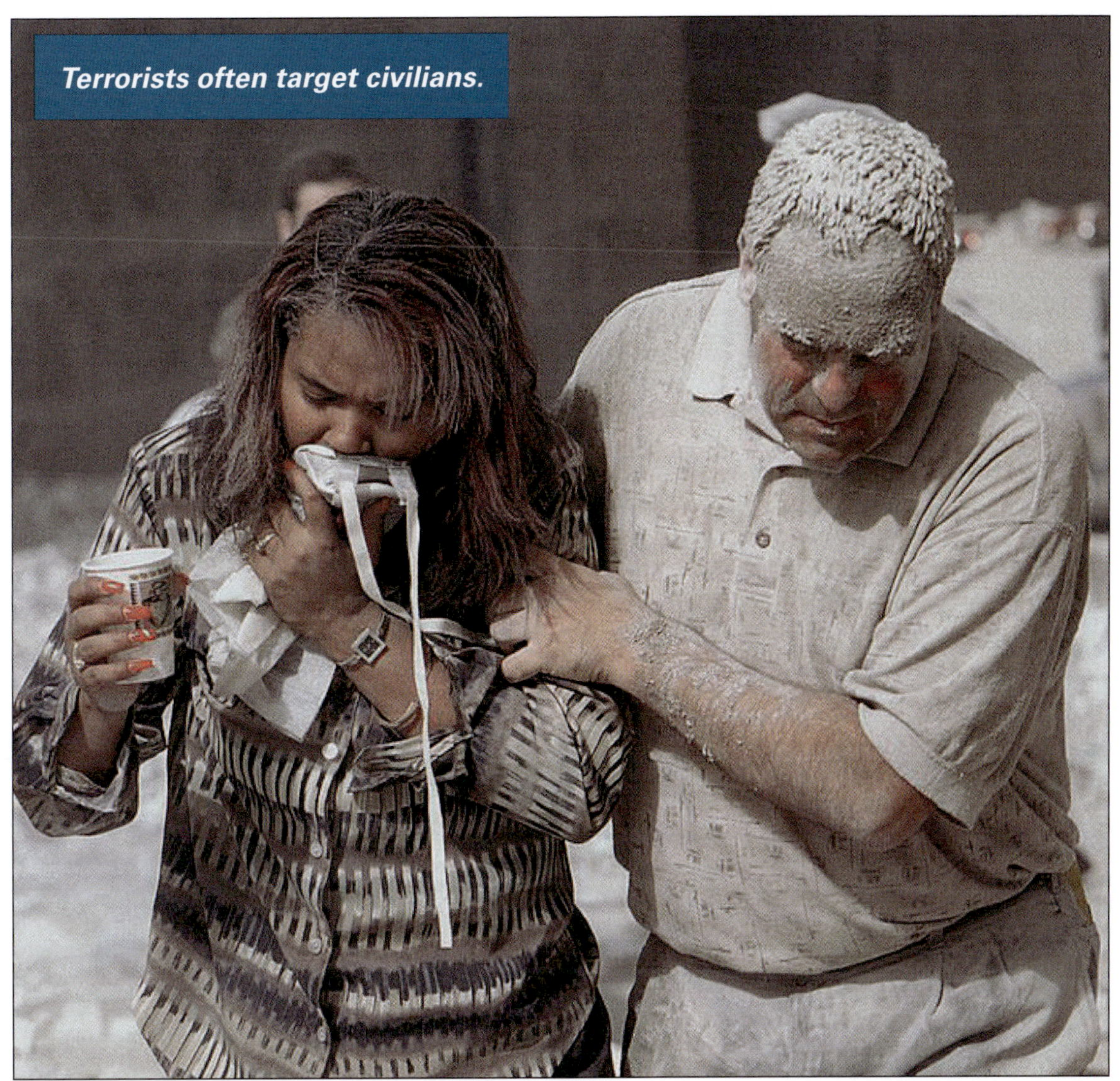
Terrorists often target civilians.

The most destructive act of terrorism was the September 11 attacks in 2001. It was carried out by Islamic terrorists. Thousands of people died. We still hear a lot about Islamic terrorism today. These terrorists cite religious reasons to commit mass murder around the world. They can attack anyone, anywhere. Terrorism can lead to full-scale war, as has happened in the Middle East.

Future of War

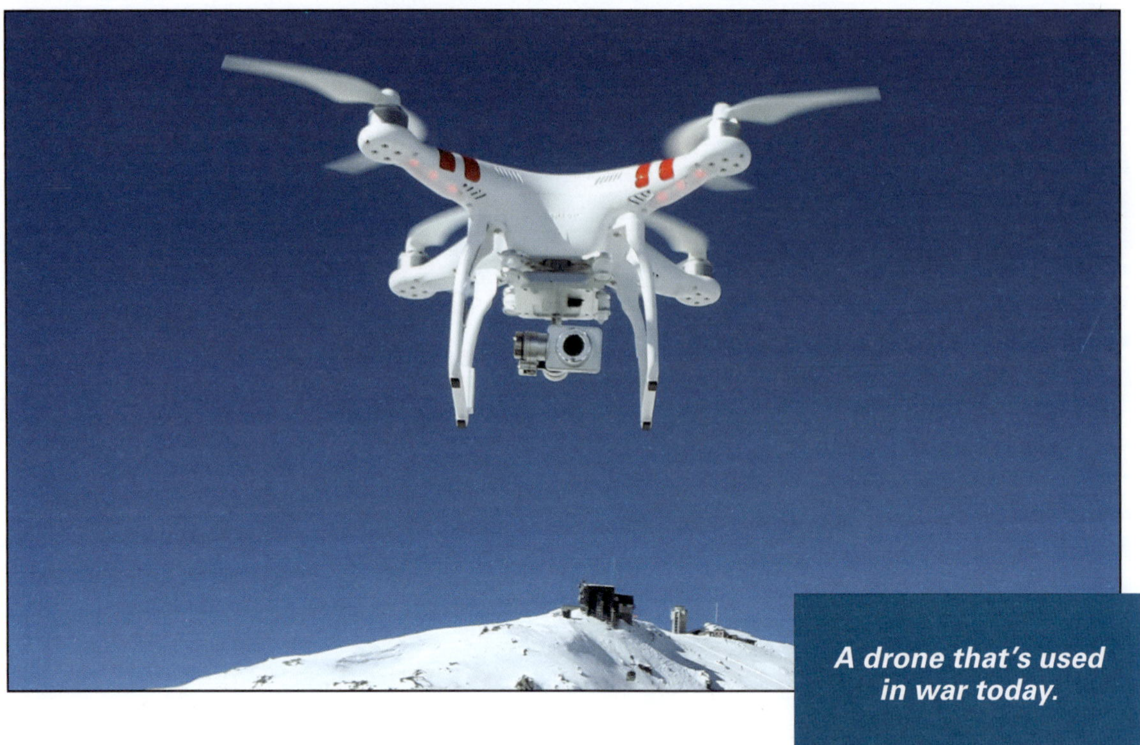

A drone that's used in war today.

New technologies have changed the face of war. Drones deliver pinpoint destruction. They're flying robots controlled remotely by computer. **Cyberwarfare** is also new. A nation attacks the computer networks of another nation. They can shut down important functions, like electricity.

Hacking into computer systems is the goal of cyberwarfare.

QUIZ

Circle the correct answer.

1. War has existed since ______ .

medieval

prehistory

bronze

2. A revolution can topple a ______ .

pyramid
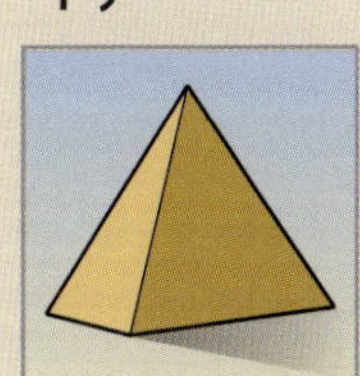

government

agriculture

3. Advanced technology in World War II led to more ______ .

settlements

plague

casualties

4. ______ is a threat today.

Terrorism

Feudalism

Pottery

5. People may start a revolution for ______.

fertile | independence | reincarnation

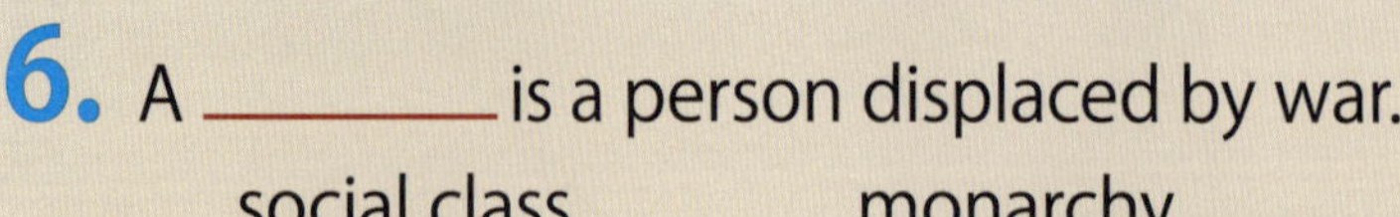

6. A ______ is a person displaced by war.

social class | monarchy | refugee

7. A nation attacking a computer network is ______.

cyberwarfare | pope | nuclear weapon

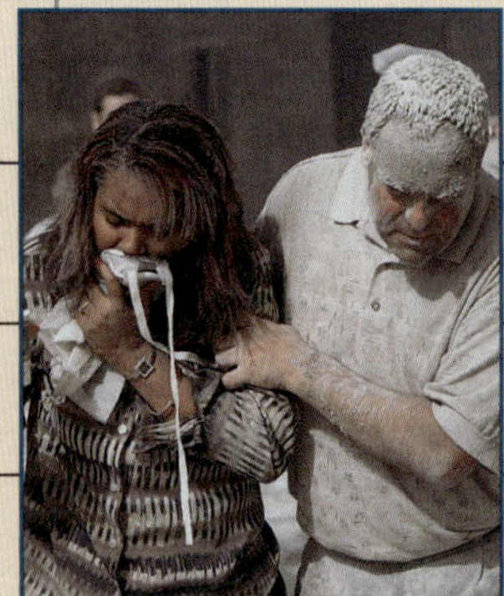

Write About It

CHAPTER
13

Modern Times

An era of history 1800 to today

Monarchies lost out to new forms of government.

Imperialism built empires that controlled weaker nations.

World war transformed the 20th century.

Technology is transforming the 21st century.

Modern Times Timeline

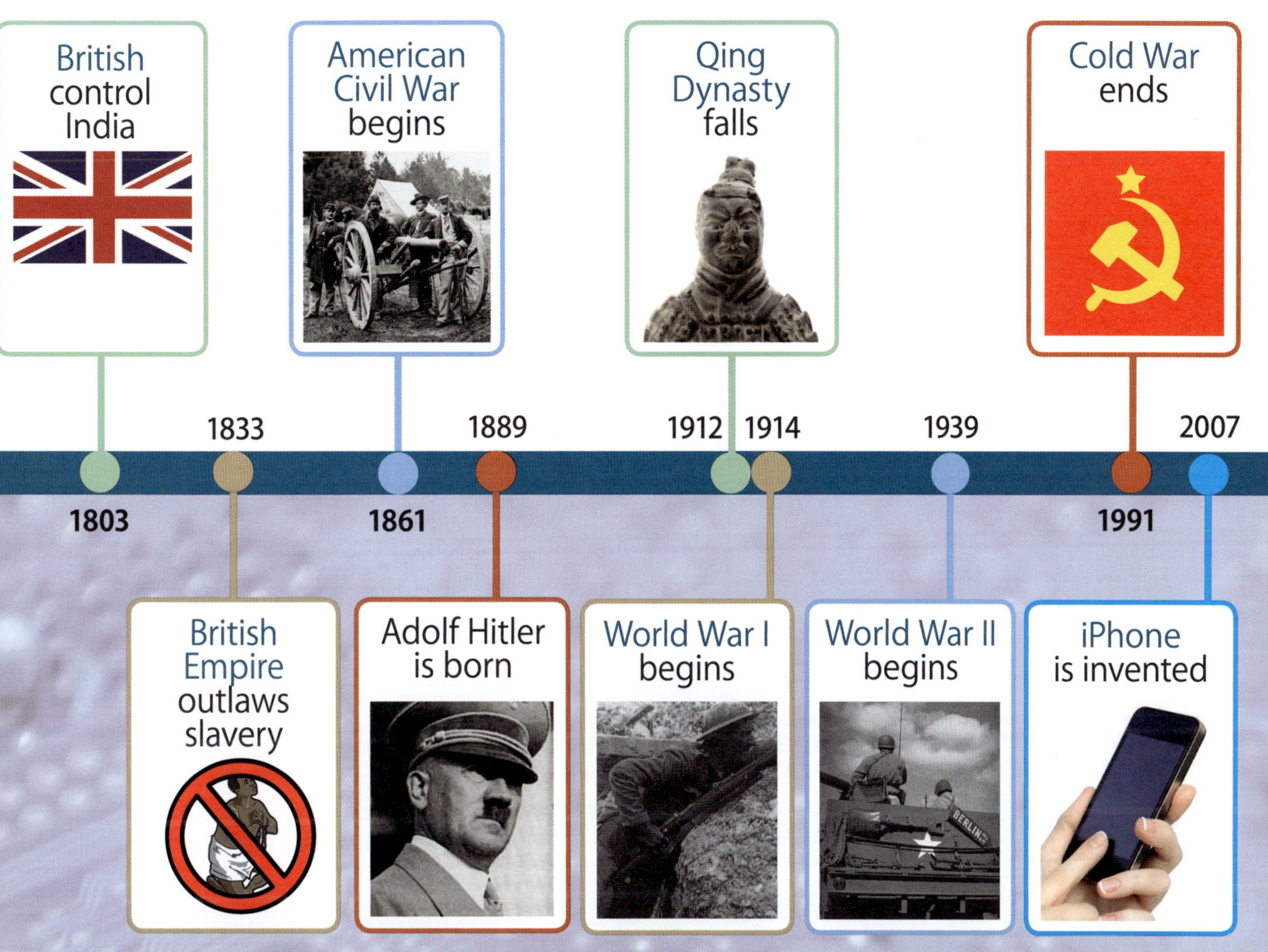

19th Century | 20th Century | 21st Century

1800 1850 1900 1950 2000 today 2100

A century is a period of 100 years. The 19th century refers to the 1800s. That's because it's the 19th 100-year period since the year zero. We are living in the 21st century.

VOCABULARY

imperialism	a powerful nation dominating weaker nations
dictator	a leader who has complete control over a nation
immigration	people moving into a new nation
Nazi Germany	when Germany was ruled by Adolf Hitler

People moving into a new nation

_ _ _ _ _ _ _ _ _ _ _

VOCABULARY

Great Depression		a period of economic hardship in the 1930s
D-Day		the Allied invasion of France during World War II
Cold War		a fight between the United States and the Soviet Union over political ideas
communism		when a government owns all the land and buildings

An Allied invasion of Europe

___-___ ___ ___

Modern Times

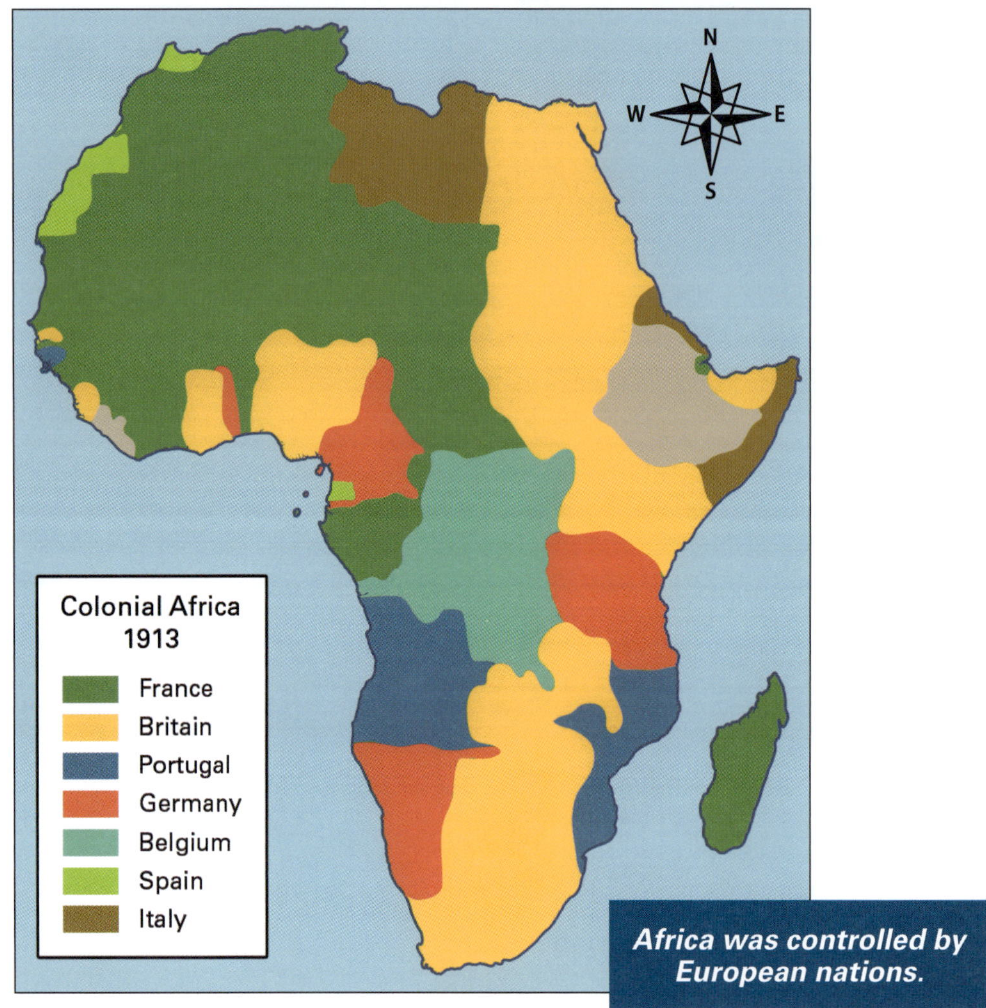

Africa was controlled by European nations.

When this era began, Europe was changing. Monarchies were losing out to other forms of government. The Industrial Revolution expanded global trade. That made some nations very powerful. European nations used **imperialism** to control almost all of Africa. Japan became imperialistic too. China's last dynasty fell in 1912. The nation struggled with war and revolution for the next 60 years.

World wars caused much suffering in the 20th century. After World War I, **dictators** seized power in Germany and Japan. Germany invaded neighboring nations. Japan bombed Pearl Harbor. World War II began. It was a long and very deadly war. Eventually Germany and Japan surrendered. Later, a cold war started between the United States and the Soviet Union. It ended peacefully.

A 1936 photograph of two dictators, Mussolini from Italy and Hitler from Germany.

中国人民解放军是毛泽东思想大学校

A Chinese poster from 1969 featuring Mao Zedong. He became China's leader after a long civil war.

Immigration

Immigration to the United States

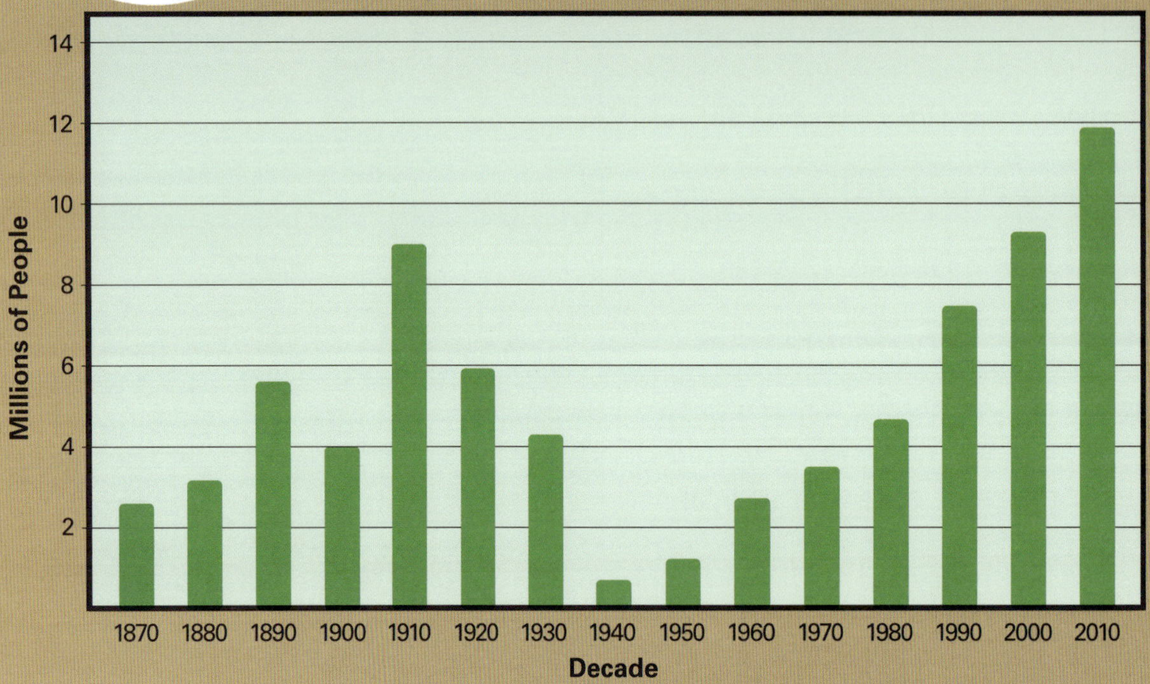

Immigration has been around throughout history. Sometimes people leave their homeland because of war. Usually people move for economic reasons. They want to make a better life for themselves and their families. Immigration increased a lot during this era.

The United States has received more immigrants than any other nation. Immigration is still an important issue today.

A wave of immigrants trying to enter Germany in 2015.

British Empire

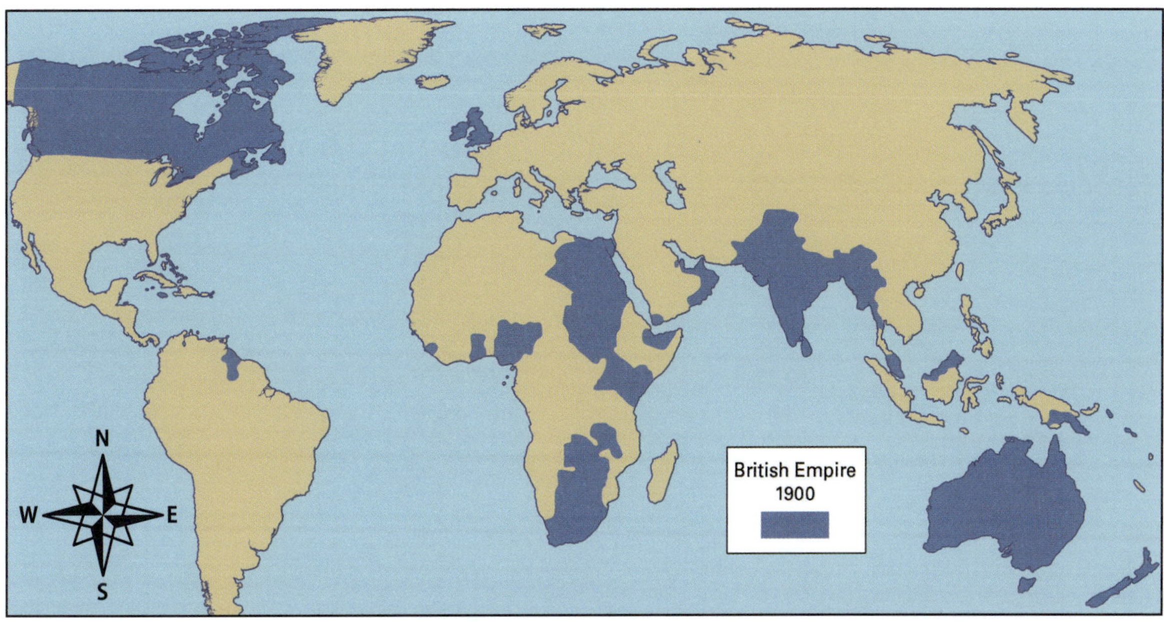

Great Britain is an island nation. To trade, it had to travel by sea. During the 19th century, the British navy became the most powerful in the world. Great Britain was also the most industrialized nation. This combination of advantages led to the world's largest empire. The British Empire controlled territories on six continents. It ruled India for almost 200 years. India became independent in 1947.

Titanic being built in 1910.

World War I
1914-1918

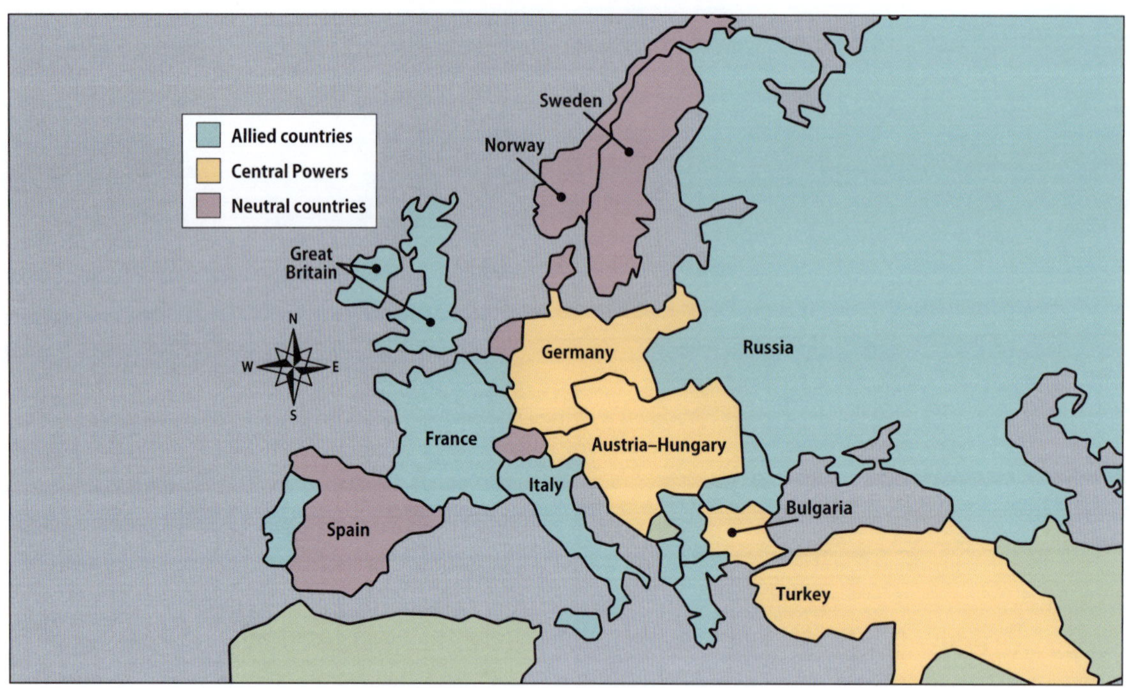

European nations divided into two groups. The Central Powers and the Allies battled each other in World War I. It was a long and very deadly war. The United States and other nations joined in. The Allies finally won, but at great cost. About 13 million people died. It was the first war to use airplanes and poison gas in battle. Unfortunately, the war didn't lead to long-term peace.

World War I armies dug trenches for protection.

Between the Wars

Adolf Hitler had many supporters in Germany after taking power.

The world continued to have troubles. Russia fought a civil war. Afterward, it became the Soviet Union. Germany's economy was in bad shape. Conditions were ripe for a government takeover. Adolf Hitler rose to become the dictator of **Nazi Germany**. The world also endured the **Great Depression**. In the United States and Europe, millions of people were out of work.

People standing in line for free soup in Chicago during the Great Depression.

World War II
1939-1945

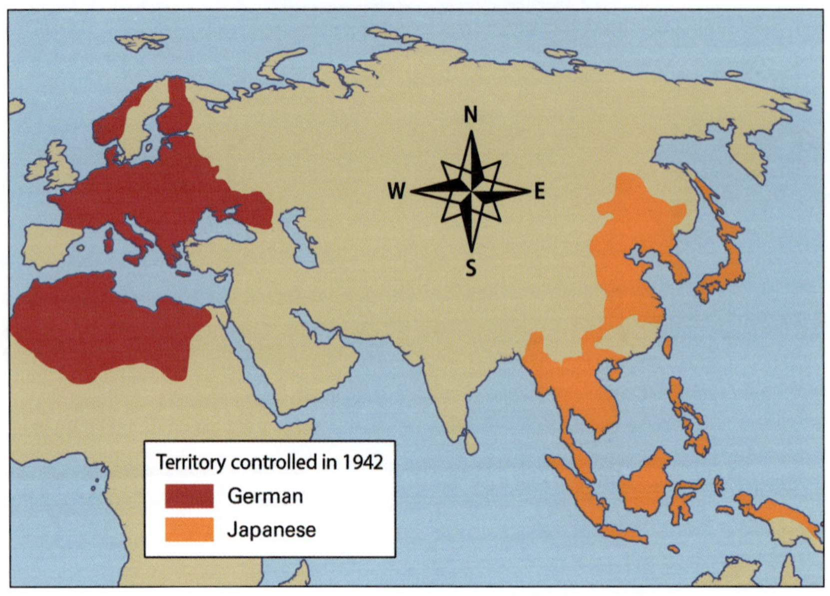

Germany and Japan started World War II. First, Japan invaded nations in Asia. Then Germany attacked in Europe. The United States declared war on both nations after Japan bombed Pearl Harbor. In 1942, Germany and Japan were in control. Then Germany's invasion of the Soviet Union backfired. Great Britain was never conquered, and the United States was winning battles in both Europe and Asia.

Axis		Allies	
	Germany		United States
	Japan		Great Britain
	Italy		Soviet Union

D-Day gave the Allies a foothold in western Europe. The Soviet Union gained control of Eastern Europe. In 1945 Germany surrendered. Later that year, the United States dropped the atomic bomb on two Japanese cities. Then Japan surrendered. World War II took a terrible toll. About 60 million people died. After the war, Europe was divided into Eastern and Western Blocs. The United States helped rebuild Japan, and they became friends.

Japan attacking Pearl Harbor, 1941.

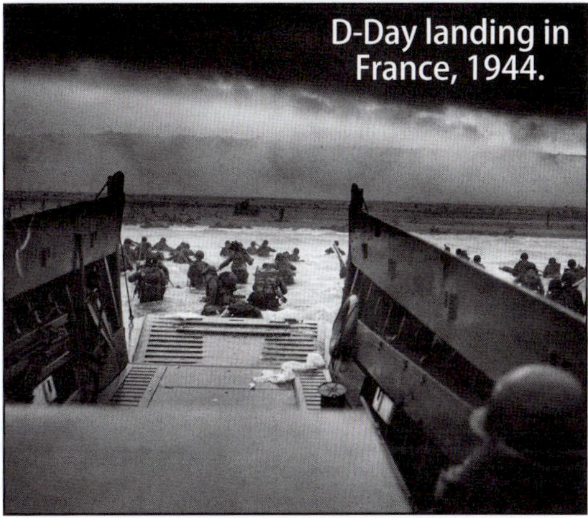
D-Day landing in France, 1944.

Effects of the atomic bomb in Nagasaki, 1945.

Survivors of a Nazi concentration camp after the war.

Cold War

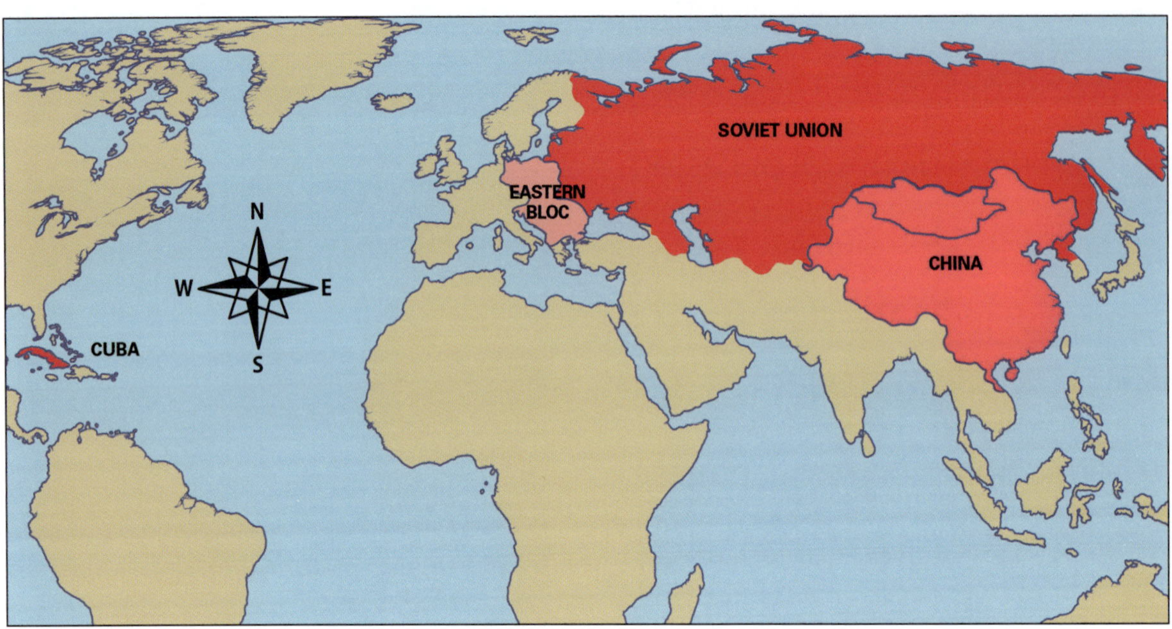

The United States and the Soviet Union were allies during World War II. Afterward, their cooperation ended and the **Cold War** began. The Soviet Union believed in **communism** and wanted other nations to be like them. Countries in eastern Europe, Cuba, and China were communist. The United States thought democracy was better. The U.S. and its allies didn't want communism to spread.

Korean War fought from 1950-1953.

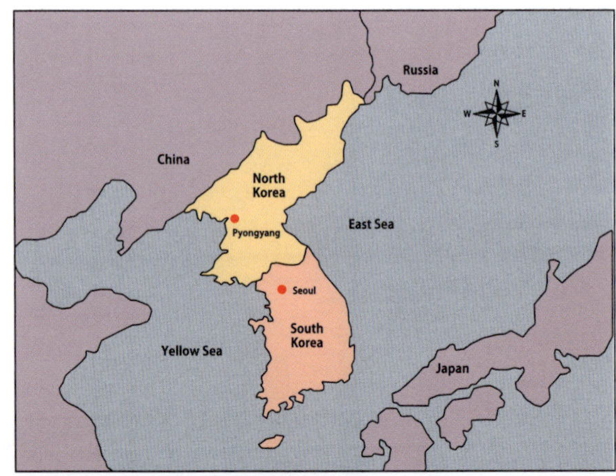

SOVIET UNION	UNITED STATES
Government owns farms.	Farmers own farms.
Government owns factories.	Companies own factories.
People have no choice about who runs the government.	People vote for government leaders.
Government controls the press.	Freedom of the press.

People were afraid of a nuclear war. The United States and the Soviet Union came close during the Cuban Missile Crisis. But the nuclear missiles were removed from Cuba and the crisis ended. There were deadly wars fought in Korea and Vietnam over the spread of communism. But the U.S. and Soviet Union never fought each other directly. The Cold War ended when the Soviet Union broke apart in 1991.

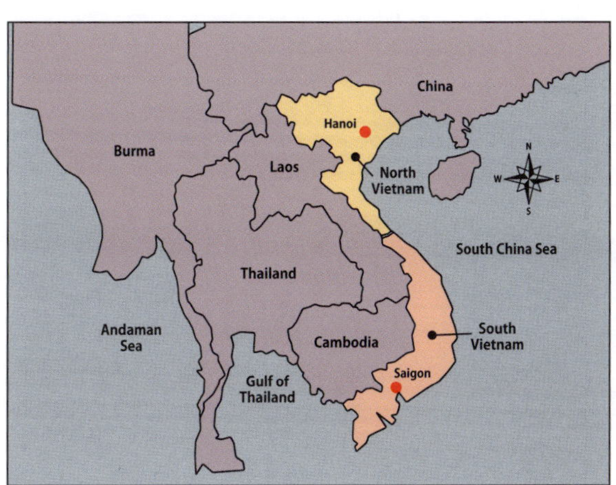

Vietnam War fought from 1964-1975.

United States Superpower

What Makes the United States a Superpower	
	Strong global currency.
	Strongest military in the world.
	Stable government with strong constitution.
	World leader in science and technology.

During the 20th century, the United States became the world's most powerful nation. It had the strongest economy. The dollar was used throughout the world. It was the only nation to land an astronaut on the moon. And it was a leader in important inventions, like computers and the Internet. The U.S. also had the strongest military. The United States continues to be a superpower today.

Photograph of an American astronaut on the moon in 1969.

Rise of China

Shanghai China, 1928

Shanghai China, 2015

China was invaded by Japan before World War II. China's military was weak and the people were very poor. In 1949, their civil war ended and China became a communist nation. Then the Cultural Revolution hurt their people and economy. In 1978, China began economic reforms. They quickly rebuilt their country. Today China is again a very powerful nation.

New Technology

TECHNOLOGY	1910	NOW
phones		
information		
entertainment		
cars		

Technology is changing quickly. The first cross-country telephone call was made in 1915. Smartphones today instantly send messages, photos, and videos around the world. Airplanes were just beginning to fly in 1910. Today we send spacecraft to Mars. Science and technology has changed how we live, for the better. How do you think technology will change the future?

QUIZ

Circle the correct answer.

1. _______ lost out to new forms of government.

Renaissance | Monarchies | Refugees

2. Powerful nations used _______ to control weaker nations.

imperialism | immigration | century

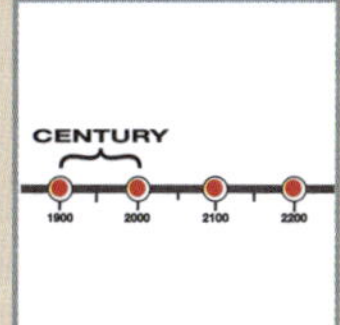

3. _______ transformed the 20th century.

Proteins | Rituals | World Wars

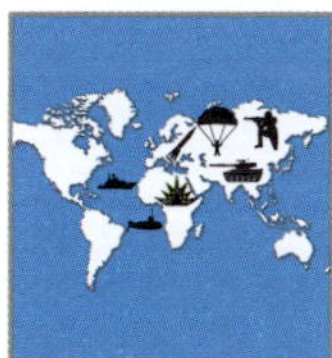

4. Growth in _______ is changing the world today.

technology | tax | writing

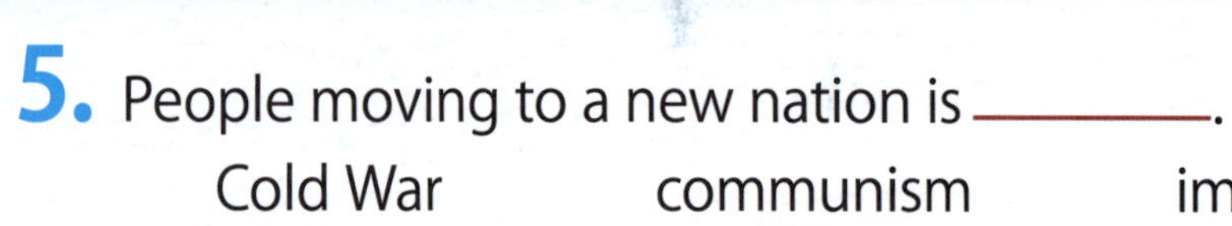

5. People moving to a new nation is ________.

Cold War | communism | immigration

6. ________ was the Allied invasion of Europe during World War II.

Dictator | D-Day | Great Depression

7. A ________ is a leader of a country with complete control.

caravan | manufacture | dictator

Write About It

CHAPTER 14

Biographies

Denisovans

Chapter 3
Early Humans

Extinct human species
When they lived: 300,000 years ago

Russia

We know about an ancient human species because of a finger bone and a tooth found in a Russian cave. The bone and tooth were evidence of a human species that existed about 300,000 years ago. Scientists named these humans the Denisovans. The Denisovans lived during the same time as another group called the Neanderthals. Scientific testing tells us that the bone belonged to a young girl. Other evidence shows that the Denisovans migrated from Africa to South Asia, where they later became extinct.

Cave Painters

France

Prehistoric artists
When they lived: 40,000 years ago

Chapter 3
Early Humans

We do not know who the prehistoric cave painters were, but their pictures tell us how they lived. Scientists think the oldest drawings are 40,000 years old. The cave pictures show people gathering food and hunting animals. Some paintings are colorful hand outlines. Cave paint was made of dirt or charcoal mixed with animal fat. For brushes, the artists used twigs, feathers, animal hair, and their fingers.

Ötzi

Chapter 3
Early Humans

Mummy
When he lived: 3300–3255 BCE

Italy

In 1991, a frozen human body was found by hikers on a glacier in the Ötztal Alps in Italy. The body had become a mummy because of the snow and ice. When a body becomes a mummy, it does not change much over time. Scientists named the mummy Ötzi the Iceman. They think he was born around 3300 BCE and lived for about 45 years. He still had food in his stomach that showed that he ate meat and grains. Ötzi wore clothing made of animal skins. He had an axe, a knife, and a bow with arrows. Wounds on the mummy show that Ötzi was killed by an arrow and a blow to the head.

What do you know?

Denisovans

1. Where was evidence of an ancient human species found?

2. How long ago did the Denisovans live?

3. What other human species lived at the same time as the Denisovans?

Cave painters

1. Who were the cave painters?

2. What did cave painters use to make their paint?

3. How did cave painters apply paint to cave walls?

Ötzi

1. What food was discovered in Ötzi's stomach?

2. How do we think he was killed?

3. Where was his mummified body found?

Gregor Mendel

Chapter 4
Agriculture

Czech Republic

Genetic scientist
When he lived: 1822–1884

Gregor Mendel used pea plants to learn how parents pass traits on to their children. These traits include height and eye color. Mendel experimented with peas because they are easy to grow. He learned that different combinations of pea plants pass along different colors and shapes. By cross pollinating the plants, he discovered that some traits take priority over others. Scientists did not agree with Mendel until after his death. Then his ideas about genetic traits were proven to be correct.

John Deere

United States

Chapter 4
Agriculture

Blacksmith and inventor
When he lived: 1804–1886

John Deere used his skills as a blacksmith to invent a new kind of plow. His steel plow could cut through the sticky soil found in Illinois. The John Deere Company was started when he sold his first plow in 1837. In 1848, he moved the company to the banks of the Mississippi River. He used steamboats to ship his plows to the North and the South. In 1858, John's son Charles Deere took charge of the business. The company still sells farm machinery.

Rachel Carson

Chapter 4
Agriculture

Author and environmentalist
When she lived: 1907–1964

United States

Rachel Carson's love of nature and ocean life led her to a career as a marine biologist. She worried that chemical pesticides were harming the environment. She wrote a book called *Silent Spring* to tell the story of how harmful chemicals had created problems for fish and birds. The book helped create important environmental laws. Rachel Carson continued fighting for new laws to protect the environment and human life for future generations.

What do you know?

Gregor Mendel

1. Why did Gregor Mendel use peas for his experiments?
2. What is a trait?
3. How did scientists first react to his scientific discoveries?

John Deere

1. Why did John Deere move his company to the banks of the Mississippi River?
2. Who did he choose to take over his company?
3. When did he sell his first plow and start his business?

Rachel Carson

1. What was the impact of Rachel Carson's book about the use of harmful chemicals?
2. How did she help create important environmental laws?
3. Why did she become a marine biologist?

Nefertiti

Chapter 5
Early Civilizations

Egypt

Queen of Egypt
When she lived: 1370–1330 BCE

Nefertiti is known as one of the most beautiful and powerful queens of Egypt. Her name means "The beautiful one has come." She was the royal wife of Pharaoh Akhenaten. Many gods were worshipped in Egypt, but Nefertiti worshipped only Aten, the sun god. Nefertiti gave birth to six daughters. Two of the daughters later became queens of Egypt.

Nebuchadnezzar

Iraq

King of Babylonia
When he lived: 634–562 BCE

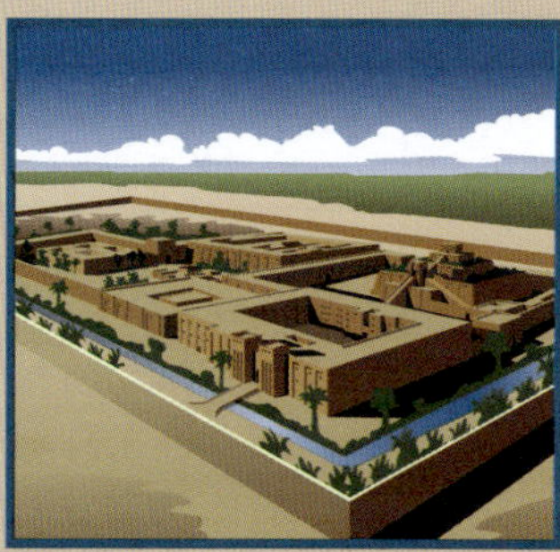

Chapter 5
Early Civilizations

Nebuchadnezzar ruled the kingdom of Babylonia. His army defeated other kingdoms and created a large empire. The city of Jerusalem was destroyed by Nebuchadnezzar's army. In the Bible, the Book of Jeremiah describes Nebuchadnezzar as a destroyer of nations. He used wealth taken from defeated kingdoms to build monuments and temples. Walled gardens in the capital city of Babylonia have been described as one of the seven wonders of the ancient world.

Confucius

Chapter 5
Early Civilizations

China

Chinese teacher and philosopher
When he lived: 551–479 BCE

For hundreds of years, the teachings of Confucius have helped people think about how to live. Confucius helped Chinese leaders learn to make good decisions. The ideas of Confucius became a philosophy based on kindness and respect. His philosophy became known as Confucianism. Many years after his death, the teachings of Confucius continue to have meaning for many people.

What do you know?

Nefertiti

1. What does the Egyptian name "Nefertiti" mean?

2. Who was her husband?

3. How many gods did she worship?

Nebuchadnezzar

1. Why did the Babylonian army defeat other kingdoms?

2. Who was described as a destroyer of nations?

3. What did Nebuchadnezzar do with wealth taken from defeated kingdoms?

Confucius

1. What is the philosophy of Confucianism based on?

2. Who did Confucius help to make good decisions?

3. Do his teachings still have meaning for people?

Plato

Chapter 6
Writing

Writer and philosopher
When he lived: 428–347 BCE

Greece

Plato was a Greek philosopher who wrote down his ideas about life and the world. He was a student of another famous philosopher named Socrates. Socrates never wrote any books. The writings of Plato include explanations of what Socrates shared with him. Plato's most famous writing was called *The Republic*. He founded his own school, called the Academy. Plato's school was the first university in the Western world.

Johannes Gutenberg

Germany

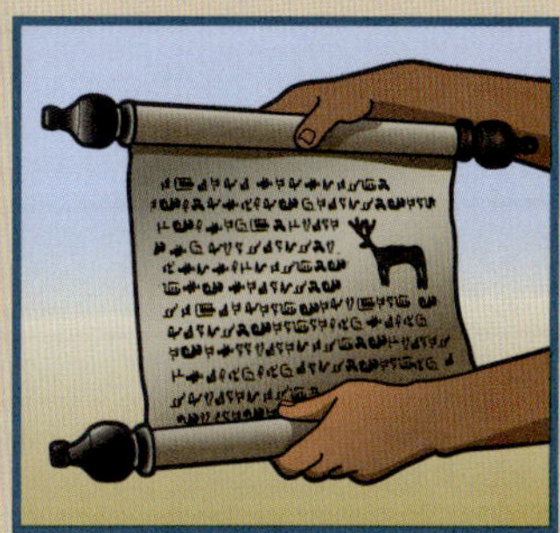

Chapter 6
Writing

Inventor and printer
When he lived: 1395–1468

Johannes Gutenberg invented a new kind of printing press in 1450. His press used movable type, which made it easier to print books. The Gutenberg Bible was the first book in Europe printed with movable type. Because of Gutenberg's printing press, more people could have books and learn how to read. During his years as a printer, Gutenberg never put his own name on his work.

William Shakespeare

Chapter 6
Writing

English playwright
When he lived: 1564–1616

England

William Shakespeare wrote many plays, including *Romeo and Juliet*, *Hamlet*, and *Macbeth*. He wrote histories, comedies, and tragedies. He started a theater in England and spent much of his time performing there. Queen Elizabeth I and King James I came to see his plays. Shakespeare died at the age of 52. He was buried in the same church he attended as a child.

What do you know?

Plato

1. What was the name of Plato's university?

2. Who did he write about?

3. How could people learn about the philosophy of Socrates if he never wrote any books?

Johannes Gutenberg

1. What book was first to be printed in Europe with the Gutenberg press?

2. How did the Gutenberg press make a difference in the lives of many people?

3. What did the Gutenberg printing press use that made it easier to print books?

William Shakespeare

1. How did William Shakespeare spend much of his time?

2. Name two people who came to see his plays.

3. What kinds of plays did he write?

Alexander the Great

Chapter 7
Classical Empires

Ancient Greek emperor
When he lived: 356–323 BCE

Greece

Alexander became a Greek king after the death of his father in 336 BCE. Two years later, in 334 BCE, Alexander and his army began conquering many cities. He became ruler of the largest empire in the world. After surviving many battles, he became sick and died at age 32. Without Alexander as a leader, his empire soon collapsed.

Cleopatra

Egypt

Chapter 7
Classical Empires

Queen of Egypt
When she lived: 69–30 BCE

Cleopatra was 18 when her father died and she and her brother became rulers of Egypt. Their father was Pharaoh of Egypt, which means he was the king. Her brother wanted to be the only ruler and forced Cleopatra from the royal palace. Cleopatra returned to become queen of Egypt when her brother died. Cleopatra helped Egypt to stay independent from the powerful Roman Empire. After Cleopatra's death, Rome took over Egypt. Cleopatra was the last Pharaoh to rule Egypt.

Constantine

Chapter 7
Classical Empires

Rome

Roman emperor
When he lived: 272–337

Constantine became a Roman leader at a time when the Roman Empire was divided into two parts. As emperor of the Eastern Roman Empire, Constantine used his army to win control of the Western Empire. He built the city of Constantinople as the new capital of Rome. Constantine created new laws to protect Christians from being treated badly. He was the first Roman emperor to join the Christian Church.

What do you know?

Alexander the Great

1. How did Alexander the Great build a large empire?

2. When did he begin conquering cities?

3. What happened to the Greek Empire after his death?

Cleopatra

1. What was the name given to a king or queen of Egypt?

2. How old was Cleopatra when she first became a ruler of Egypt?

3. Why was she forced to leave the royal palace?

Constantine

1. How did Constantine help protect Christian people?

2. What was the name of the capital city he built?

3. When did he become a Roman leader?

Phoenicians

Chapter 8
Trade

Israel

Sea traders
When they lived: 3000–65 BCE

The Phoenician people lived along the coastline of the Mediterranean Sea. Their empire had expert shipbuilders and skilled craftsmen. Phoenician glassmakers made jewelry and bottles. The Phoenicians discovered how to create purple clothing dye from snail shells. Their merchant ships sailed to Greece and Egypt for trading. The Phoenician alphabet was one of the first writing systems. After thriving for almost 3000 years, the Phoenician Empire was defeated by the army of Alexander the Great.

Marco Polo

Italy

Trader and traveler
When he lived: 1254–1324

Chapter 8
Trade

Marco Polo was a famous trader from Venice. Marco and his father traveled to Asia on the Silk Road. They were gone for 24 years. He returned to Venice and became a wealthy merchant. He traded goods between Europe and China. Marco was the first to write a book about his travels. Marco's book inspired Christopher Columbus in his discovery of the New World in 1492.

Vasco da Gama

Chapter 8
Trade

Portugal

Portuguese explorer
When he lived: 1460–1524

Vasco da Gama was the first person to reach India from Europe by sailing around Africa. He was sent by the king of Portugal to find a sea route to India. His ship left in 1497 and arrived in India ten months later. He came to India again with a military fleet in 1502. The Portuguese forces killed hundreds of people and took control of Indian sea ports. After his third voyage, Vasco da Gama became ill and died in India on Christmas Eve.

What do you know?

Phoenicians

1. What were the Phoenicians skilled at?

2. Who defeated the Phoenician empire?

3. Where did the Phoenicians go to trade their goods?

Marco Polo

1. How did Marco Polo and his father travel to Asia?

2. What did he do after he returned to Venice?

3. Who was inspired by the book he wrote?

Vasco da Gama

1. How many voyages did Vasco da Gama make to India?

2. What was the purpose of his first voyage to India?

3. What happened on his second voyage?

Charlemagne

Chapter 9
Middle Ages

King and emperor
When he lived: 742–814

Germany

Before modern countries like France and Germany existed, Charlemagne ruled most of Europe as King of the Franks. The Frankish kingdom grew larger, and Charlemagne became known as Charles the Great. In the year 800, Pope Leo III crowned Charlemagne as the first Holy Roman emperor. As emperor, he worked to grow the Christian Church. To support education, Charlemagne created a school at his palace where he taught grammar, geometry, and music.

Hildegard of Bingen

Germany

Chapter 9
Middle Ages

Visionary and writer
When she lived: 1098–1179

When she was a child, Hildegard of Bingen began having visions. In her visions, she heard messages from God. At the age of eight, Hildegard was sent to live in a monastery, where she later became a nun. She wrote books explaining her visions and describing natural methods of healing. Her writings spread across Europe. Pope Benedict XVI honored her as a saint of the church in 2012, 833 years after her death.

Zheng He

Chapter 9
Middle Ages

Chinese explorer
When he lived: 1371–1433

China

Zheng He was a Chinese explorer and military leader who led seven expeditions. On his first expedition, he sailed from China to India with over 300 huge ships. His ships made trading visits to more than 25 countries. The ships returned to China filled with goods and treasure. Zheng He served under three emperors and spent his life leading expeditions for China. The Chinese explorer died during his seventh voyage.

What do you know?

Charlemagne

1. How did Charlemagne support education?

2. Who crowned him as Holy Roman emperor?

3. Name two countries that did not exist when he ruled Europe.

Hildegard of Bingen

1. Why did Hildegard of Bingen write books?

2. What were her books about?

3. When was she honored by the church as a saint?

Zheng He

1. What was Zheng He's job on his missions?

2. Where did he visit on his first expedition?

3. How many ships sailed in the first expedition?

Francis of Assisi

Chapter 10
Religion

Italy

Catholic friar
When he lived: 1182–1226

Francis lived a life of privilege until he received a message from God that changed his life. He was told to help the sick and repair the church of Assisi. He decided to live a life of poverty and to devote himself to God. Many people wanted to help Francis with his work. By the age of 44, Francis had started a Franciscan order in the Catholic Church for people to join. He was declared a saint in 1228, just two years after his death.

Martin Luther

Germany

Religious reformer
When he lived: 1483–1546

Chapter 10
Religion

Martin Luther thought the teachings of the Roman Catholic Church disagreed with the Bible. Luther nailed a list of 95 issues on the door of the church. Catholic leaders became angry and told Luther to leave their church. People who agreed with Martin Luther's ideas about religion were called Lutherans. They started the Lutheran Church, named after Martin Luther.

Aimee Semple McPherson

Chapter 10
Religion

Missionary and preacher
When she lived: 1890–1944

Canada

When Aimee Semple McPherson was a teenager, she questioned her Christian faith. After attending a revival service, she decided to serve God in new ways. She started preaching to people of all faiths around the world. She founded the Foursquare Church in 1923. As a missionary, she created free clinics and gave food and clothing to thousands of people. Aimee preached until her death at age 53.

What do you know?

Francis of Assisi

1. What did God tell Francis of Assisi to do with his life?

2. How did he change his life after receiving a message from God?

3. When was he declared a saint?

Martin Luther

1. Who was upset with Martin Luther after word of his religious ideas spread?

2. What were the people called who agreed with his ideas?

3. What did he think about the teachings of the Catholic Church?

Aimee Semple McPherson

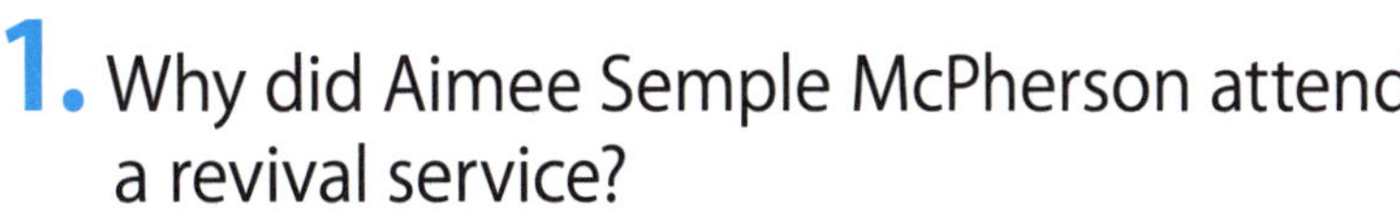
1. Why did Aimee Semple McPherson attend a revival service?

2. What church did she create?

3. How did she help people as a missionary?

Elizabeth I

Chapter 11
Early Modern

England

Queen of England
When she lived: 1533–1603

Elizabeth I claimed the royal throne of England when Queen Mary I died. Elizabeth became Queen of England at the age of 25. She is described in history as a fair and intelligent ruler. During her rule, the English navy fought and destroyed a much larger force known as the Spanish Armada. England then entered a period of peace and growth called the Elizabethan Age. Elizabeth I ruled England for 44 years. Elizabeth II became queen of England 350 years after Elizabeth I died.

Shah Jahan

India

Chapter 11
Early Modern

Emperor of India
When he lived: 1592–1666

Shah Jahan was the fifth Mughal emperor of India. The Mughal emperors ruled India from 1526 until 1857, when India was conquered by Great Britain. Historians call the time of his rule the golden age of Mughal architecture. Shah Jahan created monuments, gardens, and temples. In the capital city of Agra, the Taj Mahal was created as a tomb for his wife. The Taj Mahal took more than 20 years to complete. It is often called one of the seven wonders of the world.

Leonardo da Vinci

Chapter 11
Early Modern

Italy

Artist and scientist
When he lived: 1452–1519

Leonardo da Vinci showed artistic talent at a young age. After years of studying other artists, he became a master painter in 1478. His two most famous paintings are the *Mona Lisa* and the *Last Supper*. Leonardo was also a scientist. He filled journals with thousands of drawings and scientific theories. His projects combined both art and science. Historians believe that Leonardo was a self-taught genius.

What do you know?

Queen Elizabeth I

1. What kind of ruler was Elizabeth I?

2. Who did the English navy fight and destroy?

3. How long did she rule England?

Shah Jahan

1. What are some examples of Mughal architecture that Shah Jahan created?

2. Why did he have the Taj Mahal built?

3. How long did it take to construct the Taj Mahal?

Leonardo da Vinci

1. What are two of Leonardo da Vinci's most famous paintings?

2. How did he learn about painting and art?

3. What did his projects combine?

Joan of Arc

Chapter 12
War

Leader of the French army
When she lived: 1412–1431

France

When she was a young girl, Joan of Arc had a vision from God telling her to save France from its enemies. The message told her to help King Charles fight the English. At age 16, Joan led the French army into battles and helped defeat English forces. After being captured during a battle, she was killed at the age of 19. For her bravery, Joan was made a patron saint of France.

Suleiman I

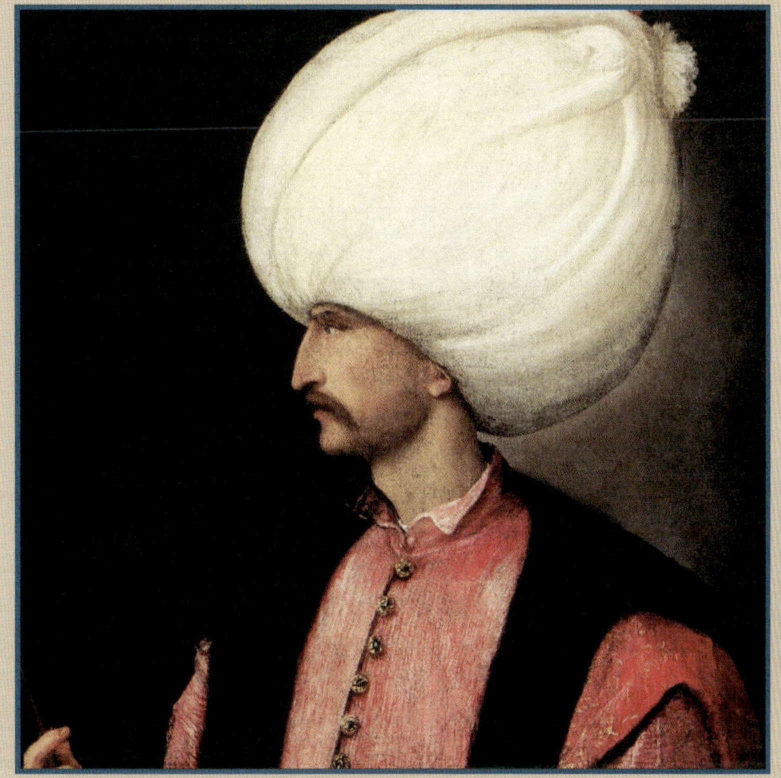

Turkey

Chapter 12
War

Ottoman sultan
When he lived: 1494–1566

Suleiman I became the tenth Ottoman sultan after the death of his father. Suleiman I ruled one of the largest and longest-lasting empires in the world. Known as "The Lawgiver," he simplified the code of laws used in the Ottoman Empire. Suleiman I was a talented poet and surrounded himself with people involved with science and art. Suleiman I died fighting in a battle at age 71.

Simón Bolívar

Chapter 12
War

Venezuela

Military leader and liberator
When he lived: 1783–1830

Simón Bolívar was a South American military leader. He spent 20 years as a soldier and leader, liberating his homeland of Venezuela from the Spanish Empire. Bolívar led his forces to victory at the Battle of Carabobo in 1821. He then helped four other South American countries gain independence. He served as leader for all of the newly independent countries. After an assassination attempt on his life, he resigned as president in 1830.

What do you know?

Joan of Arc

1. Why was Joan of Arc made a patron saint of France?

2. What was she told to do in her vision?

3. Who did she lead into battles?

Suleiman I

1. Why was Suleiman I called "The Lawgiver"?

2. How did he become the Ottoman sultan?

3. What talent did he have?

Simón Bolívar

1. Why did Simón Bolívar resign as president in 1830?

2. What battle helped liberate Venezuela from the Spanish Empire?

3. How many other countries did he help after liberating Venezuela?

Napoléon Bonaparte

Chapter 13
Modern Times

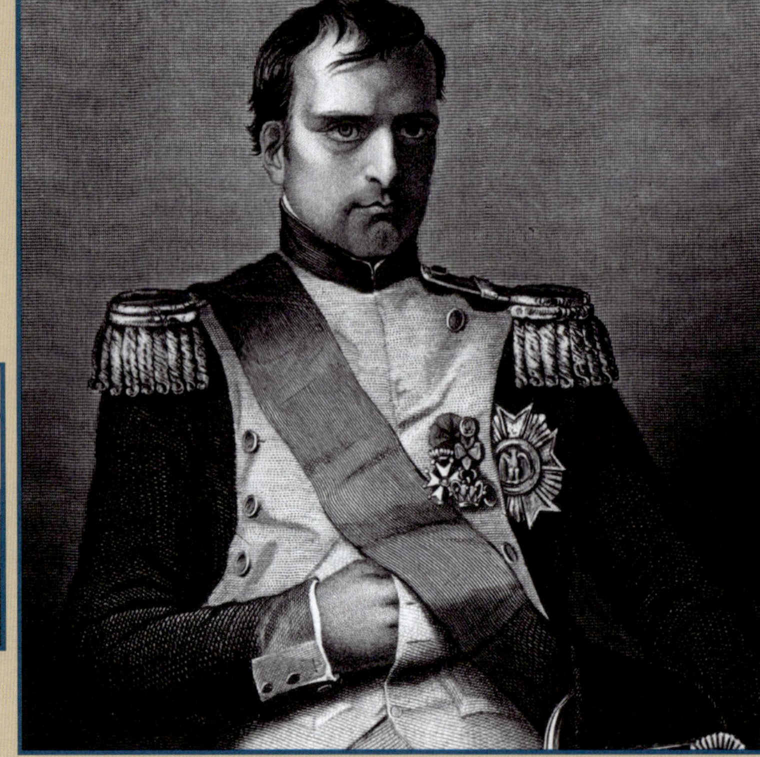

France

First emperor of France
When he lived: 1769–1821

As a military general, Napoléon led the French army to many victories. His success as a general helped France rule over other countries. In 1804, Napoléon became emperor of the French empire. In 1815, the British army defeated French forces at the Battle of Waterloo. After surrendering to the British, Napoléon was sent to an island prison, where he died at the age of 51.

Anne Frank

Germany

Chapter 13
Modern Times

Teen writer
When she lived: 1929–1945

Anne Frank and her family were Jewish. Because of their religion, they had to go into hiding during World War II. Anne received a diary for her 13th birthday and wrote about everyday life in hiding. After two years, her family was captured and sent to concentration camps, where Anne died in 1945. Her diary was later found by her father and published for all to read.

Mahatma Gandhi

Chapter 13
Modern Times

Spiritual and political leader for India
When he lived: 1869–1948

India

When Gandhi was born, his home country of India was ruled by Great Britain. After attending school in London, he lived in South Africa for 20 years. He helped improve working conditions for Indian people in South Africa. Gandhi came back home to help India become independent. He taught people how to protest without using violence. India won its independence in 1947. Gandhi's life ended violently when he was shot in 1948. His teachings of nonviolent protest influenced civil rights leaders in the United States.

Haile Selassie

Ethiopia

Chapter 13
Modern Times

Emperor of Ethiopia
When he lived: 1892–1975

Haile Selassie was crowned emperor of Ethiopia in 1930. As emperor, he wanted to modernize his country. To give more rights to his people, he created a new constitution of laws. One of his laws ended slavery. Some people in Ethiopia thought Selassie had become too powerful. He was blamed for the suffering and hunger caused by a drought. In 1974, he was forced from his throne. He died a year later while under house arrest in his palace.

Mao Zedong

Chapter 13
Modern Times

Communist leader of China
When he lived: 1893–1976

China

Mao Zedong joined the Communist party when he was 25 years old. Communists wanted factories and farms to be shared by everyone. Mao helped start a revolutionary war in China. Many people died. In 1949, the Communists won the war. As the new leader of China, Mao Zedong became known as Chairman Mao. Chairman Mao ruled China until he died at the age of 82.

What do you know?

Napoléon Bonaparte

1. How did Napoléon Bonaparte help France rule over other countries?

2. When did he become emperor of France?

3. What happened to him after the Battle of Waterloo?

Anne Frank

1. Why did Anne Frank and her family have to go into hiding?

2. What happened to her diary after it was found?

3. How long did her family live in hiding?

Mahatma Gandhi

1. Why did Mahatma Gandhi go to London?

2. Who did he help when he lived in South Africa?

3. When did India win independence from Great Britain?

What do you know?

Haile Selassie

1. Why was Haile Selassie forced from the throne?
2. How did he change the laws in Ethiopia?
3. When was he crowned emperor of Ethiopia?

Mao Zedong

1. Where did Mao Zedong live?
2. What did the Communists want?
3. What was he called when he became leader of China?

Glossary

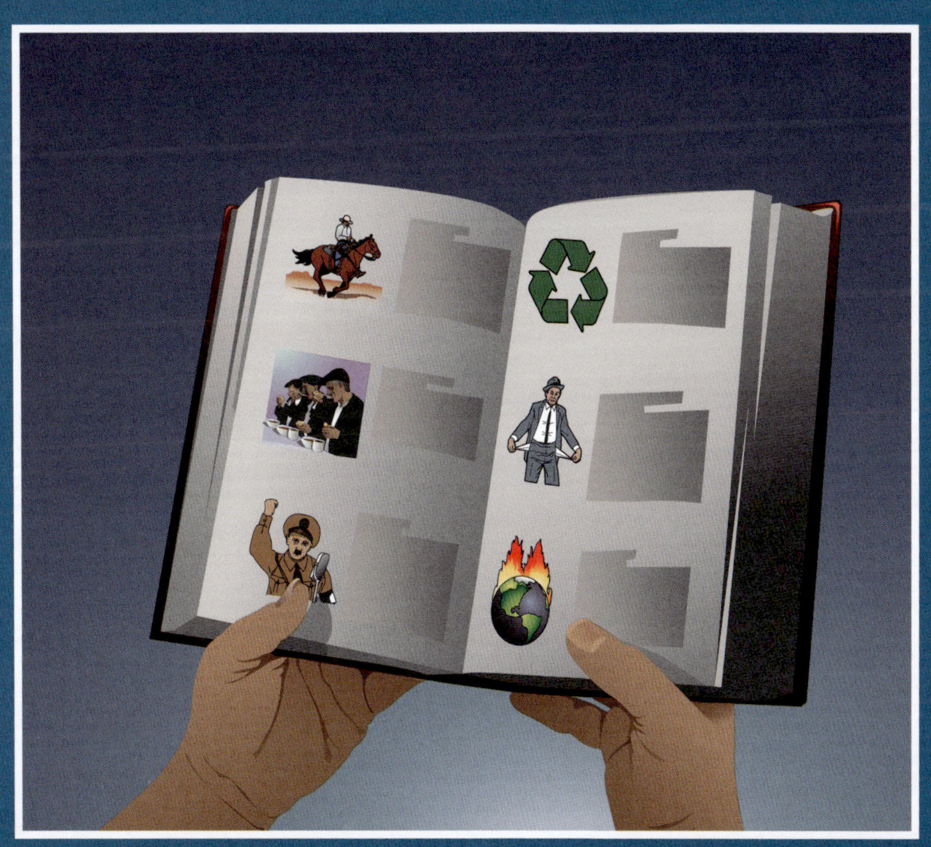

Vocabulary word	Symbol	Definition	Page
Age of Enlightenment		an era when people began to use reason and science to understand the world	189
Age of Exploration		an era when sea voyages sailed to new lands	190
agriculture		growing plants and raising animals for food	54
alphabet		letters of a language that are arranged to make words	96
archaeologist		a person who studies old cultures and artifacts	46
architecture		to design and construct buildings	112
aristocracy		a wealthy class in a society, often related to royalty	207
atmosphere		the air made of gases that surrounds the earth	27
barter		to trade goods or services without using money	131
BCE	**B.C.E.**	an abbreviation for Before the Common Era	39
breed		to control the offspring of animals	62
bronze		a metal made from copper and tin	73

Vocabulary word	Symbol	Definition	Page
caravan		a group of merchants traveling together on land for safety	126
casualty		a person injured or killed in a war	205
cavalry		soldiers who fought on horseback	154
century		a period of 100 years	109
Christianity		a major religion based upon the teachings of Jesus Christ	148
city-state		a city and surrounding territories governed as one state	70
civilian		a person not in the military	212
civilization		an advanced state of cultural and material development in a society	72
classical		judged over time to be important and high quality	108
climate		the weather conditions of an area	22
Cold War		a fight between the United States and the Soviet Union over political ideas	230
colonization		having settlements away from your homeland	191
communism		when a government owns all the land and buildings	230

Vocabulary word	Symbol	Definition	Page
continent		one of seven large land masses on Earth	13
country		an independent nation with clear borders	24
Crusades		wars for control of the Holy Land	173
cultivate		prepare and use the land for crops	56
culture		a group of people sharing similar beliefs and behavior	17
cuneiform		a writing system used in Mesopotamia	94
currency		money that's used in a culture	134
cyberwarfare		a nation attacking a computer network of another nation	214
D-Day		the Allied invasion of France during World War II	229
democracy		a system of government where people vote for leaders	110
dictator		a leader who has complete control over a nation	223
DNA		genetic code found in cells	41
document		a piece of written material that provides information	91

Vocabulary word	Symbol	Definition	Page
domesticate		to tame animals and plants for food or other uses	55
dynasty		a line of rulers from one family	152
empire		a group of states or nations ruled by one powerful government	106
equator		an imaginary line that forms a circle around the middle of the earth	20
era		any period of time	36
extinct		died out	40
fertile		land that's good for growing crops	76
feudalism		a social system that ranks people by power and status	146
genocide		trying to kill everyone of a group, like a race or religion	209
government		the power structure to represent, control, and organize a society	70
graph		organizes data into a picture	7
Great Depression		a period of economic hardship in the 1930s	227

Vocabulary word	Symbol	Definition	Page
hieroglyphics		a writing system used in ancient Egypt	92
Ice Age		a very long time with an unusually cold climate	37
image		a picture of people or objects	6
immigration		people moving to a new nation	224
imperialism		a powerful nation dominating weaker nations	222
independence		self-rule	206
Industrial Revolution		rapid development of new machines and factories	196
iron		a silver-colored metal stronger than bronze	73
irrigate		to supply crops with water to improve the harvest	59
Islam		a major religion based upon the teachings of Muhammad	148
manufacture		to produce a large number of items for use or trade	128
map		shows features of an area of land or sea	4

Vocabulary word	Symbol	Definition	Page
market		a place where goods are bought and sold	127
medieval		relating to the Middle Ages	153
military		an army of trained soldiers	107
monarchy		a government run by a king, queen, or other royalty	190
monotheism		the belief that there's only one god	168
Muslim		a follower of Islam	174
nationalism		patriotic feelings for your country	186
natural resource		a material provided by the earth that people use	128
Nazi Germany		when Germany was ruled by Adolph Hitler	227
Neanderthal		a human species that went extinct	40
New World		North and South America and nearby islands	184
nomads		people who often move from place to place	37

Vocabulary word	Symbol	Definition	Page
nuclear weapon		a bomb or missile that uses nuclear energy to make an enormous explosion	211
ocean		a vast body of salt water	16
plague		a terrible disease that spreads	158
pope		the head of the Roman Catholic Church	173
population		all the people who live in an area	26
prehistory		the time before writing was invented	90
protein		a nutrient in food necessary for survival	60
pyramid		a large structure with a pointed top	77
Reformation		a reform movement that led to the Protestant religion	173
refugee		a person displaced by war	208
reincarnation		the belief that your spirit will live again after you die	169
religion		a set of beliefs that include a higher power like god	166

Vocabulary word	Symbol	Definition	Page
Renaissance		a rebirth of art and culture	187
ritual		a religious ceremony	166
scribe		a person who writes information down	98
settlement		a small community of people who live in the same place	56
social class		a ranking of people in a society based upon their role, wealth, or job	70
stylus		a small tool used for writing or drawing	94
subject		a person controlled by an emperor or king	106
surplus		something left over, like grain after a harvest	54
table		organizes data into rows or columns	8
tax		a payment from people to the government	114
The Holocaust		mass killing of Jews and others during WWII	171
timeline		shows when events happen and the order they occur	5

Vocabulary word	Symbol	Definition	Page
trade		to exchange goods or services	126
wealth		a lot of money or possessions	135
writing		producing words that can be read and understood by someone else	90

Chapter Topic Index

Chapter 1: Study Tools

Chapter 2: Geography

Chapter 3: Early Humans

Chapter 4: Agriculture

Chapter 5: Early Civilizations

Chapter 6: Writing

Chapter 7: Classical Empires

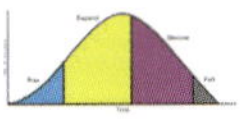

Chapter 8: Trade

Chapter 9: Middle Ages

Chapter 10: Religion

Chapter 11: Early Modern

Chapter 12: War

Chapter 13: Modern Times

Topic	Symbol	Page
Between the War		227
British Empire		225
Cold War		230
New Technology		234
Rise of China		233
United States Superpower		232
World War I		226
World War II		228

Chapter 14: Biographies

Topic	Symbol	Page
Alexander the Great		254
Bolívar, Simón		276
Bonaparte, Napoléon		278
Carson, Rachel		244
Cave Painters		239
Charlemagne		262
Cleopatra		255
Confucius		248
Constantine		256
Deere, John		243
Denisovans		238
Elizabeth I		270

Chapter 14: Biographies